WITHDRAWN

Performing
Arts
Resources

Performing

Arts Resources

edited by **Ted Perry**
with the editorial assistance of Barbara Skluth

Volume One, 1974

Drama Book Specialists / Publishers

Theatre Library Association

© Copyright 1975 by Theatre Library Association

First printing
All rights reserved

No part of this publication may be reproduced or transmitted in any form or by any means, electronic or mechanical, including photocopy, recording, or any information storage and retrieval system now known or to be invented, without permission in writing from the publishers, except by a reviewer who wishes to quote brief passages in connection with a review written for inclusion in a magazine, newspaper or broadcast.
All rights reserved under International and Pan-American Copyright Conventions. For information address: Drama Book Specialists/Publishers, 150 West 52nd Street, New York, New York 10019.

Library of Congress Catalog Card Number: 74-25848

Perry, Ted
   Performing Arts Resources
New York, New York Drama Book Specialists/Publishers
February, 1975

10-24-74

Series: Vol. 1 First in a series titled Performing
   Arts Resources With Theatre Library Assoc.

Printed in U.S.A. by
NOBLE OFFSET PRINTERS, INC.
New York, N.Y. 10003

Table of Contents

vi Robert M. Henderson .... Foreword

ix .... Preface

xi .... Notes on Contributors

1 Louis A. Rachow
   Performing Arts Research Collections in New York City

17 Anne G. Schlosser
    Film/Broadcasting Resources in the Los Angeles Area

33 Alan Woods
    A Survey of the Ohio State University Theatre Research Institute

43 Frederick J. Hunter
    Theatre and Drama Research Sources at the University of Texas at Austin

48 Nati H. Krivatsy and Laetitia Yeandle
    Theatrical Holdings of the Folger Shakespeare Library

56 Laraine Correll
    The Belknap Collection for the Performing Arts: University of Florida Libraries

66 Kay Johnson
    The Wisconsin Center for Theatre Research

74 Ray B. Browne and William Schurk
    The Popular Culture Library and Audio Center

79 James Powers
    The Film History Program of the Center for Advanced Film Studies of The American Film Institute

88 *John B. Kuiper*
   The Motion Picture Section of The Library of Congress

93 *Betty Wharton*
   The Chamberlain and Lyman Brown Theatrical Agency Collection

99 *Avi Wortis*
   The R.H. Burnside Collection of The New York Public Library

147 *Phyllis Zucker*
   The American Film Institute Catalog Project

153 *Barry B. Witham*
   An Index to "Mirror Interviews"

156 *Briant Hamor Lee*
   Theatrical Visual Arts Ephemera: Care and Protection

173 *Richard Stoddard and Frances Knibb Kozuch*
   The Theatre in American Fiction, 1774-1850: An Annotated List of References

213 *James P. Pilkington*
   Vanderbilt Television News Archive

218 *Lawrence W. Lichty*
   Sources for Research and Teaching in Radio and Television History

Foreword

THE MAJOR FUNCTION of a theatre library is to provide the resources from which the scholar can construct his analyses of past or present. That these resources for theatre research are widely scattered and underpublicized makes the scholar's task more difficult.

It is toward the solution of this problem that the Theatre Library Association directs this first annual volume, *Performing Arts Resources.* We hope that the discussion of the contents and locations of theatre collections, both public and private, will result in easier accessibility and higher standards of scholarship.

The contents of this annual will demonstrate the concern of the Theatre Library Association with the entire field of the performing arts, excepting only dance and music which are well represented in other journals.

If you are making your first acquaintance with TLA through this annual, you are invited to become a member and to become a contributor to future annuals.

Robert M. Henderson
*President
Theatre Library Association*

Preface

ATTEMPTING TO PROVIDE documentation for theatre, film, television, and popular entertainments, each annual volume of *Performing Arts Resources* will include articles on storage and use of non-print resources, studies of curatorship, indexes, bibliographies, subject matter guides to various archives and collections, analyses of individual collections and museums, descriptions of regional holdings in a particular field or subject matter, and thorough surveys of research materials, government holdings, training and programs in the performing arts. While the major portion of each annual volume of *Performing Arts Resources* will be devoted to describing and indexing resources for research, some articles will treat such issues as historiography, methodology, and states of research in the performing arts.

Each annual volume of *Performing Arts Resources* is envisioned then as a collection of articles which will enable the performing arts student, scholar, and archivist to locate, identify, and classify information about theatre, film, braodcasting, and popular entertainments.

Manuscripts for future volumes of *Performing Arts Resources* should be submitted, along with self-addressed envelopes, to the editor at 400 South Building, New York University, New York, New York 10003.

THE EDITOR WOULD LIKE to express his appreciation for the support and assistance of Brooks McNamara, Professor of Drama at New York University and Chairman of the Theatre Library Association's Publications Committee.

Notes on Contributors

RAY B. BROWNE, Director of the Center for the Study of Popular Culture at Bowling Green State University as well as Chairman of the Popular Culture Department. WILLIAM L. SCHURK is Popular Culture and Audio Librarian at Bowling Green State University, Bowling Green, Ohio.

LARAINE CORRELL, formerly Curator of the Belknap Collection for the Performing Arts located in the University of Florida Libraries at Gainesville, Florida, has become the Director of the American Theatre Resource Center of the Charles MacArthur Center for American Theatre in Tallahassee, Florida 32304.

FREDERICK J. HUNTER was Curator of the Hoblitzelle Theatre Arts Library at the University of Texas at Austin from 1960 to 1971. He has been in the Department of Drama since 1957, teaching theatre history and dramatic theory and criticism.

KAY JOHNSON was Assistant Director of the Wisconsin Center for Theatre Research from 1969 to 1973. Presently, she is finishing her dissertation in American History at the University of Wisconsin.

NATI KRIVATSY and LAETITIA YEANDLE have both been members of the Folger Shakespeare Library staff since 1957. Ms. Krivatsy is Reference Librarian. Ms. Yeandle is Curator of Manuscripts.

JOHN B. KUIPER is presently head of the Motion Picture Section of the Prints and Photographs Division of the Library of Congress.

BRIANT HAMOR LEE is Assistant Professor of the Graduate Theatre Faculty of the Speech Department at Bowling Green State University.

LAWRENCE W. LICHTY is a Professor in the Department of Communication Arts of the University of Wisconsin at Madison.

JAMES P. PILKINGTON is the Administrator of the Television News Archive located at Vanderbilt University in Nashville, Tennessee.

JAMES POWERS is Director of Publications at the Center for Advanced Film Studies of The American Film Institute in Beverly Hills, California.

LOUIS A. RACHOW is the Librarian of The Walter Hampden Memorial Library at The Players of New York.

ANNE G. SCHLOSSER is the Librarian of the Charles K. Feldman Library at The American Film Institute Center for Advanced Film Studies in Beverly Hills, California.

RICHARD STODDARD is an Assistant Professor in the Department of Drama and Theatre at the University of Georgia in Athens. FRANCES KNIBB KOZUCH formerly was a Reference Librarian at the University of Georgia. Presently she is an Acquisitions Librarian at the Roosevelt University Library in Chicago, Illinois.

BETTY (MRS. JOHN F.) WHARTON is a board member of the Theatre Library Association as well as an active staff member of the Theatre Collection of The New York Public Library at Lincoln Center.

BARRY B. WITHAM is an Associate Professor in the Department of Communication and Theatre at Miami University in Oxford, Ohio.

ALAN WOODS is Assistant Professor of Theatre as well as Managing Director of the Theatre Research Institute at Ohio State University. He also edits the Institute's publication, *Theatre Studies*.

AVI WORTIS is Humanities Librarian at Trenton State College and the author of several children's books.

PHYLLIS ZUCKER is an Assistant Professor in the Department of Library at Staten Island Community College.

LOUIS A. RACHOW

Performing Arts Research Collections in New York City

TERENCE'S PHILOSOPHICAL GEM, "nothing is so difficult but that it may be found out by seeking," is as true today as it was in the second century B. C. when those words were penned. This is evident from the wealth of information garnered for compilation and dissemination in this article. For there are, indeed, theatrical treasures of all ages to be found in Manhattan's institutions of culture and learning — and they are ours merely for the seeking and the asking — to enlighten, to enjoy, and to nourish both mind and soul.

Because of the growing interest in the performing arts as an area of scholarly research, this study endeavors to describe a few of these performing arts resources in libraries, museums, institutions, archives and collections with the exception of the widely recognized New York Public Libraries of the Performing Arts at Lincoln Center. Excellent as they are, these divisions have received extensive coverage of late; therefore, this essay is primarily concerned with the special libraries in the metropolitan area whose cultural research facilities encompass a wide discipline of the humanities including theatre and drama, dance (ballet, folk, ceremonial and modern), music, opera, moving pictures, broadcasting (radio and television), magic, burlesque and circus.

Not to be overlooked, but regretfully excluded for reasons of space, are the libraries indigenous to the Actors Studio, Juillard School, Manhattan School of Music, Mannes College of Music, and the Neighborhood Playhouse School of the Theatre; the Harkness House Library and Museum on Dance; the Metropolitan Museum of Art Costume Institute; the Motion Picture Association of America; and the schools of fashion and design libraries such as the Fashion Institute of Technology, National

Design Center, Parsons School of Design, and the Traphagan School of Fashion.

Anthology Film Archives
80 Wooster Street, 10012
Tel: (212) 226-0010.
Founded 1971.

Anthology Film Archives, the first film museum in the world devoted entirely to film as an art, was made possible through the vision of Film Art, Inc. Organized and developed out of roots and plans for the encouragement of independent filmmaking, the group's concept is "to present a cycle of selected films defining the history of cinema as an art" resulting ultimately in "a new generation of film understanding" and an ever increasing "sensual enjoyment" of total cinema. At the end of each series the cycle is repeated with additions to the repertoire as new films are received. Film-makers Kenneth Anger, Stan Brakhage, Robert Bresson, Luis Buñuel, Jean Cocteau, Carl Theodor Dreyer, Sergei Eisenstein, Gregory Markopoulos, Georges Méliès, Andy Warhol, John and James Whitney, Jonas Mekas, Peter Kubelka, and others are represented in the Archives' screenings. The films are shown only in the Invisible Cinema and are not available on a rental basis. Program information, calendars and cycles may be obtained at the box office.

The primary purpose of the library is to collect books, articles, clippings, scenarios and other documentation relating to film as an art with special emphasis on critical material on the films shown in the six-week cycles. As presently composed, the library reportedly has the largest collection of documents relating to the American avant-garde film in the world and continues to appeal to film-makers to deposit notes and associated items related to the making of their respective films. Special facilities are provided for critics writing on experimental films and for students doing advanced research in this area. Library hours are by appointment only Monday through Friday.

Cooper-Hewitt Museum of Design
Smithsonian Institution
9 East 90 Street, 10028
(Formerly The Cooper Union Museum)
Tel: (212) 860-2011. Founded 1897.

The resources of the Cooper-Hewitt Collection place it among the foremost repositories of decorative arts and design in the world, and although its primary concern is "the practical, physical, and psychological effect of design on life" there is within its holdings an excellent collection of theatrical drawings and prints, architectural fantasies, peep shows, and royal and papal "fête" designs. Allied materials include a rare 18th-century Italian marionette stage with proscenium arch along with marionettes of Commedia dell'Arte characters, various versions of Punch and Judy, Indonesian Wayang Golek puppets, and the entire Haines Marionette Company Collection which was shown from the late 1920's until recently. This group includes over two hundred marionettes, music, scripts, sets and props, all made by the donors and marionetteers Frank and Elizabeth Haines.

Italy is represented in the print department from the 16th through the 19th-centuries with a pen and brown ink "Stage Backdrop" by Scamozzi (or close follower) to actor Malagodi's stage set "Church Yard at Night". Callot's 17th-century engravings for *Soliman* and Simon Lissim's 1925 set design for the Theatre de L'Oeuvre's *Hamlet* in Paris may be found in the French collection. Eighteenth century English drawings include William Angus' engraving of Dixon's "Inside View of the Pantheon showing their Majesties Box," while 20th century designs by Eugene Berman, Gian Carlo Menotti and Donald Oenslager are representative of the United States.

Complementing the museum's holdings are the well developed resources of the library. Among these is a broad variety of books on theatre design and an especially fine group of "fête" books. Although currently closed to the public until renovations are complete, the museum and library hours are from 10 a. m. to 5 p. m. Monday through Friday by appointment.

The Hispanic Society of America,
Broadway between 155 and 156 Streets, 10032.
Tel: (212) 926-2234. Founded 1904.

The Hispanic Society of America was founded with the object of establishing a free public museum and reference library to present the culture of Hispanic peoples. The museum collections, representative of the culture of the Iberian Peninsula from prehistoric days to the present century, include paintings, sculpture, and examples of the decorative arts. The library with its thousands of manuscripts and over one hundred thousand books is an important center for research on Spanish and Portugese art, history, and literature.

Rarely publicized is the Society's superb collection of literally hundreds of manuscripts (some with stage business, notes and annotations) of the Golden Age of Spanish Drama — dramas of Pedro Calderón de la Barca, Lope de Vega, Guillén de Castro y Bellvís, and Antonio Mira de Amescua, to name a few. Complementing these holdings are numerous titles of rare 17th-century printed books on the drama and the stage, English translations of Spanish plays, and Spanish translations of international drama. Modern materials include letters and documents of the major and minor dramatists and performers from 1904 to the present day, as well as clippings.

The field of music is represented by a number of choir books, original opera scores and manuscripts including Manuel de Falla's score for *El gran teatro del mundo* and Granados' *Goyesca,* the first full-length Spanish opera to be presented in the United States. Folkloric costume and dance form an integral part of the holdings with thousands of photographs of provincial, ceremonial, and spectacular dances including the

Jota — a dance of Aragón and almost the only dance to appear on theatre programs and playbills.

The Archive of Recorded Voice contains tapes and recordings of Spanish authors reading their own works. Available on a rental basis are filmed productions of Calderón de la Barca's *La vida es sueño* and *El gran teatro del mundo* as performed by the faculty and students of Barnard College. Reading Room hours are from 1 to 4:30 p.m. Tuesday through Friday and 10 a.m. to 4:30 p.m. on Saturday. Manuscripts and early printed books may be consulted by appointment with proper professional and/or institutional identification.

The Institute of the American Musical
220 West 93 Street, 10025. Tel: (212) 787-1997 or 595-1523. Founded 1972.

The Institute of the American Musical is "a new, tax-exempt, public, not-for-profit corporation dedicated to establishing the very first study center and archive expressly devoted to a native American art form: the musical". Incorporated in 1972, the Institute houses the world's largest private collection of reference materials on the American musical theatre and motion pictures, including 20,000 phonograph records, sound tapes, and cylinders dating back to the 1890's; record catalogues to the turn-of-the-century; thousands of theatre and film programs, periodicals, sheet music and vocal scores as early as 1880; thousands of motion picture press books and over 200,000 stills from 1915 to the present; every musical comedy script published in America and dozens in manuscript form; original or photocopied materials from the archives of movie palaces, film, and record companies including discographies of many major Broadway and Hollywood stars; and thousands of books on theatre, film, broadcasting, world's fairs and other allied areas of showmanship.

A current project is the preservation and documentation of an important collection of silent 16mm motion picture footage of more than one hundred fifty Broadway musicals, actually filmed during theatrical performances from 1931 to the present. These brief excerpts, all in color from the late 1930's on, represent virtually the only record extant of how the Broadway musical appeared in motion during the last forty-two years. Funds are being raised to copy this collection, fully annotate the performers and songs in the form of screen titles, and ultimately donate complete sets to the Library of Congress and the Lincoln Center Theatre Collection, while retaining a set for its own use. The Institute is also engaged in a research project to document the little discussed but widespread practice of vocal dubbing in films.

Despite limited funding and physical facilities, the Institute is open by appointment to writers, researchers, students and educators.

International Theatre Institute of the United States, Inc.
245 West 52 Street, 10019. Tel: (212) 245-3950.
Founded 1948.

The International Theatre Institute was chartered by UNESCO in Prague "to promote the exchange of knowledge and practice in the theatre arts". Eleven nations took part in that historic meeting twenty-five years ago. Today ITI centers exist in over seventy countries around the world. The American center of the international organization is the International Theatre Institute of the United States (ITI/US), and although it has become an integral part of the United Nations of theatrical activity over the past quarter of a century, its library is relatively new to the research world.

Opened in 1970, the collection consists of a library and archives documenting all aspects of modern theatre throughout the world since World War II. Its holdings cover six continents, one hundred six countries, and seventy-one ITI centers or affiliates. Here one can find with ease and delight foreign materials not generally available in this country — books, plays, newspapers, periodicals, yearbooks, pamphlets and monographs, articles, programs, brochures, production schedules, newsletters and house organs — nearly all of which are gathered through an international exchange program. American theatre is covered by current files on theatres and theatre groups across the country, more than fifty regularly received periodicals, books on management, design, stagecraft, theory and biographies, and playscripts.

The library owns one thousand American plays and two thousand five hundred foreign dramas in manuscript or published editions, in collections and anthologies, and in periodicals — all cataloged by author, title, and country of origin. Two hundred fifty theatres across the country are documented with current schedules, press releases, and programs. Expanded through grants from the New York State Council on the Arts, the ITI collection is available Tuesday through Friday from 10 a.m. to 3 p.m. by appointment.

The Museum of Modern Art Film Archives
11 West 53 Street, 10019. Tel: (212) 956-6100.
Founded 1935.

The Museum of Modern Art Film Archives was established in May 1935 as a separate corporation "to create a consciousness of history and tradition within the new art of the motion picture". Then, as now, its purpose was "to trace, catalog, assemble, preserve, exhibit and circulate to museums and colleges single films or programs of all types of films, so that the film may be studied and enjoyed as any other one of the arts is studied and enjoyed". It was the pioneer in a field of study and scholarship which has since become international.

Although films had been included in the museum's original prospectus, the museum did not aspire to a centralized film and film material collection such as the British Film Institute, and its service is primarily to its departments rather than to the public. In addition to the library's highly selective book and periodical holdings, based on the needs relevant to the museum's varied activities, it is extremely active in the publishing and reprint fields and in special services and cooperative ventures with institutions here and abroad — not to mention its ever enlarging film preservation projects. The Department of Film Circulating Programs is constantly meeting "a continuously expanding demand from colleges and universities in the United States for significant examples of film classics, documentaries, and current experimental work.

The Study Center of the Department of Film provides the following facilities and services to the "serious student of film": a reader and a 16mm projector upon which films from the museum's collection can be viewed; an extensive collection of screenplays and dialogue continuities, stills, clippings on films and film personalities; film catalogues and yearbooks; a collection of collateral material including books and plays which have been made into films, as well as records and tapes. To qualify for research the student must currently be enrolled in a film course and must present a letter from an advisor stating the nature and validity of the project. The researcher must also present a brief outline of the paper or thesis. Writers and authors may also use the facilities in which case a letter from the respective publisher is to be presented. In each instance the museum retains the right of approval or disapproval of the individual project. An appointment is necessary to use the facilities of the Film Study Center, and appointments for viewing films must be made at least one week in advance. The hours are from 1:30 to 5 p.m. Monday through Friday.

The Museum of The City of New York
Theatre and Music Collection
103d Street and Fifth Avenue, 10028. Tel: (212) 534-1672

The Theatre and Music Collection of the Museum of the City of New York comprises an outstanding collection of theatrical memorabilia illustrating the dramatic and musical events in New York from colonial times to the present. Of particular historical interest are the photographs and information on theatre buildings and architecture from the John Street Theatre to the Palace renovations to the Uris, one of the newest of the three Broadway theatres housed in a skyscraper complex. Its aim continues to be collecting and preserving material in every theatrical media and making it available to students and professional researchers. Complementing this aspect is the planning and arranging of frequent exhibitions for the purpose of bringing "alive the people, the writings, and the examples of this special form of culture".

In the field of design research there are the original scene and costume drawings of the Dazian Library for Theatrical Design; the Charles W. Witham drawings, unique in that they are the only designs for the American stage in existence between 1869 and 1880; the more recent originals of Robert Edmond Jones, Donald Oenslager, Boris Aronson and Oliver Smith; and a number of actual stage models representative of the 19th and 20th-century designers, the latest being Ming Cho Lee. The manuscript and orchestration holdings contain playscripts and promptbooks of George M. Cohan, Eugene O'Neill, Harry B. Smith, E. A. Sothern and Julia Marlowe, in addition to those by actress Kate Claxton, stage managers and producers. Portraits and caricatures are represented by artists John Singer Sargent, William Cummings Chase, Henry Inman and Alex Gard among others. The costumes range in period from the early part of the 19th-century to Edwin Booth's Hamlet to Lauren Bacall's Margo Channing and encompass theatre, opera, dance, musical comedy, motion pictures and television. Highly prized are the Léon Bakst costumes for the 1916 Hippodrome production of *The Sleeping Beauty* executed by Dazian. Special attention is also being given to design and fabric analysis, theatrical importance, and original designers and manufacturers.

The music department boasts of an almost complete record of Bagby Concerts plus published music of the late 18th and early 19th-centuries. Other special collections are those of William A. Brady, Howard Dietz, Charles and Daniel Frohman,

Lillian Gish, Helen Hayes, Jenny Lind, the Lunts, Mary Martin, Ethel Merman, the Civic Repertory Theatre and the Yiddish theatre. Recent exhibitions include *Ziegfeld, Musicals of the 1930's, George and Ira Gershwin* and *Stars of the New York Stage 1870-1970*. Library hours are 10 a.m. to 4:30 p.m. Monday through Friday by appointment.

New-York Historical Society
170 Central Park West (77 Street), 10024
Tel.: (212) 873-3400.
Founded 1804.

Although long recognized as one of the major libraries and museums of American history whose purpose was "to collect and preserve whatever may relate to the natural, civil or ecclesiastical History of the United States in general and of this State in particular," the New-York Historical Society's holdings reveal some extremely interesting, invaluable, and amusing items in the performing arts. Highlights of the manuscript collection are the scripts, diaries, and correspondence of such luminaries as William Dunlap, Baltimore theatrical manager John Thomson Ford, playwright Annie Elizabeth Burke, actor Charles Walter Couldock, and monologist Ruth Draper. Even more rare and diverse are Jabez Peck's 1786 manuscript prompt copy of *Columbia & Brittannica* as performed at the Clinton Academy in East Hampton; the 1778-1779 Account Book of the Theatre Royal managers; the property book of Richard Gray Riddle (c. 1828) listing plays and properties for the Salem Theatre, Massachusetts; Henry Wadsworth Longfellow's holograph manuscript of his play *The Spanish Student*; the manuscript of a drama written by a Mr. Kellog, who was taken prisoner of war by the Confederate Army at the first Battle of Bull Run, and acted by his fellow prisoners probably in 1861; the autobiography of Mrs. Tom Thumb; the diaries of Gertrude

Kellogg (1863-1902); the papers of playwright and dramatic critic Andrew Carpenter Wheeler; and Voltaire's manuscript of his dramatic *Charlot ou La Comtesse de Givry.*

Aside from the manuscript materials are the playbills of the Baltimore Theatre for the years 1782 and 1783; manuscripts and comprehensive programs of the concert performances of Emma Thursby; 19th-century "Dramatic, Musical and Literary Journals" such as *Figaro, The Critic,* and *The Histrionic*; an extremely outstanding representation of 18th and 19th-century newspapers throughout the United States including the almost unattainable *Royal American Gazette*; a collection of historical material on "Hotels, Taverns, Restaurants and Theatres" prior to 1942; and 19th and 20th-century musical scores, librettos, sheet music (piano and solo instrumental) and programs; the Strobridge Collection of Lithograph Posters of Theatre and Circus; and the Bella C. Landauer Collection of playbills, sheet music, trade cards, bookplates and numerous other items.

Mention must also be made of the Phineas Taylor Barnum circus holdings concerning Barnum's activities as well as those of the circus in general: a sizeable collection of manuscripts, letters, pamphlets, advertising matter, photographs, broadsides, programs, tickets and clippings. Least expected is the E. S. Boughton Collection of Biographies of Silent Screen Actors and Actresses containing press releases, "general information regarding the motion picture business," and a listing of "Motion Picture Actors and Acresses having Large Incomes (1927)". The library is open from 10 a.m. to 5 p.m. Monday through Saturday. There is a nominal charge for non-members of the Society.

Pierpont Morgan Library
29 East 36 Street, 10016
Tel: (212) 685-0008. Founded 1924

The Pierpont Morgan Library is noted for its illuminated manuscripts dating from the sixth to the 16th centuries, its master drawings and Rembrandt etchings, its early printed books and literary first editions, and its autograph manuscripts of such works as Dickens' *A Christmas Carol,* Thackeray's *Vanity Fair* and Balzac's *Eugénie Grandet.*

Foremost in the theatrical holdings is the superb Gilbert & Sullivan Collection, probably the most extensive of its kind and a truly representative example of a collaborative art form of humor, satire, and music of the Victorian age, with its hundreds of manuscripts, pictures, posters and programs. The Mary Flagler Cary Music Collection contains nearly two hundred autograph musical manuscripts including those of most of the great European composers. A Bach cantata, the Beethoven "Geister" trio, the First Symphony of Brahms, the "Goldschmidt" manuscript of Handel's *Messiah,* Gluck manuscripts, a Chopin mazurka, Mozart's violin and piano sonata K. 376, Ponchielli's draft of his opera *La Gioconda,* Schubert's song cycles *Winterreise* and *Schwanengesang* and his quartet "Death and the Maiden," *Don Juan* by Richard Strauss, Schoenberg's *Moses und Aron,* the Diaghilev manuscripts of Stravinsky's *L'Oiseau de Feu,* and an unknown aria for Verdi's *Ernani* (which has now been performed) are but a few of its treasures.

The more than three thousand autograph letters and documents include those of composers, performing artists and individuals associated with the world of music. On deposit are books and manuscripts of the Heineman Foundation, a library particularly strong in French literature of the 18th and 19th centuries and in musical manuscripts, especially Mozart. There are also letters or manuscripts of Goethe, Heine, Rousseau, Napoleon and Maupassant and of 20th-century artists Adolf Busch, Bronislaw Hubermann, Lotte Lehmann and Joseph Szigeti. The library itself has a comprehensive collection of letters of dramatists and actors in its English Autograph Miscellaneous Letters Dramatic Collection. Library hours are Monday through Friday by appointment.

Performing Arts Research Collections 13
in New York City

*Television Information Office
of the National Association of Broadcasters
745 Fifth Avenue (between 57 and 58 Streets), 10022
Tel: (212) 759-6800. Founded 1959.*

The Television Information Office (TIO) was established to provide "a two-way bridge of understanding between the television industry and its many publics," and is supported by the three major television networks (ABC, CBS, NBC), individual commercial stations and groups, educational stations and the National Association of Broadcasters. It provides a continuing information service to meet the needs of educators, students, government agencies, the press, the clergy, librarians, allied communications professionals and the general public, as well as broadcasters.

TIO maintains the nation's most extensive public library and information center covering the social, cultural and programing aspects of television. Its services are sought by individuals within and outside the industry who rely on the library for access to books, periodicals, articles, theses, dissertations, speeches, debates, and other materials. Among the library holdings are extensive research studies, serials, pamphlet and clipping files, and government documents. In addition to its research activities, the library continues to develop and publish a series of annotated bibliographies; e.g. *Television and Education; Television in Government and Politics;* and *Television Careers* which are available at a minimal cost. The TIO library does not, however, cover the technical aspects of the broadcasting industry. Library hours are by appointment Monday through Friday.

*The Walter Hampden Memorial Library at The Players
16 Gramercy Park (East 20 Street between Park Avenue
South and Third Avenue), 10003
Tel: (212) 228-7610. Founded 1957.*

The Walter Hampden Memorial Library evolved from the founding of The Players in 1888 by Edwin Booth — a club where actors and dramatists of repute mingle in good fellowship with craftsmen of the fine arts as well as those of the performing arts. In addition the Club was formally charged with the primary duty of building up "a library relating especially to the history of the American stage, and the preservation of pictures, bills of the play, photographs and curiosities". Booth's nucleus of one thousand volumes has been augmented by hundreds of additions, and the library is now permanently chartered under the Education Law of the State of New York. Its doors were opened to the world of research in 1957 at which time it was renamed in honor of the Club's fourth president.

Included in the Booth papers and correspondence are records dealing with his theatre experience and theatrical business matters; ledgers, account books and journals of Booth's Theatre; the Booth-Barrett and Booth-Modjeska tours; and numerous promptbooks and scripts, letters, photographs and scrapbooks. The Walter Hampden Collection of promptbooks and scripts, letters, photographs, notices and reviews, programs, ledgers, blueprints and drawings also includes the Hampden Theatrical Company records, leases, contracts and route books. At least a third of the John Mulholland Magic Collection is made up of privately circulated material including periodicals issued and edited by magicians which provide the greatest source of biographical and historical data of the past seventy-five years. The thousands of books, letters, programs photographs and advertisement material substantiate the claim that it is one of the country's outstanding collection on magic as a performing art.

The American 20th-century burlesque collection of Chuck Callahan, comedian and script-writer, consists of nearly three hundred burleycue scripts and vaudeville skits, music in manuscript, photographs and a typescript biography of Callahan. Unique to the library is the collection of Players Pipe Night Tapes dating from 1962 honoring individuals of the performing arts. The first program to be recorded was the Lunt-Fontanne Night followed by Maurice Chevalier, Victor Borge, James Cagney, Danny Kaye, Frederic March and Florence Eldridge, and Jack Benny among others. The Union Square Theatre Collection is heavily illustrated with portraits, views, autograph letters, programs, biographies and autobiographies, obituaries, contracts and other contemporaneous material. Other holdings too numerous to describe are the William Henderson Collection of 18th-and-19th-century English playbills and the collections of Tallulah Bankhead, George M. Cohan, Maurice Evans, Max Gordon, Muriel Kirkland, Newman Levy, and Robert B. Mantell. Library hours are from 10 a.m. to 5 p.m., Monday through Friday by appointment.

Yivo Institute for Jewish Research
1048 Fifth Avenue (86 Street), 10028
Tel: (212) 535-6700. Founded 1925.

The YIVO Institute for Jewish Research "engages in research in the Jewish sciences and humanities; collects and preserves documentary and archival material pertaining to Jewish life; trains younger scholars; disseminates information to universities, organizations and the public and publishes scholarly books and periodicals". Its archives consist of records and materials that "revolve primarily around all phases of life of Jewry in Eastern European countries and in all other countries of the world in which Eastern European Jews reside". Among its major fields of specialization is the Yiddish culture, with particular emphasis on its language, literature, press, education and folklore. There is a comprehensive coverage of the Yiddish drama, both in the original and in English translation from its 19th-century beginnings to the present, including folk and juvenile plays. Materials on the history of the Yiddish theatre — its beginnings in the folk plays of the Middle Ages, its modern development in Czarist Russia, the Yiddish theatre in the Soviet Union, and the theatrical activities in the ghettos during the Nazi regime — are available in monographs and periodicals. Specialized periodicals and newspaper items dedicated to theatre and moving pictures are represented as well as biographical and bibliographical sources.

In addition to many manuscripts of Yiddish playwrights, which include texts of published and unpublished dramas and correspondence, there exists the special dramatic collections of Sholem Perelmuter, Mendl Elkin, Maurice Schwartz, Abraham Goldfaden, Jacob Gordin and Mark Schweid — all containing numerous plays in manuscript and printed form, programs, posters, announcements, advertisments, photographs and critics' reviews. Augmenting these holdings are the records of the Union of Jewish Actors in Poland between the two world wars; the Vilna YIVO Collection of posters, playbills and photographs; materials on Boris Tomashevski and Jacob Adler; recordings of theatre songs from 1903 to the present; and the extensive music collection with its scores and sheet music. The above mentioned collections are available for legitimate research to qualified users except in the case of donor-imposed restrictions. Library hours are from 9:30 a.m. to 5:30 p.m., Monday through Friday, except the Jewish and civil holidays.

Film/Broadcasting Resources in the Los Angeles Area

ANNE G. SCHLOSSER

IN RECENT YEARS film and television has become an acceptable scholarly pursuit. The "toy" as it was once called has today become one of the basic forms of communication, a major industry, and one of the most popular forms of creative expression. It has become the only original art form to emerge out of the twentieth-century. Thus, the mass media has come to gain a certain amount of academic respectability. Across the United States, there are various libraries which can support an historical/critical inquiry into the origins and development of film and television. The two main areas for research are New York/Washington, D.C. and Southern California, although there are a number of other valuable collections. In the East there are the magnificent collections at the Museum of Modern Art, the Lincoln Center for the Performing Arts, the Television Information Office, the George Eastman House, and the Library of Congress. In the mid-west a major collection is at the Wisconsin Center for Theatre Research. This article devotes itself however to the research collections in Southern California. Los Angeles is a large place, and it would be helpful to the scholar to know what awaits him before he arrives. There are of course many collections, private and public. This article limits itself to the public, albeit some are open only on a very limited basis.

Margaret Herrick Library
Academy of Motion Picture Arts and Sciences
9038 Melrose Avenue, Los Angeles, Cal. 90069
Head Librarian: Mildred Simpson.

THE MARGARET HERRICK LIBRARY of the Academy of Motion Picture Arts and Sciences is unquestionably the best and largest library in Los Angeles for the study of American film history. Founded in the early 1930's, the Library's prime function was, and still is, to collect data for the annual Academy Awards. The open stack collection contains approximately 9,000 volumes mostly in the English language, covering every aspect of motion pictures: history, criticism, and biography. Foreign language publications are restricted to significant reference works. Only the major technical publications are acquired. Similarly for radio and television only those English language publications of a historical and/or reference nature are purchased. Over 100 current periodicals are received. Included are most of the important U.S. film magazines and trade papers, and selected British periodicals. The Academy Library is well known for its extensive back runs of early motion picture trade magazines. There is a complete set of *Views and Film Index* (1906-), the first industry trade magazine, and a good run of *Bioscope, Motography, Edison Kinetogram* and *New York Clipper.*

Other areas where the collection is especially strong are in the clipping files, periodical indexes, and screenplay collection. For over thirty years, the staff has been clipping pertinent film and television articles from the major trade magazines (e.g., *Variety, Hollywood Reporter*, and *Box Office*) and other general magazines (e.g., *Life, New Yorker, TV Guide, New York Times Sunday Edition, Los Angeles Times*). The Biography File covers all persons associated with the film and television industries. The Motion Picture File includes production articles, reviews, cast and credits, programs, as well as stills, on over 35,000 films. The General File contains articles on countries, genres, and other subjects. Other fascinating files are:

Awards File (excluding Academy Awards), Film Festival Awards File, Guilds and Union File, Independent Producers and Production Companies File, and the very helpful Story Purchase and Title Changes File.

The Theater Arts Reading Room offers students, writers and scholars all the important film and television reference works, a large clipping and biography file on both film and television, stills from major motion pictures including the large Twentieth Century-Fox Collection, and the J.C. Jessen Collection of early (1905-1930) publicity photographs documenting the motion picture industry in Southern California. The FIAF Periodical Indexing Service is also available in the Reading Room. The script collection covers equally well both film and television. Over 3,000 film scripts and continuities are available from such films as *The Friendly Persuasion, The Champion,* and *On the Waterfront.* A marvelous set of scripts are those from the noted cinematographer Gregg Toland, fully annotated with lenses, filters and camera set-ups. Like USC, the UCLA collection has a sizeable number of MGM scripts. The Theater Arts television collection has grown significantly due to the establishment of the National Academy of Television Arts and Sciences-UCLA Television Library. All manuscript material received by the Archive is deposited in the Reading Room. Thus, for example, the collection has a complete set of all *Star Trek* scripts including voluminous production records as well as some 200 to 300 scripts from other television series.

Housed in the Department of Special Collections are the personal collections of such film personalities as Albert E. Smith (founder of the early Vitagraph Company), John Houseman, King Vidor, Kenneth MacGowan, and Dudley Nichols. The George Johnson Collection provides an unparalleled collection of clipping files, indexes, and other data on early Negro films, actors, and actresses, and production companies. The Harold Leonard Film Collection is another important clipping file which covers the period of the U.S. film from

1940 to the early 1960's. This collection was originally designed as source material for the second volume of *The Film Index* (compiled by the WPA and edited by Mr. Leonard). The Oral History Department deposits its transcripts in the Department of Special Collections. Included are interviews with George Cukor, W.W. Hodkinson (founder of Paramount), and Edmund DePatie (former vice-president of Warner Brothers). For radio and television scholars, the Department can offer among other items a large collection of the *NBC Matinee Theatre* radio scripts (1955-1958), Stirling Silliphant papers including scripts from *Route 66*, the Ernie Kovacs Collection, the David Wolper Collection of television scripts and notes from the series *Biography*. Finally there is the great Jack Benny Collection of scripts and records from nearly all of his shows on radio and television.

The UCLA Theater Arts Collection is open to all students, writers, and qualified scholars. A borrowers' card or reference card is necessary but readibly procured at the University Research Library circulation desk. Xeroxing and photographic facilities are amply available.

UCLA *(University of California, Los Angeles)* Film Archive
405 Hilgard Avenue, Los Angeles, Cal. 90024
Director: Howard Suber. Curator: Robert Epstein.

National Academy of Television Arts and Sciences – UCLA Television Library
Theater Arts Department, Room 1438 Melnitz Hall,
University of California, Los Angeles, 405 Hilgard Avenue,
Los Angeles, Cal. 90024.
Director: Ruth Schwartz.

Just a short walk up the UCLA campus the scholar will find the UCLA Film Archive and the National Academy of Television Arts and Sciences — UCLA Television Library. Both archives contain the visual print materials so necessary to complement the book and manuscript collections. The Film Archive was founded in 1967 and has already been accepted as a corresponding member of the International Federation of Film Archives. Out of a 2,100 print collection, the Archive can offer such outstanding items as the studio print collection of Twentieth Century-Fox and Paramount covering the years 1927 to 1953, as well as the personal print collections of Stanley Kramer and Preston Sturges. This archival collection is open to all qualified researchers on request. All prints must be viewed on the UCLA campus.

The magazine index is an invaluable reference source for scholars, as most film magazines are notorious for bad or nonexistent indexing. On a regular basis, all film reviews and articles appearing in the major motion picture magazines are indexed on a card file. One outstanding aspect of this index is that it includes *Photoplay* from 1914 onward. Other magazines indexed are *Sight and Sound, Film Comment, American Cinematographer,* and *Film Quarterly.*

The screenplay collection numbers approximately 1,000 production scripts and continuities from U.S. motion pictures. Included are such titles as *Alice Adams, The Scarlet Empress,* and *The Hunchback of Notre Dame.* Recent acquisitions cover the personal script collection of the late Isobel Lennart and 334 Paramount scripts. For the radio historian the Academy can offer a complete set of the Lux Radio Theatre scripts covering the years 1936 to 1953. Other special collections of which the Library can boast are: the Richard Barthelmess scrapbooks of press clippings, documenting the actor's motion picture career; the Thomas Ince scrapbooks containing stills, cast and credit information and often a synopsis for all the director's pioneering films. Then there are the personal records of prominent motion picture individuals such as Col. Selig and Mack Sennett. In addition there is also the magnificent Paramount Stills Collection, packed in 375 cartons. Due to a severe space shortage, however, this collection is not available for use at the moment.

One of the primary research centers for the study of the U.S.

film, the Margaret Herrick Library is open Monday through Friday, 9 a.m. to 5 p.m., to all Academy members and others engaged in motion picture research. The collection is non-circulating, but xeroxing and photographic facilities are readily available.

UCLA and USC, the two major universities in Los Angeles, complement and supplement the Academy's holdings as both are rich in primary and source materials on the American film. However, by actively collecting foreign language materials, both university collections expand the resources available in Southern California for the study of the European film. And as will be discussed further on, UCLA also offers one of the finest research centers for the television historian.

Department of Special Collections
Doheny Library
University of Southern California
University Park, Los Angeles, Cal. 90007
Department Head: Robert Knutson.

The cinema collection at the University of Southern California is housed in the Department of Special Collections in the Doheny Library. The closed stack collection numbers 6,000 books and 130 currently received periodicals. All aspects of film are included: history, criticism, biography, and technical. The salient feature about this collection results from USC being designated as the Farmington's Plan repository for cinema. For the last 20 years, USC has been acquiring all foreign language materials especially East European publications. Such a collection of Czech, Polish and Russian film books is unequaled in Southern California. Regarding television, all major English language books and periodicals are acquired on a regular basis, but housed in the main stacks of the Doheny Library.

The Performing Arts Collection, as it is called, also offers large and varied clipping files, stills files, scrapbooks, and files of posters/programs/press books. The Library subscribes to the FIAF Periodical Indexing Service, thus providing coverage of some 65 motion picture magazines in all languages. In addition there is a smaller magazine index furnishing references to *Variety* film reviews (1961-1964) and a subject index to the British magazine *Film* (1954-1966). Also on file is an interesting tape collection of lectures, interviews and discussions held with prominent film and television personalities and USC cinema students.

An outstanding script collection is also housed in the Performing Arts Collection. It includes some 7,000 scripts from U.S. sound films, especially from MGM and Twentieth Century-Fox, but also from Warners, Universal, Paramount, etc. There is, in addition, a sizeable number of radio and television scripts such as those from the Amos n' Andy radio show. As for personal papers, USC can offer the scholar the working records of Hal Roach, Albert Lewin, Louella Parsons, Robert Wise, William DeMille, Maurice Jarre, Edward Anhalt, Burns and Allen, and Jerry Lewis, just to mention a few items in this rich collection. Access to the USC cinema holdings is available to all qualified writers and scholars. But one should remember that this too is a non-circulating collection.

Theater Arts Reading Room
University of California, Los Angeles (UCLA), University Research Library
405 Hilgard Avenue, Los Angeles, Cal. 90024.
Librarian: Audree Malkin.

At the University of California in Los Angeles, the Theater Arts Library was founded in the mid-1940's. As a separate branch library the collection covered theater, film, and radio-television. In recent years however the books and periodicals have all been incorporated into the main collection of the University Research Library. The various non-book and special materials are housed in either the Theater Arts Reading Room or in the Department of Special Collections (both also located in the University Research Library). The book and periodical collection numbers some 7,000 volumes on every aspect of motion pictures, both historical/biographical and technical. Current subscriptions are placed for over 170 of the major film and television magazines. The acquisition policy emphasizes the purchase of French, German, and Italian publications. Therefore UCLA provides a good cross section of secondary materials on the West European film. Esoteric as it may seem, it is still worth noting that the Oriental Library does acquire the major works on the Asian film industry written in the Chinese and Japanese scripts. Since the Theater Arts Department has an active program in radio-television production, the Library acquires all English language literature published on the mass media. The major broadcasting periodicals and journals are currently received in the periodicals section of the University Research Library, including *TV Guide*, the only complete record of television programing in Southern California.

The Television Library is a joint project of the National Academy of Television Arts and Sciences and the University of California Regents. Founded in 1965, the Library has become one of the largest and most varied archives devoted to commercial programing. The collection is excelled only by those archives at the Library of Congress and the individual networks. The NATAS Archive acquires a large range of television programing on a local, regional, and network level, from documentaries to drama to comedy to sportscasts, even to commercials. Only a representative sampling of each is acquired; comprehensiveness is not the goal. The 2,000 print collection includes video tape (2", high and low band, b/w and color, and cassettes, and half inch), film (16 and 35 mm, b/w and color) and kinescopes. Outstanding items are 163 program titles from *The Hallmark Hall of Fame* (1952 to 1972), a nearly complete set of *Ralph Story's Los Angeles,* and D.W. Wolper's *Making of the President* series from 1960, 1964, and 1968, plus other Wolper documentaries. Finally, of interest to political scholars as well as media specialists, is the John F. Kennedy Collection. It consists of some 5,000 pieces (speeches, travels, interviews, etc.) documenting the late President's rise from the Senate to the highest office in the land. As previously mentioned, all manuscript materials received with the print collections are deposited in the Theater Arts Reading Room. Such script materials can be borrowed from the Reading Room and taken to the Archive when viewing the related visuals. Access to the Television Library is on an appointment basis only, and materials are restricted to use on the UCLA campus in connection with research and teaching.

Charles K. Feldnan Library
The American Film Institute
501 Doheny Road, Beverly Hills, Cal. 90210
Librarian: Anne G. Schlosser.

The American Film Institute's Center for Advanced Film Studies houses the fourth film research collection. Founded in 1969, the Charles K. Feldman Library was designed to serve the needs of the Center's film study program. The 2,500 volume collection contains all the important film and television reference works and the major publications on history, criticism, and biography. In addition there is a play collection and a short story collection, both of which are used in the directing and writing classes. Emphasis however has been placed on the acquisition of all materials relating to the technical aspects of film and television. Available are books and pamphlets on motion picture production, distribution, financing, copyright and other legal aspects; publications on new video processes and equipment; and information on cable programing, services and regulations.

The special collections program centers around the screenplay collection numbering over 1,500 scripts. These include Mitchell Leisen's annotated shooting scripts, continuities from

John Ford films, scripts from pictures directed by William Wellman, produced by Pandro S. Berman and written by Nunnally Johnson and Robert Riskin. Like UCLA and USC, the Feldman Library also has a large collection of outstanding MGM scripts, as well as 36 scripts from major Twentieth Century-Fox productions. A small working collection of television scripts includes *All in the Family, Columbo,* and *Lassie.* The scrapbook collection includes the Buster Keaton Scrapbook when the comedian was still a child in vaudeville; and the Mike C. Levee Scrapbooks on the ill-fated Screen Guild (1932) and the First National Studios. The Columbia Stills Collection is the only photographic collection at the Feldman Library. It complements the Paramount Collections at the Academy and the Twentieth Century-Fox Collection at UCLA. Finally mention should be made of the 13 volume set of the *Radio Flash,* the house organ of RKO covering the years 1932-1955.

The American Film Institute's Oral History Program funded by the Louis B. Mayer Foundation deposits with the Feldman Library all its tapes and transcripts undertaken in the project. Available are oral history interviews with Pandro S. Berman (producer), Geoffrey Shurlock (MPAA Code and Rating Administration), Allan Dwan (pioneer director), Lee Garmes (cinematographer), and Leo McCarey (director). These transcripts provide the scholar with first hand accounts of the development of the U.S. film industry. The Library is currently cross indexing all the transcripts into a master file of names, titles, and subjects. This will of course produce a more comprehensive reference source for the scholar using these oral histories.

Although relatively small, the Feldman Library can offer the scholar some valuable source material on film and television. The Library is open on a non-circulating basis to all qualified scholars, writers, historians, and industry personnel. Hours of service are Monday through Friday, 9 a.m. to 5:30 p.m.

In addition to the four major film and television research collections mentioned above, Los Angeles has several other important special libraries of which the researcher should be aware. These collections are limited in scope but definitely of importance to any one doing in-depth research in this area.

Industrial Technology Department
Los Angeles County Museum, Exposition Park, Los Angeles, Cal. 90007
Contact: Norwood Teague.

The first collection is located at the Los Angeles County Museum in Exposition Park. Housed in the Industrial Technology Department is a magnificent array of early motion picture projectors, cameras, and other apparatus, as well as catalogs of early equipment, supplies, and parts. Accompanying this collection are back runs of early directories and trade magazines such as the *Society of Motion Picture and Television Engineers Journal* (vol. 1, no. 1-to date), and the *International Photographer* (vol. 1, no. 1-to date). There is also a set of patents for motion picture apparatus covering the period 1860 to 1917. The photographic collection consists of early cameras and other technical equipment as well as stills from silent films and portraits of early actors and actresses. The six volume set of complete Biograph stills is, however, the outstanding item in the photographic collection. Available to researchers is also a small but rare set of correspondence, patents and letterheads from Thomas Edison, Jenkins and Armat (an early Southern California motion picture pioneer); one drawer of production scripts from the 1920's and early 1930's; and numerous film posters and programs.

Very little has been acquired in the television field, but a good collection of radio equipment and other artifacts is preserved. It is probably the largest such collection in Southern California. A valuable set of early technical radio journals complements these pieces, along with a number of supplies and equipment catalogs. For a technological history of the mass media the Department of Industrial Technology is a must.

However, due to limited staff and space the collection is closed except by appointment.

Cecil B. DeMille Collection
2010 DeMille Drive, Los Angeles, Cal.
Contact: Florence Cole.

For the Cecil B. DeMille scholar, the producer-director's personal production records as well as his numerous awards and citations are an incredible resource. These records are all preserved in his personal office at home, located in the old Los Feliz section of Los Angeles. Downstairs next to his Academy Awards are his leather bound, fully annotated shooting scripts for all seventy films. Upstairs there is a small room packed full of stills and photographs from most all of his productions. It should however be pointed out that this is not in any sense a regular library, nor does it pretend to be one. Supervisory staff and reproduction facilities are not available. Therefore access to this DeMille Collection is severely restricted to highly bonafide scholars working on a specific project. A letter of introduction stating one's research needs is necessary before arriving. Another item to be pointed out to the scholar is that DeMille's personal collection of film prints has been deposited with the George Eastman House in Rochester, New York.

Walt Disney Productions Archives
500 South Buena Vista Street, Burbank, Cal. 91505
Archivist: David Smith.

On the studio lot out in Burbank, the Walt Disney Archives was established in 1970 to collect, preserve, and make available for use the Company's historical records. It is the first and only such studio archive in existence. The period covered is that of Walt Disney's career, as well as the company he established and all of its activities, past, present and future. Three types of archival records are preserved:

a. Creative records: drawings, sketches, art work, designs, models, blueprints, etc., for Disney films, television shows, comic books, and all other products and/or enterprises.
b. Business records: personnel and accounting records, surveys, annual reports, as well as production and distribution records.
c. Products: motion picture and television films, stills and photographs, sheet music, character merchandise, and books, articles and other publications on Walt Disney and his films.

In addition to the necessary biography files and credit listings, there are extensive clipping files dating back to 1924 and publicity scrapbooks on every motion picture produced. The screenplay collection includes scripts and continuities for all feature and animated films, as well as shorts, documentaries, and films produced for television. For the animated films, the "drafts" (a more precise term for the script) are especially fascinating. They describe each sequence and cite who directed it and who worked on it.

The personal papers of Walt Disney formed the basis for the archival collection. These papers comprise some 46 file drawers of correspondence, notes, memorabilia, in addition to the 51 Academy Awards won by Disney or Disney films. Other personal collections are those of Carl Barks, Burton Gillett (director of *Three Little Pigs*) and Robert Feild (author of *The Art of Walt Disney*). The Barks Collection is delightful as it consists of his fan letters plus copies of his replies. These replies describe early animation techniques and the development of creative ideas. The Feild Papers cover the period while he was working on the now famous book and include a personal diary he kept while at the studio.

Preserved in the studio film vaults are nearly 100 of the early silent cartoons and almost all of the post-Mickey Mouse (circa 1928) productions. These include of course all films made for television along with the World War II training films. It is important to note that this print collection is not yet generally available for viewing by researchers.

At present the Walt Disney Archives is located in somewhat

limited quarters. But plans are well along on a building specifically designed to house the archive and its magnificent records. This unique studio archive is open to all qualified scholars on an appointment basis only.

Hollywood Center for the Audio-Visual Arts
412 South Parkview, Los Angeles, Cal. 90057
Director: Clarence Inman.

The Hollywood Center for the Audio-Visual Arts offers another research collection for the American film historian. With the demise of the Hollywood Museum in 1965, the City of Los Angeles assumed control of the materials and gave them to the Hollywood Center (a division of the city's Department of Recreation and Parks). The collections range from books and periodicals, to personal papers and scripts, to stills and early motion picture equipment to film prints themselves. The books and manuscripts are currently housed at the Lincoln Heights Jail! As a sampling of the rich resources, there is a complete run of *Photoplay*, the magnificent Frank Borzage Scrapbooks, and the personal records of the early film pioneer Carl Laemmle. Being on nitrate stock, the film prints are stored in the commercial vaults at Bekins and the Hollywood Film Company. While the resources are indeed large and varied, there is no catalog of holdings available for use, and there is no staff member supervising the collections on a full-time basis. Consequently, the Center's materials are to all intents and purposes closed to the general public and to students. However, access is available to serious scholars on a limited basis, if an appointment is made in advance.

First Federal Savings and Loan Association of Hollywood
Hollywood and Highland, Hollywood, Cal. 90028
Contact: Bruce T. Torrence, Senior Vice President.

One looking for stills of early Los Angeles and the emerging film industry should not miss the following two collections. The First Federal Savings and Loan Association of Hollywood offers a sizeable (3,500-4,000) array of still photographs devoted to Hollywood as a community. In this collection there is a special section devoted to motion picture studios. Here of course the boundaries of Hollywood have been extended to include the San Fernando Valley, Edendale, Western Los Angeles, and Santa Monica. Some 500 photographs include Inceville, Tiffany-Stahl, Metro, Christie, Nestors and the old Fox studio. Many of the pictures are aerial shots showing the layout of the various studios over the years. Accompanying these photographs are narrative chronologies of each studio's history. This documentation covers dates founded, original owners and transfers of ownership, and major additions and changes to the studio lot. The Association will make these materials available to any researcher making an appointment in advance. Reproduction facilities are available.

Security Pacific National Bank, Head Office, Los Angeles, Cal.
Bank Historian: Victor R. Plukas.

The California History Collection at the Security Pacific National Bank includes some 250,000 photographs covering the state from San Francisco down to San Diego. One file drawer is devoted to motion pictures — the personalities, the films, sundry technical equipment, sets, and the studios. Included are some unique early photographs of the Los Angeles area before and during the development of the motion picture industry. This collection is also open to the public on an appointment basis.

Finally, attention should be called to the many local commercial enterprises concerned with film and television. In addition to the libraries and special collections, these business concerns can, for a price, offer a wealth of material to the writer and historian.

Most everyone knows about the Larry Edmunds Book Store with the "world's largest collection of books on the cinema." Located at 6658 Hollywood Boulevard in Hollywood, California 90028, Larry Edmunds does have a seemingly inexhaustable stock of books, periodicals, posters, programs, and stills, concerning motion pictures and television, from the early years to the latest item just off the press. But there are also other good stores in town besides Edmunds. For example, a few blocks down the street is Bennetts Book Store, 6763 Hollywood Boulevard, offering most of the current English language film and television publications, along with a vast collection of stills, posters, programs, etc. This latter advertising and publicity material is fast becoming a special emphasis for Bennetts. Stills are also available at the Cherokee Book Shop, P.O. Box 3427, 6607 Hollywood Boulevard, and Eddie Brandt's Saturday Matinee, 6501 Lankershim Boulevard, North Hollywood, California 91609. The latter store is off the beaten track in the San Fernando Valley, but well worth the trip. Eddie Brandt has a mammoth collection of stills and photographs on any person, place, film, or studio. Finally, in a slightly different line of interest, one looking for legal and copyright information on film and television should not miss the Seven Arts Press, 6430 Sunset Boulevard, Hollywood, California 90028. This company has a good collection of books, catalogs, and card files on entertainment law. These are the people who recently published *Your Introduction to Film-TV Copyright, Contracts and Other Law* and *Film Superlist, 2000 Motion Pictures in the Public Domain.* Use of this library is available to any one with serious interests in this area. An appointment is necessary, however.

A Survey of the Ohio State University Theatre Research Institute

ALAN WOODS

IN 1950, PROFESSOR JOHN H. MCDOWELL of The Ohio State University faced a major dilemma. As Director of Theatre within the university's Department of Speech, he guided doctoral candidates preparing dissertations, but found a persistent and growing difficulty in the little research material locally available: Ohio State is located in Columbus, Ohio, which, while the state capital and possessing rich collections of materials pertaining to Ohio's history, had little to offer the theatre scholar. The university's library was fully professional and more than adequately supported undergraduate and graduate class work, but it did not contain significant primary sources specifically usable by the would-be Ph.D. in theatre.

McDowell's response to his problem was creative: instead of attempting to obtain a large (and expensive) collection of primary documents or training a generation of students as local theatre historians — both of which would have been valid approaches — McDowell founded the Ohio State University Theatre Collection. Based on his firm belief that primary materials could be obtained on film and that the study of the filmed documents (judiciously supplemented with research trips to examine the actual material itself) would prove possible, McDowell began amassing large quantities of microfilm. Initial acquisitions included filmed copies of the Donald Oenslager scene design collection, obtained through Oenslager's kind assistance, and large numbers of promptscripts from The New York Public Library's Theatre Collection, then headed by the late George Freedley.

By 1973 when Professor McDowell retired, his original plans had succeeded astoundingly. The OSU Theatre Collection had grown in the intervening twenty-three years both in amount of material and in function. Recently renamed The Ohio State University Theatre Research Institute, McDowell's creation serves as the major graduate research facility for the university's Department of Theatre (itself the result of a recent university reorganization) and the College of the Arts. Although the Institute and its work are widely known abroad, its potential benefit for American theatre researchers has not yet been generally recognized. This essay attempts to provide a brief summary of the Institute's holdings as well as to give some information about the Institute's role within the university's theatre program.

The collections of the Ohio State University Theatre Research Institute are in three discrete, yet interrelated, units: the John H. McDowell Film Archives, the OSU Theatre Museum, and the Print and Document File. All three are presently housed at the Institute's research center in OSU's Thompson Library.

The John H. McDowell Film Archives

The McDowell Film Archives constitute the core of the Institute's holdings. Over four hundred thousand frames of 35 millimeter microfilm are currently catalogued, with more film continually being added. All of the film, stored either in reels or in strips enclosed in protective acetate jackets, is the product of a vigorous acquisition program and is instantly available for study at the Institute.

The film has been obtained through the courtesy of over fifty American and European museums and libraries since 1950. Although in some instances direct orders are placed with institutions who have published catalogs of their holdings (notably the British Museum and The New York Public Library), the major portion of the filmed documents has been selected by researchers working directly at the original library or museum; the lengthy list of such researchers included in each issue of *Theatre Studies*, the Institute's annual journal, gives some indication of the scope of this continuing operation.

To make the rich material on film readily available for research purposes, Professor McDowell and his staff developed the unique *Research Classification System*, which provides a six-digit code for each frame of microfilm. A specialized catalog card was also developed to permit the use of extensive cross-reference files created by reproducing the original card.[1] Files, therefore, exist not only for the *RCS* code, which permit the retrieval of similar materials for comparative studies, but also for *artist, theatre,* and *play title.* A researcher can thus draw upon the *RCS* file to study similar types of scene designs[2] or to trace the development of a specific theatrical form;[3] the *artist* file permits studying the work of any individual;[4] while the *theatre* file aids analyzing the history of physical theatres[5] and the *play title* file brings together material relating to an individual play.[6]

The exhaustive catalogues at present exist solely in card form in Columbus.[7] Several short lists of materials have been published, however, which provide some indication of the scope and range of materials within the McDowell Archives.[8] These various handlists and checklists reveal two of the McDowell Archives' major areas of strength: festival books of the late Renaissance, and the materials from the nineteenth century theatre, especially that of England. The McDowell Archives are particularly rich in festival books depicting royal entries, marriages, funerals, and various state celebrations; the materials have been drawn from repositories throughout France, the Netherlands, Germany, and Italy. As the Cooperman handlist indiates, the McDowell Archives also include great quantities of promptbooks (well over a thousand from English authors alone) and playscripts from the nineteenth century. In addition to English plays, the McDowell Archives include promptbooks from Vienna's Burgtheater, the National Theatre of Hungary, the Comédie Française, and from various American cities.

One of the richest areas within the McDowell Archives not

indicated by handlists thus far published is that of scene and costume designs. The detailed classification system for scene designs with the *RCS* only hints at the wealth of material gathered from Italian, French, Dutch, English and Scandinavian sources, among others. The hundreds of designs generously donated by Donald Oenslager now form the heart of an enormous number of filmed designs. As is the case with most of the materials housed within the Theatre Research Institute, the McDowell Archives are richest in designs from the sixteenth through the nineteenth centuries, although significant amounts of materials exist for other historical periods. Similarly, large numbers of costume designs have been filmed, both from original plates and from rare books of engravings. Photographic developments in recent years have made it possible to film most recent acquisitions in color, making the filmed costume plates even more valuable. Numerous textual materials have also been included in the McDowell Archives: diaries, treatises on scene design, descriptions of festivals, critical materials from rare newspapers and journals, and various manuscript sources.

The John H. McDowell Film Archives were created for the sole function of providing a research resource; the examination of primary documents on film is at best only a preliminary stage of research, and many of the projects begun at The Ohio State University Theatre Research Institute are completed only after traveling to examine the actual materials. The goal in developing the McDowell Archives, however, has been to permit initial study at a readily accessible site in the United States, study which will allow the researcher to make more efficient use of time at the great theatrical research libraries and museums of the world. To this end, materials have been filmed throughout Europe, making it possible for the researcher to compare materials from widely separated locations.

Acquisition has, of course, depended on the cooperation and gracious assistance of the museums and libraries possessing the original documents. To permit acquisition to continue, the Theatre Research Institute has adopted strict rules governing the uses of the microfilm it holds. The firm principle that the Institute's filmed copies exist solely for research purposes has been successfully maintained since the McDowell Archives were established: film is copied only with the express written permission of the institution owning the original material. This rule applies to all reproductions of filmed documents, whether for unpublished work (theses and dissertations) or for published articles and books. The McDowell Archives are not a repository of rare original documents, but rather copies of such documents; the ultimate control over the film's reproduction rests not with the Institute but with the original library.

The OSU Theatre Museum

Although the vast majority of material within the collections of the Theatre Research Institute is contained in the John H. McDowell Film Archives, the Institute does possess a small number of original materials. Most of these collections — the Armbruster Collection, the Harmount *Uncle Tom's Cabin* Collection, the several scrapbook collections — are outlined in Young[9] and therefore will not be detailed here.

The OSU Theatre Museum consists of these collections and of other materials: an extensive playbill collection, documents tracing the history of the OSU Theatre Department's productions, and similar items. Also included in the Museum are a large number of models reconstructing important theatre and technical devices. Used primarily as instructional devices, the models of the Theatre Museum make it possible to graphically demonstrate the workings of the *changement-à-vue* system, several different kinds of nineteenth-century traps, and a seventeenth-century wave machine. All of the technical models and many of the theatre reconstructions have been built from rare plans and documents found in the McDowell Archives.

The Print and Document File

In addition to the original materials collected in the OSU Theatre Museum, the Theatre Research Institute also maintains an extensive collection of secondary research documents, including journals, articles, books, clippings, photographs, brochures. These documents are housed in the Print and Document File, and are catalogued with the microfilmed sources. The Print and Document File does not attempt to serve as a drama library; the Theatre Research Institute draws upon the excellent collections of the Ohio State University Main Library resources, and has consciously attempted not to duplicate materials readily available through that system.[10]

Virtually all the material in both the OSU Theatre Museum and the Print and Document File has been acquired by gift or donation. The models in the Museum and the background work on filmed materials in the Print and Document File are the results of ongoing work within the Institute itself. In the latter category are included numerous bibliographies of holdings within the University Library and the McDowell Archives, catalogues of the various collections, promptbook analyses, and various other unpublished reports of the research work performed by Institute staff members and students.

This brief survey of the research materials held within The Ohio State University Theatre Research Institute given above, it is hoped, provides some hint as to the range of the Institute's collections. The role of the Theatre Research Institute within the Department of Theatre at Ohio State is perhaps apparent from the amount and type of materials included in the McDowell Archives. The Archives, Museum, and Print and Document File are the basic materials which the Institute employs in its function as a research and service facility for the Department of Theatre, the College of The Arts, and for the University.

The primary role of the Theatre Research Institute is, as its name states, theatrical research. Through its collections, it provides the basic materials for most of the theses and dissertations written at OSU in the field of theatre history. The Institute also furnishes support for advanced student research in other theatre fields, supplying desk space within the library, assistance in locating and obtaining material for study, and general advisement. In addition, the Institute annually publishes *Theatre Studies* to report on research in progress at Ohio State. First issued in 1954, *Theatre Studies* is distributed without charge to interested scholars, libraries, and museums around the world; it has a circulation of fourteen hundred.

On several occasions, issues of *Theatre Studies* (until 1971 *The Ohio State University Theatre Collection Bulletin*) have been devoted to single subject areas: royal festivals, Juvarra's playhouse built for Cardinal Ottoboni, and Dumont's theatrical activities in the Jesuit college of Rome are three recent examples. The last mentioned issue (No. 16), published in 1969, is perhaps the clearest example of the continuing work sponsored by the Institute: the project began in 1962 and is still in progress. It has involved visits to Rome and other European cities, as well as research trips to New York, London, and Paris. Several advanced seminars have been held to explore various aspects of eighteenth-century Jesuit theatre and technical production practices. Thus a single project, prompted by the four unidentified engravings in Dumont's *Parallèle des plus belles salles de spectacle d'Italie et de France* (Paris, 1763), has resulted in a widening series of related explorations involving theatrical architecture, production, and repertory in the late eighteenth century. The Dumont research is not unique; similar projects have been in progress at the Institute since its founding, with their results apparent both through publication in *Theatre Studies* and in the appearance of numerous theses and dissertations.

In addition to scholarship of the traditional kind just outlined, the Theatre Research Institute also sponsors production research. Several plays presented by the Department of Theatre — most recently Molière's *School For Wives*, which drew upon several promptbooks from the Comédie Française — have been carefully researched by Institute staff and departmental designers in preparing for actual performance. Similarly, a production of Bulwer-Lytton's *Richelieu*, scheduled for perfomance in 1974, will be adapted from the Institute's filmed copy of William Macready's promptbook for the 1839 premiere. Staff of the Institute are also working with the OSU Center for Medieval and Renaissance Studies, preparing a production of *The Play of Herod* from the Fleury manuscript. If current plans are realized, such productions will occur on a more regular basis in the future.

The Theatre Research Institute also functions in a service capacity for the Department of Theatre, providing direct instruction for a series of thirteen courses (on various levels) in theatre history. The Institute supplies instructional support through the several thousand slides in its collection, the maintaining of a reserve shelf for students in the Master of Fine Arts program, and through the use of models from the Theatre Museum. Staff members provide program notes and general background materials for departmental productions. Occasional displays of rare items from the Theatre Museum and Print and Document File are held in the University theatre building as well as in the Institute itself. The Theatre Research Institute also schedules a series of *converzationi* with students, staff, and visiting scholars; topics scheduled for the 1973-1974 academic year range from Classic vase paintings of theatrical music instruments to the origins of the Spanish *zarzuela*. These informal meetings permit a free interchange of theories and information, and materially assist the Institute's instructional program.

In the previous discussion I have attempted to provide a brief general overview of The Ohio State University Theatre Research Institute, its holdings and its functions as the major research facility of OSU's Department of Theatre. It remains only to mention that the Institute's staff is pleased to provide whatever assistance possible to scholars and researchers who wish to employ the Institute's resources for preliminary stages of their work. As indicated earlier, material from the McDowell Archives cannot be copied without consent of the institution holding the original document, a factor which in most instances means that researchers must come to Columbus to fully utilize the Institute's holdings. If, however, that procedure simplifies necessary trips to many different repositories of theatrical materials around the world, an essential aim of the Theatre Research Institute will have been realized.

Notes

1. The *RCS* system is explained in John C. Morrow, "OSU Theatre Collection: A Unique Facility," *Players Magazine*, No. 41 (November 1964), 57-58.

2. Cf. Roger Allan Hall, "Neo-Classic and Romantic Destruction: Scene Designs of Ruins From 1700 to 1850," *Theatre Studies*, No. 19 (1972-1973), 7-15.

3. Cf. Louis Otto Erdmann, "The Printed Festival Book: A Study of Northern Continental Festivals in the Late Sixteenth Century" (unpublished Ph.D. dissertation, Ohio State University, 1966).

4. Cf. William Henry Zucchero, "The Contributions of James F. Neill to the Development of the Modern American Theatrical Stock Company" (unpublished Ph.D. dissertation, Ohio State University, 1964).

5. Cf. Konrad Zobel and Frederick E. Warner, "The Old Burgtheater: A Structural History, 1741-1888," *Theatre Studies*, No. 19 (1972-73) 19-53.

6. Cf. John David Burke, "The Stage History of London Productions of George Farquhar's *The Recruiting Officer*, 1796-1964" (unpublished Ph.D. dissertation, Ohio State University, 1971).

7. Planning is currently under way to produce a printed catalogue of the McDowell Archives; the project is now in the beginning stages.

8. Cf. Allan S. Jackson and John C. Morrow, "Handlist of Acqua-Dramas Presented at Sadler's Wells, 1805-1824, *OSTUC Bulletin*, No. 9 (1962), 40-48; Richard L. Grupenhoff, "The Lord Mayor's Shows: From Their Origins to 1640," *Theatre Studies*, No. 18, (1971-72), 13-22; Corwin A. Georges, Jr. and Konrad Zobel, "Entrances and Exits in the *Theatrum Mundi*: A Checklist of Documentation of Entries and Funerals in the OSU Theatre Research Institute with a Postscript on the Social Aspects of Courtly Festivals," *Theatre Studies*, No. 18 (1971-72), 23-33; Gail B. Cooperman, "A Handlist of British Drama in the McDowell Archives of The Ohio State University Theatre Research Insti-

tute, 1800-1850: Part I," *Theatre Studies*, No. 19, (1972-73), 60-73; Alan Hedges, "The Henry Betty Promptbooks: A Survey," *Theatre Studies*, No. 19 (1972-73), 77-83.

9. William C. Young, *American Theatrical Arts* (Chicago: American Library Association, 1971), p. 100.

10. This reliance upon the University Library has permitted The Theatre Research Institute to concentrate upon the acquisition of filmed primary source documents; reference works necessary for the full utilization of the McDowell Archives are housed in the Library. It is for this reason that the Institute itself is located within the University's Main Library building. Hugh Atkinson, University Librarian, and his staff have always been most cooperative in assisting the Theatre Research Institute through book and serial acquisition. In turn, the Institute's journal, *Theatre Studies,* is an increasingly requested element in the library's exchange program.

FREDERICK J.
HUNTER

Theatre and Drama Research Sources at the University of Texas at Austin

WHILE THE THREE ORIGINAL COLLECTIONS of rare books and manuscripts at the University of Texas — the Wrenn, Aitken, and Stark collections — contain much that is valuable to students of drama and theatre, the past two decades have seen a marked increase in library sources in this extensive field of cultural history.

In June, 1954, the Hoblitzelle Foundation (under the direction of Karl Hoblitzelle, a Dallas philanthropist and theatre owner) deposited at the University, on permanent loan, the James Orchard Halliwell-Phillips edition of Shakespeare (1853-1865): sixteen volumes of plays and sixteen portfolio volumes containing two thousand illustrative plates for the plays. In 1956, the library of William James Battle (for many years Professor of Classical Languages at the University), with some 10,634 volumes, became a part of the classics library. In this gift there came some important editions of classical drama, including the complete Plautus with commentary by Lambinus printed in Geneva in 1620, and another edited by Gronovius and printed in Leipzig in 1760.

The holdings of the classic libraries together with the acquisition of the E.A. Parsons collection made available the early editions of nearly all classical drama from Aeschylus to Seneca. The 40,000-volume Parsons collection, which arrived in June, 1958, includes a sizable section on the history of art, architecture, and design, including early prints of Leonardo da

Vinci, Benvenuto Cellini, and twenty-nine folio volumes of the work of Giovanni Piranesi, the eighteenth century architect and stage designer. This collection, assembled over the past eighty years in New Orleans, came to the University of Texas through the contributions of Mr. and Mrs. St. John Garwood of Austin, Mr. and Mrs. Will Clayton, and the M.D. Anderson Foundation of Houston.

On November 17, 1958, the T.E. Hanley Library of 150,000 items was purchased by the University. This famous collection consists of first editions, presentation copies, and manuscripts of many nineteen and twentieth century authors, English and American. Of particular interest to scholars of the drama are manuscripts and correspondence of Yeats, Wilde, Galsworthy, Barrie, and Eliot. It also contains one of the largest bodies of Shavian dramatic materials in the United States.

As early as February, 1956, the Hoblitzelle Foundation had presented to the University the Albert Davis collection of theatrical artifacts, including posters, programs, and photographs which had been assembled diligently by Mr. Davis between 1874 and 1942 in Brooklyn, New York. It was with this collection that the library acquired the first materials on the history of motion pictures in the United States. Its movie stills, books, and early photographs, when augmented by the more recent additions of the Interstate Circuit, the E.V. Richards, and the Ernest Lehmann collections, make a good beginning for the motion picture division of the Theatre Arts Library. The Albert Davis collection was also the first one here to contain sources and original documents for the study of American theatre history. Rather than "fugitive materials" as they are sometimes described by librarians, these artifacts such as programs, clippings, photographs, cash books, and production contracts become in this context the fundamentals for objective theatre research.

In June, 1958, the Messmore Kendall theatre collection, including those materials gathered by William Winter, Augustin Daly, Thomas McKee, and Harry Houdini, became a part of the Theatre Arts Library, and is still the richest of any in auto-graphs, engravings, programs, and extra-illustrated books. It is particularly rich in materials on the Kembles, David Garrick, P.T. Barnum, Edmund Kean, Charles Matthews, and the Bacon-Shakespeare controversy. This controversy was also extensively covered in the library of Frank Woodward of London which was purchased for the University from Dr. Burnell F. Ruth in 1959. Likewise, the collection of opera librettos in the Kendall Library was considerably augmented by those purchased with the Edwin Bachmann collection of music in June, 1958.

Three months later, in September, 1958, the Edgar G. Tobin Foundation of San Antonio purchased and made the gift of the complete Norman Bel Geddes Collection of Design to the University, which placed it for restoration, preservation, and cataloguing in the Theatre Arts Library. Mr. Robert L.B. Tobin, president of the Edgar G. Tobin Foundation, among his many activities, has served as a director and impresario of opera in San Antonio and Santa Fe; has been the leader of the Arts Festival of Spoleto, Italy; and was one of the first persons to be aware of the great theatrical value of this huge collection. *The Catalog of the Norman Bel Geddes Theatre Collection* by Frederick J. Hunter has recently been published by G.K. Hall press.

Through the efforts of Chancellor Emeritus Harry H. Ransom, the Robert Downing Theatre Collection was purchased in 1965 to give major support to the Hoblitzelle Theatre Arts Library with its additional research potential. The Robert Downing Collection contains not only five thousand books on the history and theory of the theatre but also a large collection of photographs, typescripts of plays, the Lacy acting editions, and many American plays inscribed by the authors. There are also sketches and floor plans from the productions for which Mr. Downing was stage manager.

During the next year, the John Gassner Collection was acquired, and it included not only the manuscripts and notes made by the critic himself but all his sources in books, articles, and plays which he had used. It is an extensive collection of materials in the area of dramatic theory and criticism.

Since that time, a number of other collections, both large and small have been acquired by the Theatre Arts Library and the Humanities Research Center as a whole. They include dissertations on theatre and drama reproduced on microfilm and out-of-print plays contributed by the Department of Drama, the Leo Perper playbills and Dance collection for the period 1930 to 1965, the Simon Lissom collection, Jule Styne musical scores, the Ernest Lehmann motion picture manuscripts, the George C. Howard collection of manuscripts and nineteenth century acting editions of plays, and the Elmer Rice collection of production notebooks and historical sources.

These collections, when taken together, contain many thousands of unique and irreplaceable items. Altogether, they encompass the performance history in such theatrical centers as London, New York, Boston, and Philadelphia over the past two hundred years and give some data on most of the performers of any note during that period. The Theatre Arts Library alone contains at least two hundred thousand playbills from the period, fifty thousand engravings and photographs of performers and scenes from plays, ten thousand clippings, twenty thousand pieces of sheet music, and five thousand original letters which tell of theatrical performances from London to Australia. In addition, there are at least ten thousand bound volumes of theatrical history and biography, one thousand pamphlets and unbound books, dozens of account books of theatres, and scrapbooks of many players and playgoers.

When coordinated with materials in other collections in the Humanities Research Center, such as the Hanley collection of George Bernard Shaw, the Parsons collection, the Wrenn and Aitken collections, the Stark collection, and the manuscripts of modern American playwrights (Maxwell Anderson, Lillian Hellman, Arthur Miller, and Tennessee Williams), there can be little doubt that continuing contributions and purchases at the

University of Texas will make it an outstanding repository of research materials for the study of theatre history and dramatic literature.

Theatrical Holdings of the Folger Shakespeare Library

NATI H. KRIVASKY
LAETITIA YEANDLE

THE FOLGER SHAKESPEARE LIBRARY is a research institution devoted to the study of the Renaissance with special emphasis on the humanities. Its collections cover the sixteenth and seventeenth centuries and are strongest in all aspects of British civilization. There are however many supplementary works dealing with life on the Continent.

Since the original collection was formed around Shakespeare, theatrical holdings are particularly strong. The Folger contains the world's largest collection of original editions and reprints of Shakespeare's works. The works of sixteenth and early seventeenth century writers, Shakespeare's contemporaries, are also well represented. The large collection of the works of Restoration playwrights is especially strong in John Dryden, Thomas Shadwell and Nahum Tate, with their adaptations of Shakespeare's works, e.g. the adaptation of the *Tempest* by Dryden in conjunction with Sir William D'Avenant. The Library's eighteenth century theatrical holdings are dominated by David Garrick (1717-1779), who produced many of Shakespeare's plays in his own version during his long management of Drury Lane Theatre. There are many collections of nineteenth century plays, including Inchbald's *The British Theatre* (125 plays), Oxberry's *The New English Drama* (113 plays) and Lacy's *Acting Edition of Plays* in 100 volumes. In addition, the Folger Library has a large collection of Continental plays, numerous Neo-Latin dramas and an extensive collection of Italian plays, listed in Louise Clubb's bibliography *Italian Plays (1500-1700) in the Folger Library* (1968).

The original editions of the plays and other theatrical source materials are supplemented by more recent scholarly editions of the same works and facsimile reprints. The Library has a comprehensive collection of reference works concerning the plays, their authors, the theatres where they were performed, and other aspects of theatrical history. An attempt is made to acquire all currently published scholarly works having relevance to the civilization of the sixteenth and seventeenth centuries.

Of great historical importance and immediate theatrical use are the approximately 3000 promptbooks — Shakespearean and non-Shakespearean — mainly pre-1920, including most of the Smock Alley books. The Smock Alley Theatre in Dublin, also known as Ogilby's Theatre, opened after the Restoration in 1662. The new theatre was built by John Ogilby (1600-1676) who obtained the patent for Master of the Revels in Ireland from Charles II on May 8, 1661. These Smock Alley promptbooks are made up of leaves from a Third Folio. According to G. Blakemore Evans, *Shakespearean Promptbooks* (1960-   ), they date from about 1676 to 1685. The eighteenth century promptbooks include those of Garrick, manager of Drury Lane Theatre from 1747 to 1776. These promptbooks supplement the Library's large collection of Garrickiana described below in the survey of theatrical manuscripts. John Philip Kemble's promptbooks relate to Covent Garden Theatre, of which he was manager from 1803 till 1808. The nineteenth century brought many changes and innovations to the theatre; the great productions of this period are reflected in the promptbooks of actor-managers William Charles Macready, Samuel Phelps, and Charles Kean. May of these are illustrated with drawings of set designs. Charles Kean wanted his productions to be as historically accurate as possible and had people carry out research for him at the British Museum and elsewhere.

The American promptbooks date from the nineteenth century, including Augustin Daly's. Daly (1838-1899) was a playwright, producer, author and adapter of plays, lessee of the Fifth Avenue Theatre and Daly's Theatre in New York City from 1869 to 1899. His company and productions were celebrated for taste and Daly's was the first American company to visit England. The promptbooks of John Moore (1814-1893) who had been with Daly for twenty three years as stage manager, prompter and actor, are also present. A rich source of information about Daly's productions are the extra-illustrated volumes of Shakespeare's plays, as produced at Daly's Theatre, containing portraits of actors and actresses, watercolor sketches of costumes, photographs of scenes and playbills.

Other nineteenth century American promptbooks include some of George Becks' (1835-1904), actor and theatrical collector; a set of Edward Sothern's (1859-1933) and Julia Marlowe's (1866-1950); and a group of Henry Jewett's (1862-1930). Jewett directed in Boston the first civic repertory theatre in the United States.

All Shakespeare promptbooks have been listed by Charles H. Shattuck in *The Shakespeare Promptbooks* (1965).

There are some 250,000 playbills of the English and American stages, arranged and listed by city, theatre and season. They start about 1692 and the strongest period is from 1820 to 1870. The London playbills date mainly from the middle to the end of the nineteenth century, but there are strong holdings in the late eighteenth century. Provincial theatres are also represented: Theatre Royal in Bath, Theatre Royal in Birmingham, Queen's Theatre in Dublin, Adelphi Theatre in Edinburgh, Theatre Royal in Edinburgh, Theatre Royal in Manchester, Theatre Royal in York — to mention only a few.

The American playbills are mostly from the 1810's to the 1910's, the strongest period being the second half of the nineteenth century. There are playbills of the Philadelphia, Boston, New York theatres and a number of others.

Supplementing these collections are the 50,000 literary and theatrical prints, engravings, photographs, drawings, watercolors, etc., mainly from the nineteenth century. A group of late eighteenth century engravings contains portraits of actors and actresses in various roles. The costume designs include one hundred original pencil and watercolor designs by John Seymour Lucas for Sir Henry Irving's production of Shakespeare's *King Henry VIII*, on January 5, 1892, at the Royal Lyceum Theatre in London. There are also costume designs by Lucas for *Hamlet, King Lear* and *Macbeth*. Charles Kean's (1811?-1863) costume books include about 900 watercolor drawings of costumes, scenes and scenery used in Shakespearean productions.

A large part of the art is cataloged and listed by artist, engraver and subject. Work is in progress on remaining pieces in the collection.

The scrapbook collection covers approximately the years 1750-1920 and its main emphasis is on theatrical history and Shakespeare. The scrapbooks contain mostly clippings from newspapers and magazines; some also have portraits of actors, playbills and manuscript notes added.

The manuscript collection is strong in theatrical material. One of the most important sources for the history of the stage in the sixteenth century is the Loseley collection. Sir William More (1520-1600) of Loseley Park in Surrey was an executor of the will of Sir Thomas Cawarden (d. 1559), Master of the Revels under Henry VIII, Edward VI, Mary and Elizabeth, from 1545 until his death. Among Cawarden's papers are many letters, warrants, inventories, bills and receipts, accounts and regulations of this office. The Master of the Revels was responsible for the entertainment given at Court, the most prolonged and elaborate being provided during the twelve days of Christmas, at Shrovetide, and to celebrate the coronation of a sovereign. Sir Thomas Cawarden had profited from Henry's dissolution of the monasteries. He had acquired property in the Black Friars monastery on the edges of the city of London and on his death it came into the possession of Sir William More. Some of its buildings became in Elizabeth's reign the home of two well-known theatres, the first Blackfriars Theatre, 1576-1584, and the second Blackfriars Theatre established in 1600. The deeds, surveys, accounts, depositions and other documents in the Loseley collection have proved to be a mine of information on these early theatres. Albert Feuillerat transcribed many of them in his *Documents Relating to the Revels at Court* (1914), and Mr. Irwin Smith used them to try and reconstruct the design and dimensions of the rooms used for the theatre in his *Shakespeare's Playhouse* (1964).

There are over fifty manuscript plays of the seventeenth century, and a dozen of the later sixteenth century. Some of these are fragmentary. The only fifteenth century plays are in the Macro manuscript — "Mankind", "Wisdom" and "The castle of perseverance". The plays have been listed by Alfred Harbage and S. Schoenbaum in *Annals of English Drama* (1940) and its supplements (1966-1970). One group of eight plays belonged to the Lambarde family of Kent. The earliest known manuscript copy of a play of Shakespeare's, a condensation of *King Henry IV*, Parts 1 and 2, was written about 1620 for the Dering family of Kent to be used in one of its private theatricals. The Library has published facsimile editions of the Macro manuscript and the *Henry IV*. A play known as "The Country Gentleman", acquired in 1947, was recently identified by Mr. A.H. Scouten and Mr. R.D. Hume as a nearly contemporary copy of a "lost" play written by Sir Robert Howard with a scene added by the Duke of Buckingham. It had been hastily withdrawn by Charles II for political reasons in 1669 before it was ever performed and had been known only from a few references in contemporary manuscripts. There are also several copies of William Henry Ireland's play *Vortigern* which he alleged to be by Shakespeare.

As stated above, David Garrick figures prominently in the Folger. Not only was he famous in his theatrical career, he also was a friend of many of the leading men and women of his time. The Library has about 300 of his letters, innumerable prologues and epilogues, a considerable quantity of verse and several plays he wrote or adapted, sometimes with the cooperation of

George Colman the elder. Some are copies with or without his corrections, some are drafts. Garrick was the first to honor Shakespeare with a festival and his papers give many glimpses of this "Jubilee" held at Stratford-upon-Avon in 1769.

Few English dramatists or actors and actresses of any consequence are not represented in the manuscript collection. There are some plays and diaries, but mostly letters — from Mrs. Siddons, Mrs. Cibber, Mrs. Abington, George Frederick Cooke, Mrs. Clive, Mrs. Pope, George Colman the elder and George Colman the younger, Thomas King, Hannah More, Richard Brinsley Sheridan, Richard Cumberland, William Smith, Samuel Foote, Edmund Kean, John Philip Kemble, Charles Kemble, Fanny Kemble, Edwin Forrest, William Charles Macready, Sir Henry Irving, Ellen Terry and many others. All of the material complements the promptbook collection. The partbooks of J.P. Kemble occupy half a shelf, and the value of the material on Fanny Kemble was enhanced greatly when Mrs. Walter Stokes of Pennsylvania gave the Library four large volumes of the letters of her ancestor. The mass of material relating to Charles and Ellen Kean is very varied. It includes the letters she wrote home during their tour of the United States during the Civil War.

One of the richest sources for the history of the eighteenth and nineteenth century stage in England is a long run of the records of Drury Lane Theatre, 1766-1880. They include the official journals and nightly accounts (1766-1852), ledgers, paybooks, agreements entered into between the theatre and performers, inventories, registers of subscribers, lists of plays and a volume of plans for the rebuilding of the theatre by Benjamin Wyatt in 1812 after it was destroyed by fire. They are most complete for the period when Garrick and, after him, Sheridan, were the managers. There are bills and receipts for the early part of the eighteenth century when Barton Booth, Colley Cibber and Robert Wilks managed the theatre together, and a list of plays acted at Lincoln's Inn Fields and Drury Lane from 1714 to 1723. Two prompters, Richard Cross and later

William Hopkins, kept a list of the plays given from 1747 to 1776 and from time to time jotted down comments on their reception and anything of exceptional interest that occurred during the performances.

The records of Covent Garden Theatre are sparse by comparison. They are mainly journals and nightly and weekly accounts of the period 1740 to 1851.

Another source of stage history in the eighteenth and nineteenth centuries is the notebooks of James Winston (1773-1843). The Folger is but one of several libraries where his voluminous notes are to be found. He culled newspapers, playbills, letters for his material and if a reader is willing to wade through them he will find much information. Winston seems to have been preparing a history of the stage but was anticipated by John Genest.

For the majority of its manuscripts on the theatre in the United States of America the Folger is indebted to two people, Augustin Daly and William Winter (1836-1917). Daly seems to have kept every letter that he ever received from established and aspiring actors and actresses, playwrights and adapters, agents in Europe, and friends — Edwin Booth, John Drew, Mrs. Gilbert, the Davenport family, Ada Rehan, Lawrence Barrett, Charlotte Cushman, Agnes Ethel, Wilkie Collins, Bronson Howard, Joseph Jefferson, Richard Mansfield, Brander Matthews, Helena Modjeska, A.M. Palmer, Sir Arthur Pinero, E.A. Sothern, Sir Arthur Sullivan, William Terriss, J.L. Wallack, "Mark Twain", Dion Boucicault, Victorien Sardou, Sir Henry Irving, Ellen Terry, to name a very few. There are over 4000 letters besides some of his own letters, volumes of playbills, contracts, a few volumes of receipts, and other documents. Daly negotiated with Lord Tennyson to put on the first production of "The Foresters" in 1893. Daly was also a collector. Some of the most interesting theatrical material of the eighteenth century in this library, such as many of the Drury Lane records and several volumes of the Garrick manuscripts, once belonged to him.

William Winter was for most of his professional life the

dramatic editor of the *New York Herald Tribune*. He conducted an enormous correspondence with countless people connected with the theatre and it has supplemented many existing holdings as well as adding significantly to their interest. Over three fifths of the 500 letters of Edwin Booth were addressed to William Winter.

After the early twentieth century there are few manuscripts to illustrate the history of the theatre. The manuscripts are concentrated in the preceding four centuries.

Library holdings in printed books and manuscripts are listed in the catalogs published by G.K. Hall: *Catalog of Printed Books of the Folger Shakespeare Library* (1970) and *Catalog of Manuscripts of the Folger Shakespeare Library* (1971).

The Belknap Collection of Performing Arts: University of Florida Libraries

LARAINE CORRELL

THE BELKNAP COLLECTION for the Performing Arts is the new name for the Dance, Music and Theatre Archives located in the University of Florida Libraries at Gainesville, Florida. As a performing arts library, the Belknap Collection accepts depositories of the ephemera of the performing and recorded arts, preserving the materials for scholars and enthusiasts, present and future. The ephemera includes all non-book materials pertaining to theatre, dance, music and the cinema which are frequently lost or thrown away, such as playbills and programmes, heralds, posters, scrapbooks, designs, photographs, prints, clippings, news letters, events calendars, press releases, in-house publications and even advertising circulars. In short, any material is sought which documents the arts activities of professional and amateur performing companies, arts organizations and schools. Concentration is mainly on the United States and Canada, but some materials are regularly received from Europe and Latin America. While a few items date back to the fifteenth century, most of the holdings are from the mid-nineteenth century to the present.

The Belknap Collection is very deliberate about collecting current ephemera. Five hundred organizations regularly supply the collection with up-to-date materials and information about themselves. The majority of all new acquisitions are received through the mail in this manner, averaging about twenty items each day. Each organization, company or school is asked to send whatever they feel they can afford in terms of time, postage and cost of materials. Without exception response to these requests is most generous and, incidentally, most unpredictable as to exactly what will be sent. Many companies must limit their donations to performance programmes for each show, either sending the material on an item-by-item basis or waiting until the end of the season to send everything at once. Occasionally only calendars of events or season subscription brochures are sent. Even less frequently the Collection receives color slides of shows or beautiful souvenir publications. The Canadian Broadcasting Corporation faithfully sends their daily programing notes.

In addition to solicitations, the Belknap Collection is fortunate to have exchange programs for duplicate materials with other performing arts libraries, notably the Crawford Collection from Yale University, The New York Public Library Theatre Research Collection, and the Wisconsin Center for Theatre Research. Except for regional material which is saved to offer in exchange, duplicate items go on to such collections as the new American Theatre Library-Museum at Florida State University. Of course, many thoughtful individuals present mementos they have been saving all their lives, or perhaps those which they have assembled from a recent vacation. Occasionally items are purchased for the collection from a small acquisitions budget.

The Belknap Collection was originally founded in 1953 as the Dance and Music Archives, "Theatre" was added to the title later. New York librarian Sara Yancey Belknap was deeply devoted to the arts and throughout her lifetime had collected ephemera of the performing arts. On her retirement she moved to Gainesville, Florida, and decided to offer her considerable collection to the Special Collections Department of the University of Florida Libraries. For the next ten years Mrs. Belknap stayed on as the Dance, Music and Theatre Archives' first curator. During this period she began her index series, *Guide to the Performing Arts*, and most of the items she used to compile this series were added to the collection. Crowded conditions in the Special Collections area forced most of her "treasures" into boxes which were stacked around her or hidden away in remote library storage areas, making public service almost impossible. Undaunted, however, Mrs. Belknap continued her efforts to secure additional materials for the collection and initiated the present practice of direct solicitation of performing arts organizations for current materials.

In 1967 a new library building was completed and the Special Collections Department moved into the fourth and fifth floors. Mrs, Belknap was no longer the curator, but the Dance, Music and Theatre Archives had continued to grow slowly under her guidelines. Her "treasures" were at last removed from storage and placed in special cabinets designed to hold 12 by 15 inch suspension files. Some materials were best kept in the traditional metal vertical file cabinets. Fortunately, all the shelving was slotted with removable metal dividers, an enormously versatile storage system for such types of materials. With physical space and storage containers now available for the collection's materials, attention was immediately focused on the bibliographic control of the collection. Mrs. Belknap had been severely handicapped in the arrangement of the collection when it had been in boxes and crowded file cabinets. She had devised a basic geographic approach which brought the collection needed cohesion. However, the collection had now grown and become more complicated. The geographic approach was cumbersome and relied on inadequate cross-referencing. Under that system an item was entered first by the name of the city with which it was associated, followed by the name of the theatre, producing organization, school, company, publisher, subject or individual. This had the only advantage of bringing together on the shelf all materials pertaining to each city. Duplicate and inaccurate entries abounded, unfortunately. Cities in the Los Angeles area were a special problem: there were two sections of folders for the Hollywood Bowl, for instance, one under "HOLLYWOOD, CALIF. HOLLYWOOD

BOWL" and the other under "LOS ANGELES, CALIF. HOLLYWOOD BOWL"; a pamphlet on the theatre publications of University Microfilms was entered: "ANN ARBOR, MICH. THEATRE"; colleges and universities were arranged alphabetically by the city in which they were located, without cross-references; individuals had to be entered by a city with which they might be associated. "HAVANNA, CUBA. ALICIA ALONSO" seemed logical enough, but the entry "NEW YORK. VALERIE BETTIS" was not helpful. The whole system was awkward.

Many changes have taken place in the collection since 1970 when the present curator was employed to take charge of the Dance, Music and Theatre Archives. At that time the library was anxious to broaden the collection's base of services to the public and wanted to begin publicizing the collection's resources. In 1971 the collection was given departmental status, and an annual acquisitions budget was assigned. The decision was also made to change officially the name of the collection to the Belknap Collection for the Performing Arts.

Probably the most significant change to occur, however, was the reorganization of the bibliographic structure of the collection. Most collections of the performing arts materials center around one specific art form, usually dance, music or theatre, and the classification system is tailored to that one art form. A system which would successfully integrate a collection comprised of two centuries of all the performing and recorded arts was clearly needed. The challenge to devise such a system was made clearer when work began to construct a new subject authority file, now composed of six hundred terms and headings. The reorganization of the entire collection was designed to be people-oriented rather than librarian-oriented, at least as much as possible. Patrons are allowed, with initial assistance from the curator, to browse in the collection and search for information themselves. It should be pointed out, however, that the Collection has a reader seating capacity of four and all work is done under the supervision of a clerk or the curator.

Materials are non-circulating, with some exceptions which will be noted later.

Two other principles guided the reclassification. The first was that main entries would be reassigned by actual names of theatres, organizations and individuals, although, because of the generality of some materials, geographic subject headings, such as "INDONESIA: DANCE", would be allowed. The second principle was that instead of forcing one encompassing system on the entire collection, certain materials should be removed from the core collection and set up as satellite collections with internal arrangements of their own. A large number of non-regional performance programmes were removed and rearranged into Theatre Programmes, Opera Programmes, Cinema Programmes, Music Programmes and Dance Programmes. Miscellaneous entertainments such as magic, circus, puppetry and ice shows remained in the core collection. The theatre, opera and cinema programmes were filed on open shelves by title of production, since seven out of ten patrons requested this material by titles rather than by authors, specific city, or theatre. They are, of course, cross-referenced in the card catalog. Dance and music programmes were arranged basically by format or by country; typical entries are "MUSIC PROGRAMMES: CHAMBER ENSEMBLES" and "DANCE PROGRAMMES: FOLK DANCING". The materials of all specific performing companies were retained in the core collection under such entries as "TULSA LITTLE THEATRE" or "SAN FRANCISCO OPERA HOUSE".

There were many requests for Shakespearean materials, so all programmes, promptscripts, company and festival files and prints relating to Shakespearean productions were brought together. Another popular request dealt with film materials, although there is only a small amount of this type of material in proportion to the other arts. All film, radio and television scripts were filed together in a vertical file next to the Cinema Programmes Collection and then the miscellaneous cinema materials were grouped in adjacent cabinets. This is a favorite place for patrons to browse for their own amusement and information.

College and University Arts Activities, one of the most frequently used collections, was already arranged separately from the core collection, but its arrangement was awkward. The main entry was the city in which the particular school was located. This collection was re-shelved by States and the folders within that division filed alphabetically by the name of the school. Thus a desirable geographic orientation was maintained and materials from one school were kept on the shelf, including schools with branch campuses in different cities. To aid the many organizations in the Gainesville, Florida area who are producing shows, production information materials were removed from the core collection, sorted into broad subject categories such as "LIGHTING" and "COSTUMES", and placed alphabetically in Hollinger boxes by the manufacturer's or distributor's name. A collection of performing arts bibliographies were similarly arranged.

The following is a more detailed account of the Belknap Collection's holdings as they are now arranged. The staff does all the processing and cataloging, with the exception of a small number of books, periodicals and microfilm, which are handled by the library's Catalog Department. Within the Belknap Collection there is the equivalent of a sixty drawer card catalog. However, the only items which are listed in the public union catalog are the books, periodicals and microfilm.

International Performing Arts Archives

This is the core collection consisting of six thousand main entries. It contains past and current materials from all the performing and recorded arts, represented in the form of performance schedules, season brochures, press releases, clippings, histories, pamphlets, announcements, posters, newsletters, flyers, and in the case of performing companies, their programmes and souvenir booklets. The shelf arrangement is by main entry (personal, corporate or geographic).

College and University Arts Archives
There are materials from five hundred schools representing all fifty states. The types of materials a school will send are catalogs, descriptions of academic arts programs, calendars of campus events, posters, brochures, clippings and programmes. Materials for each school are sorted into four categories: dance, theatre, music and general, with special categories as needed. The slotted shelving has fifty large markers designating each state, and each school is filed alphabetically within the markers.

Book Collection and Microfilm
There is a small book collection and periodical collection of seven thousand volumes as well as a growing microfilm collection of two hundred reels. These items are cataloged by the library staff using the Dewey Decimal System. Acquisitions of books is restricted due to space problems and because students do not have access to them when the collection is closed for the day or on weekends.

Performance Programmes
Non-regional playbills, flyers, clippings, souvenir and regular programmes in this collection number about 50,000. They are filed on open slotted shelving in regular file folders and sorted into separate collections of theatre, dance, music, opera and cinema. All regional performing company programmes are filed in the core collection.

Production Information Files
This section contains twelve linear feet of current catalogs and information sheets as well as older research catalogs from businesses dealing with costuming, lighting, scenic design, publicity and all phases of production in any art form. They are

filed by subject in Hollinger boxes, and then by name of manufacturer.

Performing Arts Bibliographies
Current and antiquarian catalogs, bibliographies, discographies, filmographies and rental catalogs dealing with the performing arts are contained in this section. Placed in Hollinger boxes by subject and then filed by publisher or book dealer, they are considered a part of the Production Information Files.

Photographic Collection
This collection consists of 10,000 opera, ballet, theatre, radio, television and film photographs. They are placed in acid-free folders with tissue paper between them and kept in tightly packed metal vertical files. The arrangement is by title of production, company or celebrity.

Prints and Engravings
This is a small collection of 1,000 prints and engravings of famous theatrical personalities, including an original William Hogarth engraving of Garrick as Richard III. It will be indexed and arranged in alphabetical order in print boxes.

Ringling Museum Theatre Collection
Acquired from the Ringling Museum of Art fifteen years ago, this is a small but extremely rich collection of theatrical materials from the nineteenth and early twentieth centuries, although some scripts and other items date from the fifteenth century. The playbills and heralds number about 150,000. They are chiefly from the British Isles and America, arranged roughly by country, city and name of theatre. They require delicate handling and since no adequate storage containers are available, the collection is not yet cataloged. Limited use of the materials is allowed. In addition, there are 8,000 photographs of performers from the nineteenth and early twentieth century, many in their

theatrical costumes, and most of them are autographed. They have been placed in acid-free boxes and indexed by personal name. This collection also has about 2,000 programmes, several hundred scripts and a number of scrapbooks from the period.

Shakespearean Collection
All materials in the Belknap Collection pertaining to Shakespeare, production of his plays, and the major Shakespearean companies and festivals have been brought physically together for the convenience of researchers. In addition to programmes and company information, 150 copies of promptscripts of early Shakespearean productions and a small collection of prints and engravings has been added to this unit.

Green Collection of American Sheet Music
Although the Music Study Center normally houses all the scores for the library system, this particular collection of 1,000 illustrated scores was acquired for two reasons: first, because the music reflected the home entertainment of a Florida family from 1830 to 1950, and second, a great deal of the music is popular burlesque and Broadway show tunes which parallel other materials in the Belknap Collection. The music is now sorted chronologically. It is a very popular collection.

Archival Depositories
A special project of the Belknap Collection has been to collect and preserve information on the activities of the arts and cultural groups in Florida so that these records may be a part of any records of social and political history. In addition to receiving miscellaneous materials from over three hundred Florida arts groups, an archival depository service is offered for their important documents, correspondence, financial records and other archival materials. The largest holdings are from the Florida Music Educators Association and from the Florida League of the Arts.

Reference books are kept in the Reference and Bibliography section of the main library. Books on the theatre are shelved in the general stacks in the building and there are several branch libraries on campus that hold related materials. The Music Study Center houses scores and recordings; the Architecture and Fine Arts Library has music and art; the Physical Education Reading Room includes dance; and the Journalism and Communications Reading Room holds materials on film and broadcasting. Within the Division of Special Resources, the Department of Rare Books and Manuscripts holds books and documents of interest to the patrons of the Belknap Collection, as does the P.K. Yonge Library of Florida History. The Latin American Collection has many items on Latin American arts.

Materials from the Belknap Collection are taken to schools and to arts groups in the region. Currently, the staff is also helping the Florida League of the Arts survey the arts in Florida and acting as a clearing house for arts funding information for local and state groups.

This twentieth anniversary year is being celebrated by renaming the Dance, Music and Theatre Archives for the founder and first curator, Sara Yancey Belknap, who now lives in Texas and still collects and sends materials. Twenty years ago the original collection was cramped, unindexed, and boxed in a small alcove as part of the Special Collections Department. Today the Belknap Collection, three times its original size, is an independent department in a new library building, providing extensive services and resources to students and scholars of the performing arts.

KAY JOHNSON

The Wisconsin Center for Theatre Research

THE WISCONSIN CENTER for Theater Research was founded in 1960 as a cooperative venture of the University of Wisconsin and the State Historical Society of Wisconsin. Drawing on the strengths of both institutions the Center has become, in little more than a decade, one of the nation's leading repositories of primary source materials in theatre, film, television and radio. Continually growing, the Center's archive now includes more than 150 collections of individuals and organizations in the performing arts.

The rationale for the establishment of the Center is, in general terms, identical to the rationale of all special collections — history has many facets, and the records of all kinds of human activity must be preserved so that they can be studied and understood. Only within the last fifty years have American historians come to realize that the pursuit of their craft demands more than the study of political documents; that "history" also includes, among other subjects, the way men make a living, the gods they choose to worship, the classes into which they are divided, and the arts which they produce. The arts were not often thoroughly investigated, however, because documents relating to them were unavailable. Scholarly research depends to a large extent on what archives hold, and only recently have documents in theatre, film, television and radio been collected consistently and with foresight, anticipating future research interests.

The specific rationale for the Center's establishment, then, is that the modes of man's artistry and his means of communica-

The Wisconsin Center for Theatre Research

tion shed revealing light on his existence. Man's participation in the drama is age-old, but his sophisticated use of film, television and radio is a unique aspect of the twentieth century. Even theatre has matured in the United States only since the 1920's. So the Center's decision was to collect primary resources — correspondence, scripts, financial and legal records, photographs, designs, films, tape recordings — relating to American theatre, film, television and radio in the last half-century.

The Center invites individuals and organizations to donate their papers, and the collections are organized by an archival staff trained in both history and the arts. Thorough cataloging results in a detailed inventory of each collection; these inventories are available to researchers, who use the collections in the manuscripts reading room and the film archive of the State Historical Society.

The materials collected are extensive and diverse, providing rich and even endless opportunities for research. The lists below are offered with the understanding that they are selective and not exhaustive. In addition, the categories — theatre, film, television and radio — are not mutually exclusive; that is, artists work within several media, so that in a playwright's collection there might well be much information regarding his work as a screenwriter. Indeed, the Center attempts to document an individual's career and his personal life as completely as possible, so that almost all of the collections contain biographical as well as professional information.

Theatre

Collections of playwrights and composers — S.N. Behrman, Marc Blitzstein, Edna Ferber, George S. Kaufman, Arthur Kober, Morrie Ryskind, Howard Lindsay and Russel Crouse, Moss Hart — provide in-depth studies of theatre in the 1920's, 30's and 40's. Sometimes only a finished script is available; often — as in the thick, scrawled diaries of Behrman — one can see the evolution of a work, from the notes that reflect the beginning of an idea, through the outlines and several revisions, to the final prompt-script. Blitzstein's large collection, 78 boxes, contains correspondence that reveals not only the mind and heart of the man, but his relation to the times in which he lived. Of course, an abundance of scores illustrate the work of this innovative composer and lyricist.

These collections are important in and of themselves. They also form the background for studying the men and women who followed — Paul Osborn, Frances Goodrich and Albert Hackett, N. Richard Nash, Sheldon Harnick, Joseph Stein, Jean Kerr, Gore Vidal, Murray Schisgal, Ulu Grosbard, Michael Stewart, Stephen Sondheim. Just as Blieztein's *The Cradle Will Rock* catches the tension of the depression thirties, so do Sondheim's lyrics for *West Side Story* capture the complexities of urban America in the 1950's.

Different perspectives on the theatre are provided by the papers of Broadway's foremost producers: the Playwrights' Company, Dwight Deere Wiman, David Merrick, Herman Levin, Kermit Bloomgarden, Michael Myerberg, David Susskind, Herman Shumlin, Richard Myers, Hillard Elkins, and Gilbert Cates. Contracts, budgets, financial statements and box office receipts of the Playwrights' Company, for example, illustrate the changing nature of Broadway economics, from the days when it was possible to mount a show for less than $25,000, to 1960 when the cost had risen astronomically and necessitated new methods of financing. Voluminous documentation on *The Music Man* and *My Fair Lady* shows this condition aggravated in the case of musicals, and these successes always have their counterparts in costly failures. It would be virtually impossible to study the economics of modern American theatre without the data in these producers' collections. Further, they also illumine the artistic facets of production, since they contain correspondence with playwrights, scripts and various revisions, prompt scripts with directors' notations, designs — all of the modifications that help interpret an original work for the audience that watches it.

Still other aspects of the theatre are featured in the collections of directors like Alan Schneider, actors like Hal Holbrook, set designers like Wolfgang Roth and Albert Johnson, lighting designers like Jean Rosenthal, critics like Walter Kerr, regional theaters like the Milwaukee Repertory Theatre, and politically-conscious groups like the San Francisco Mime Troupe.

Film

In 1971 the Center opened its United Artists collection, the single largest film collection ever given to a research institution. This collection is the foundation of the Center's Film Archive and provides a wealth of raw material on film history, never before available in one place. Contractual arrangements with producers, domestic and foreign exchange records, correspondence, legal briefs, minutes of the board of directors, and advertising campaigns make up the corporate records of United Artists, 1919-1950. They reveal the economic operation of the distribution company and provide a microcosm of the motion picture industry.

The Warners, RKO and Monogram film libraries are an integral part of the UA collection. The Warners library covers the years 1913-1950 and includes production files; legal files; 50 silent features; 800 sound features; 1,500 short subjects; 300 cartoons, 19,000 stills; and 150 pressbooks. 700 RKO sound features cover the years 1929-1954. Two hundred sound features (1931-1946) in the Monogram film library are supplemented by 6,000 still negatives and 80 pressbooks.

It is possible to examine in the United Artists collection the role of producers whose films the company distributed. Other collections offer even broader dimensions to this study. In the papers of the Aitken Brothers, for instance, are correspondence and business records that detail the production, financing and distribution of both silent and sound films over a period of four decades, 1900-1939. Twenty-six file cases from Walter Wanger extend the production documentation into the sixties; there is comprehensive information on the films this illustrious producer made during a thirty-year period. Correspondence and scripts in the Dore Schary collection illustrate the changing career of a writer who became the head of a studio. And nearly

100 boxes of Kirk Douglas' papers reveal the problems and satisfactions of an actor who formed his own production company.

The United Artists collection contains the work of such directors as Orson Welles, Michael Curtiz, William Wellman, John Ford and Jean Renoir and thus provides a comparative basis for the discrete collections from contemporary directors like John Frankenheimer, Abraham Polonsky, George Seaton, Robert Altman and Norman Jewison. Nor are the achievements of screenwriters neglected, for the Center holds the collections of I.A.L. Diamond, Howard Koch, Dale Wasserman, John Wexley and others, as well as many playwrights who journeyed to Hollywood and wrote for motion pictures.

A significant portion of the Center's Film Archive is devoted to the blacklist as it operated in the motion picture industry. The collections of five of the Hollywood Ten — Alvah Bessie, Herbert Biberman, Albert Maltz, Samuel Ornitz and Dalton Trumbo — are available for research, as well as a small collection from Ring Lardner, Jr. An important supplement are the papers of attorneys who represented the Ten — Robert W. Kenny and Robert S. Morris, and Arthur Galligan and Ben Margolis. The papers of Gordon Kahn and Nedrick Young also contain information pertinent to this infamous period, as do those of several other men and women who were directly affected by the blacklist. Further information on the political mood of Hollywood in the 1940's and 1950's is available in the documents and tape recordings donated by the Hollywood Democratic Committee.

Other political and social concerns are apparent in the work of documentary filmmakers like Emile de Antonio, Shirley Clarke and Lionel Rogosin. De Antonio's collection is particularly rich; its variety and depth make it valuable to students of history, political science, sociology and art as well. A wide selection of de Antonio's personal and professional papers; 128 tape recorded interviews dealing with the 1968 presidential campaign and the Vietnam conflict; kinescopes of the televised

Army-McCarthy hearings of 1954; and hundreds of thousands of feet of film dealing with the political career of Richard Nixon, and with modern art in the United States — here is "political theatre" at its finest.

Finally, within the Center's Film Archive is an iconographic resource of more than one million items. The collection of theatre and film historian Daniel Blum comprises the foundation; added to it are more than 100,000 still negatives from the United Artists collection and large general still collection.

Television and Radio

Over the past quarter-century the quantity of information and entertainment which the American public digests has increased enormously because of television; all of our lives reflect the influence of this particular channel of mass communication and mass culture. Understanding this, the Center has committed itself to collecting documents relating to television.

The Ziv television library (1948-1962), acquired by United Artists, is the largest collection of non-network programing in the country. Ziv Television Programs, Inc. was a major producer and packager of original dramatic programs for first-run syndicated use, and its library contains 2,000 episodes — prints and negatives — from thirty-eight television series, such as *I Led Three Lives, East Side/West Side*, and *Yesterday's Newsreel*; 2,000 shooting scripts and 38,000 still negatives complement the films. Three other collections also have large numbers of films. Nat Hiken's papers include sixty-nine programs from the Sergeant Bilko show, *You'll Never Get Rich*, 1955-1957, and seventy films from other series he either wrote or produced. Among the Reginald Rose papers are 132 films, the complete *Defenders* series, which ran for five consecutive seasons beginning in 1960. A smaller number of films in the David Dortort papers illustrate *Bonanza* throughout its long run, 1959-1973. The collections also include, of course, manuscript materials for these and other series.

In the collections of other writers and producers are illustrations of television programs ranging from early live broadcasts to the present taped shows. The careers of many writers — David Victor, William Spier, Hal Kanter, Alvin Boretz, Max Ehrlich, David Harmon, Ernest Kinoy, Jerome Ross — began in radio and continued into television, as the child outgrew the parent. One hundred and fifty scripts from *Suspense*, 250 from *The Adventures of Sam Spade*, and 90 from *The Big Story* — many of them annotated and with related production materials — provide examples of radio's output during the forties; and outstanding examples of television's "Golden Age" in the fifties are found in the papers of Paddy Chayefsky, Rod Serling, Howard Rodman, and David Davidson, in addition to the writers listed above. Television's capacity for producing live drama is illustrated in documents from *Playhouse 90, Studio One, The U.S. Steel Hour, The Hallmark Hall of Fame, Armstrong Circle Theatre*, and many other series. More recent popular shows like *Dr. Kildare, Mr. Novak, Ironside, The Untouchables* appear in the papers of writers and producers like E. Jack Neuman, Norman Katkov, Loring Mandel, and Winston Miller.

Television's unique potential for providing the public with a perspective on historical questions, and for analyzing contemporary problems, is reflected in the collections of documentary writers and producers Richard Hanser, Donald Hyatt, Burton Benjamin and Ernest Pendrell. Information on *The Twentieth Century, Project XX*, and *Victory at Sea* is extensive; many of the scripts of *Victory at Sea* are supplemented by films.

Specialized television collections are those of Ed Sullivan, which provides information on the host's long-running variety show; Peter Dohanos, which contains many designs from *The Bell Telephone Hour*; Arthur Cantor, which shows the work of a publicity agent for television shows; and Clark Jones, which reveals the complex and highly technical nature of the work of a director. In addition, the Center's sister organization, the Mass Communications History Center, holds the massive collections of NBC and NET.

In summary, then, the archive of the Wisconsin Center for Theatre Research enables researchers to study the arts — as creative expression, important in and of themselves; as social comment, a product of the times in which they were created; as business, often subject to rigorous financial considerations; or as technology, requiring skilled men and sophisticated equipment. The collecting of primary sources, it is hoped, will aid inquiry into past and present, bringing a breadth of vision and a depth of understanding to both.

RAY B. BROWNE
WILLIAM SCHURK

The Popular Culture Library and Audio Center

THE POPULAR CULTURE LIBRARY and Audio Center at Bowling Green State University's Center for the Study of Popular Culture began with a gift of various materials (books, phonograph records, artifacts, etc.) worth approximately $100,000 fom Bill Randle, Cleveland, Ohio, radio personality. Since 1969, when the library opened, the collection has grown to more than 250,000 items worth over half a million dollars. ture as an academic discipline, however, the purpose has grown far beyond these original boundaries. Scholars, laymen, and college, public and special libraries are becoming aware of the specialized holdings and are making heavy use of the collection. The goal always has been and continues to be that of making the collection into the finest working library in Popular Culture in the world.

Included in the Popular Culture Library are both hardcover and paperback books, magazines and a myriad of non-book materials. Nothing circulates, and only Xerox copies are available on interlibrary loan. This policy has had to be enforced because of the special nature of the materials within the collection. Not that any items are particularly rare, but much is ephemeral in nature, brittle, poor by construction, and frequently unavailable in replacement copies.

Books include both fiction and non-fiction. Novels from all periods and countries are represented, but emphasis is placed on Anglo-American imprints. Classic fiction is included but the more "popular" writings are most sought after.

These include mysteries, science-fiction, romance, adventure, war, and juvenile series. The collection is especially strong in the series writings, including large holdings of *Bobbsey Twins*, *Tarzan*, *Lone Ranger*, *Elsie Dinsmore*, *Tom Swift*, and *The Boy Scouts*, plus hundreds of lesser known series.

Paperbacks are just as, if not more, important than hardbound books, principally because of their gaudy jacket artwork and also because many were never published in any other form. (On many occasions jackets were designed to coincide with a contemporary movie version of the book.) Holdings in the Library number over 5000 items.

Non-fiction includes such subject areas as the occult and supernatural, etiquette and grooming, cookery, games and sports, popular histories and biographies, wit and humor, graphic art and cartoons, and the performing arts (dance, movies, TV, radio, music, and theater). Non-fiction materials include cartoon books, old grammars, popular reference works, hymnals, pornography, and popular juveniles.

Non-book collections include posters, comic books, Big Little Books, pulp fiction, dime novels, scrapbooks, photographs, picture postcards, matchbooks, cigar bands, newspapers, baseball and other trading cards, pamphlets, portraits, dealer and manufacturer catalogs, political memorabilia, pennants, souvenirs, movie pressbooks, theater programs, and much more.

A number of magazines are received on subscription (*Playboy*, *Variety*, *Mad*, *National Police Gazette*, *Photoplay*, and others), but long runs have also been received as gifts (*Life*, 1936-1964; *National Geographic*, 1920-1970; *Playboy*, 1958-1970; and *Esquire*, 1932-1946). There are also short runs and sample issues of over 500 titles, including *Male*, *True Confessions*, *Eros*, *Lunatickle*, *Shadowland*, *Motor Trend*, *Custom Rod*, and *Front Page Detective*.

The American Antiquarian Society has just recently donated hundreds of old popular, joke, and girlie magazines from their backfiles. Also received from another source were one person's newsstand purchases made in 1943, covering all types of magazines popular at that time.

One area in which the Popular Culture Library is making considerable thrust is in collecting manuscripts, page proofs, galleys, notes, correspondence, etc. Nearly one hundred authors are represented in the holdings. Undoubtedly the largest single collection is that of Irwin Wallace. These manuscript collections are the subjects of numerous research papers, Master's theses and Ph.D. dissertations.

Because of an inadequate annual budget, buying for the collections is usually done in a most unorthodox manner (at least for libraries). Second-hand stores are constantly scoured in the Toledo-Cleveland-Detroit area, and conferences are always welcome because new sources can be tapped. The collections rely heavily on the Goodwill Industries, the Salvation Army, St. Vincent De Paul, and Volunteers of America.

Garage sales are always investigated and auctions are sometimes attended. Antique stores can be good sources at times but their prices can frequently be quite out of range.

Some libraries have been most generous in allowing members of the staff to browse through their gift stacks and select books for the collections. Three major sources thus far included the Cleveland Public Library, the Toledo-Lucas County Public and the Bowling Green Public Library.

The Audio Center is a vital part of the Popular Culture Collection.

Subject materials on record include jazz, blues, gospel, comedy, musical, movie and television soundtrack music, documentary, poetry, prose, drama, folk music and folklore, popular music (rock, rhythm and blues, country and western), dance bands, and juvenile (i.e. commercial kiddie).

The Center also houses a collection of approximately 1000 reels of tape and about 100 pre-recorded cassettes. One of the special collections on tape includes over 600 hours of old radio shows such as *The Shadow, The Green Hornet,* and *Jack Benny.* The Bowling Green State University Living Archives, also on tape, consists of interviews with writers, musicians, vaudeville performers, and other performers, and other persons of a popular nature. A third major tape collection includes a 400 hour accumulation of old-time and bluegrass music dating from the early 1920's to the present.

Virtually every type and subject of recorded material commercially and non-commercially available is sought to be included in the Center's Collection. By item count the Center has approximately five hundred cylinder recordings, thirty-five thousand LP albums, sixty thousand 45 rpm discs, and fifteen thousand 78 rpm records.

Unique holdings include, among other items, a large collection of bootleg rock recordings, most of which will soon be quite rare since the new copyright laws forbid these from being either manufactured or sold. There are also special collections of jazz air-shots (recorded from radio) from the 1940's, and over 1000 radio spot ad discs dating back to the early 1950's.

One wish has always been that every record company would deposit one copy of each 45 rpm single and LP album which they release for the Center's files. This is probably too optimistic; however, the Audio Center would be a most logical clearing house for storing such primary sources.

A supporting collection of reference books, periodicals, and various files is also maintained in the Center. The reference materials include among other items, biographical directories, discographies, and numerical listings: Magazine subscriptions include such titles as *Rolling Stone, Downbeat, Blues Unlimited, Muleskinner News,* and *Record Exchanger.* Files are kept for portraits, biographies, manufacturer and dealer catalogs, release notices, and LP record inner paper sleeves and 45 and 78 rpm outer paper sleeves.

A number of years ago BMI agreed to supply the Audio Center on a continuing basis with all record release notices which they received. These have been put in order in file cabinets and now serve as a most valuable reference tool. They also donated large backfiles of records, catalogs, magazines, and biographies.

Donations of materials are encouraged at all times. No item is too ephemeral for consideration. In fact, the more insignificant an item may appear, the more value it may have for either of these two collections.

The Center appeals to the public at large to donate whatever they have, and especially to libraries for their duplicates and discards and for those items which are proposed to them for which they have no real use or room.

Members of the Popular Culture staff will be pleased to travel, within a distance of 150 miles, to talk to groups such as Friends of the Library, Library Trustees, Library Directors or Librarians, or individuals with sizable collections.

For further information please write to Mr. William L. Schurk, Popular Culture and Audio Librarian, University Library, Bowling Green State University, Bowling Green, Ohio, 43043. (Telephone: (419) 372-2855), or Ray B. Browne, Director, Center for the Study of Popular Culture, Bowling Green State University, Bowling Green, Ohio, 43403. (Telephone: (419) 372-2610).

JAMES POWERS

The Film History Program of the Center for Advanced Film Studies of The American Film Institute

THE MAKERS of American films have been characteristically American: careless of the present and heedless of the future. In a way they cannot be blamed. At the beginning nobody took films very seriously. They were considered an item of commerce by their makers and by the public a rather disreputable item of commerce. Although there was some attempt at preservation of film for purely financial purposes, more often once a film had played out its run, it was discarded.

What was true of American films was true of American filmmakers. Except for known and famous exceptions, the literature about films for the first generation of their life in America demonstrated the contempt or disinterest in which films were held. The histories, biographies and stories about American film in this early period are almost all "fan" orientated material. They are almost all concerned with "stars," that is, the better known players.

The British Film Institute was founded in 1933. The American Film Institute was founded in 1965 and made operative in 1967, 34 years after the British counterpart. Film Institutes and

Archives in many countries outside the United States, countries which had been far less important in the history and development of film, all preceded the United States in adopting a national position on this art and entertainment form.

Serious film scholarship, of course, preceded the founding of The American Film Institute and the eventual entrance of the AFI into this field. But one aspect of the Congressional Charter creating the AFI is important to note in this respect. The AFI was charged with — among other things — "preserving the American film heritage." Through the AFI's archival program, it has done that in a most direct manner by seeking out, receiving through purchases or gifts, and depositing with the Library of Congress more than 8,000 American films, many of them previously considered lost. This work goes on.

Allied to this project is a history program about the makers of films. This began in 1969 with a grant from the Louis B. Mayer Foundation which had previously been involved with UCLA in a similar program. The first grant from the Mayer Foundation to the AFI was in 1969 and was for $150,000 in yearly increments of $50,000 for a three-year period. The grant, under the same terms, was renewed by the Mayer Foundation on the completion of the first grant in 1972. The second three-year program is now in effect.

The Mayer grant is administered by the Center for Advanced Film Studies of The American Film Institute in Beverly Hills. Its purpose is primarily to seek out the raw material of film history so that it will be available to film scholars. The grants are made each year to a number of Oral Historians who may have one or more subjects.

Its purpose is to obtain what amount to oral autobiographies of important film figures. Although the grant by the Mayer Foundation is generous, it obviously has its limitations. Policy, which is guided by a Film History Advisory Committee of film scholars and historians not in the employ of the AFI, has been to concentrate on major figures not otherwise covered in books, articles or other data. It has also, to some extent, been keen to the fact that time is an enemy. To be blunt: The program has made priorities of filmmakers of advanced age.

In its first three years the Film History Program completed 44 Oral Histories. Among the subjects have been Nunnally Johnson, Leo McCarey, Allan Dwan, Donald Ogden Stewart, Wilbur Crane. The Oral Histories in progress have developed a certain shape and form. The AFI-Mayer program does not consider a single interview an Oral History.

Before considering the form an Oral History takes, it might be useful to consider how they are done. As noted above, decisions on the Oral Histories to be commissioned are decided by a Film History Advisory Committee. This committee is at present made up of Andrew Sarris, Charles Champlin, Arthur Knight, David Bradley, William Everson and Peter Bogdanovich. Casey Robinson was on the committee originally but asked to resign in 1972 because he planned an extended stay in Australia. The Committee instead asked that Robinson take a leave of absence with the hope that he might rejoin the group at a later date. At that time, Bogdanovich was asked to serve on the Committee and agreed to do so. Also participating on the committee are Daniel Selznick, vice president of the Mayer Foundation; James Powers, administrator for the AFI of the Film History Program; and Rochelle Reed, Program Coordinator.

This committee meets once or twice a year to consider application for funds. In addition to the Oral Histories, the AFI-Mayer program normally makes one or more larger grants for what it calls a Research Associateship. This differs from the Oral Histories in scope and nature. An Oral History is the record of an extended interview, usually covering several months and running in transcript to about 500 pages. A research Associateship is a more comprehensive project, usually covering a whole field (animation) or an era (the early Hollywood studios; the Laemmle years at Universal). The Research Associate usually expects to produce from this study a finished work of some kind, such as a book or a film.

Although the primary responsibility of the Program is the production of raw data, several finished works have resulted. Among these are Gavin Lambert's *On Cukor,* David Cherichetti's *Hollywood Director,* and Jon Halliday's *Sirk on Sirk,* all based on Oral Histories. Donald Knox's *The Magic Lantern* was based on a Research Associateship and study of the MGM studio system.

Most of the projects considered and approved by the Film History Advisory Committee have been proposed by scholars and journalists. The Program has not made a practice of generating its own projects and assigning them. It has, from time to time, made suggestions to applicants about amending or combining projects as it seemed practical.

The Oral Historians are offered a full supportive program. The three screening rooms of the Center for Advanced Film Studies are available to them. The Film Librarian handles all requests for films for such screenings. The office of the Program Administrator is available for consultation, for help in locating materials and source subjects. If the Oral Historian prefers not to transcribe his tapes, the Program Coordinator arranges for that. Incidentally, if the Oral Historian elects to prepare his own transcript, as most do, he is paid an additional fee.

The grants generally range from $500 to $1,500, depending upon the complexity of the project, whether it is for more than one subject or for a single subject of unusual length. If, after the grant is made, circumstances arise that necessitate adjustment upward, that is considered and has been done.

The Oral Historian working in Los Angeles has available the full facilities of the AFI Center for Advanced Film Studies. The Program Office seeks to locate films germane to his project. They are booked at the screening rooms. The Charles K. Feldman Library, which includes hundreds of film research books and periodicals as well as a collection of some important film scripts, is also a workroom for the Oral Historian. The Librarian will also direct him to other film resources in the area and elsewhere if they are not available at the Center.

The Historian may also take advantage of the full program of the Center such as the regular seminars for the Fellows, screenings for the Fellows and Staff and whatever other events are available and of interest.

The Oral Historian need not be based in California. Several projects have been granted to persons elsewhere in the United States or abroad if that is where the subject is located. In addition to these projects, the Program also occasionally makes small grants directly to film persons. These are designed to aid in a small way with autobiographies. Some of those who have received such grants are Clive Brook, Bessie Love, Rowland V. Lee and Howard Estabrook. In some of these cases their autobiographical material was not such that it was likely to be professionally published. But the information was valuable to the scholar and it might not exist in any other form. These manuscripts are placed in the Center Library with the other Film History material.

The Research Associate, who receives either $4,500 or $9,000, depending upon the project, is asked to make himself a more intimate part of the Center. He may conduct seminars for the Fellows if the subject is a particular part of his expertise and otherwise participate in a manner — hopefully — enriching for him and the Fellows.

The Film History Program figures as a general rule that about half the funds available are spent in grants and research associateships and half in supportive measures; screenings, transcriptions etc.

At present, two books are being prepared for Little, Brown with whom the AFI has a special publishing contract. These books will draw to some extent on the Oral Histories although more liberally from the seminars held at the Center. Tentative titles for these books are *On Directing* and *The Directors' Collaborators*. The first is drawn from interviews and seminars with directors; the second — from the same source — covers the other artists and craftsmen who contribute to films, the producers, writers, cinematographers, production designers, etc.

The method of operation for Oral Historians generally follows rules suggested by the Oral History Association. The AFI-Mayer program has some special problems, however, probably not consistent in other such programs. For one thing, almost all subjects likely to be interviewed for the AFI-Mayer program are already public figures. This has both advantages and disadvantages. The advantages are that the subjects are accustomed to talking about themselves, so they are not reluctant or hesitant in expressing their thoughts and in responding to questions. On the other hand, the more famous of them have been interviewed many times, some of them in careers that stretch over decades, and there is a hazard that part of their story has fallen into a stereotype.

Oral History of course is an outgrowth not only of increased interest in film history but a direct result of technological developments, specifically the now ubiquitous tape recorder. While a tape recorder may at first inhibit the subject, its simple operation and infrequent demands tend also to make it less intrusive than other kinds of verbatim transcription.

The AFI-Film History program has a second problem not unique to it, but inherent to its special nature: most of its subjects are elderly, some very old. Priorities are, in fact, that efforts be made to secure the important Oral Histories from those filmmakers who are unlikely to be available for very long. There are obviously special problems in dealing with the elderly, especially the famous elderly.

Memory for the elderly is likely to be keen on an occurence of 40 years ago, somewhat dim on last week. A good rapport is vital between the subject and the interviewer, indeed these professional relationships often blossom into personal friendships. A certain pattern has been discovered that is most fruitful in doing these extended interviews. Individual sessions should not generally run more than two hours. They are frequently tiring and demanding. Sessions are usually scheduled about a week apart. It has been found that the individual sessions stir memory and the space between sessions is a period when the memory refreshes and is ready for further probing.

Another aspect of this same area is the showing of films associated with the subject, whether a director, writer or composer. If the subject agrees, the subject and interviewer will watch the subject's films together, sometimes discussing them as they watch. For many subjects the sight of films made 20, 30 or 40 years ago will be another powerful stimulant to memory. On the other hand, for some subjects it is not productive. A subject will very often confess to remember absolutely nothing about the making of a particular film, even after seeing it.

Nevertheless, although the subject claims not to be stimulated by the viewing of an old film, Oral History interviewers report that the next taping session will produce some unexpected benefits. A memory stimulant may not produce exactly the response expected, but it will often stir the mind so that it produces other facts.

The mechanics of the Oral Histories follows a set pattern, altered only when it suits the convenience of the subject. Usually the Oral Historian transcribes his interviews as he goes along, sometimes referring to them for the next interview. Often an unexpected area will open up in an interview and the interviewer may very well not recognize it at the time the conversation is being taped. Quick transcription and reading of the transcription will usually bring this out more clearly and the interviewer in the next session can return to this particular point for elaboration.

One thing might be stressed. Very often scholars, thoroughly prepared in their material, will not be alert to what is being said in an interview, incongruous as that may sound. The interviewer who has prepared himself will often have a complete set of questions by which he hopes to lead the subject through his life and career. It cannot be said too strongly that the interviewer must listen to answers. This seems obvious and rudimentary but a reading of some transcripts indicates that it is not. The interviewer in some cases is only too obviously thinking of his next question while his subject is responding to the previous question. Often the subject will respond to the question obliquely or in terms other than the interviewer expected. Unless the interviewer is alert — unless he truly listens — he may miss some very important, indeed crucial material, or hints of material. This can be caught in the next interview, after the interviewer has reviewed his transcript. But if the subject happens to open a new and untapped area it is far better to pursue it at the time.

It should be remembered that the interviewer is basing his questions on previously known material. He should not be bound by that material. What he hopes to get is new or expanded material. If what he hears is at variance with previous knowledge he should gently probe the areas of difference. It should also be taken into consideration that just as eyewitnesses of an event may see it differently, so participants in a film career may have differing opinions.

The ideal situation in Film History would be to have the recollections of several participants in the same event — a film, a period of film history. It has happened that the subject will cling determinedly to his viewpoint even though an opposite one is pointed out. The Oral Historian should faithfully record what the subject says, what he believes, and leave the interpretation to the writer or scholar or teacher who takes this raw material and evaluates it.

The method by which the Oral History is completed is to take the entire transcript back to the subject. The subject then has the right to edit according to personal dictates. It may be he feels that he has been too blunt or unfair. He is allowed to edit what he subsequently feels is not something he wishes preserved. As to the mechanics of the conversation, the AFI-Mayer program follows the general rules of the Oral History Association. Only minor editing is done, solely for purposes of clarity. The personal speaking habits of the subject are preserved as nearly as possible. It gives the Oral History a spontaneity that is most interesting. To complete his work, the Oral Historian does a filmography, a bibliography, and an index of the work. He writes a brief biography of the subject and generally describes the conditions under which the interviews were conducted.

The Film History Program of the Center for Advanced Film Studies of The American Film Institute

The Oral Histories are at present only available in the Library of the AFI's Center for Advanced Film Studies in Beverly Hills, California, although plans are underway to make them available in selected collections in other parts of the United States.

Although the means are necessarily limited, the program represents a living memorial to Louis B. Mayer. It is also the most concentrated effort now underway to obtain and preserve genuine history of the American film.

JOHN B. KUIPER AND
STAFF
Motion Picture
Section

The Motion Picture Section of the Library of Congress

THE LIBRARY OF CONGRESS motion picture collections began, literally, with a sneeze. In 1894, the moving picture "Edison Kinetoscopic Record of a Sneeze," better known as "Fred Ott's Sneeze," was deposited for copyright. Because there was no provision in the copyright laws for the registration of moving pictures, "Fred Ott's Sneeze" and other early films were treated as pictorial material and deposited in the form of photographs printed on rolls of paper. In 1912 the laws were amended to permit the registration of motion pictures as a distinct form. During the next 30 years, however, because of the difficulty of handling the highly flammable nitrate film used at the time, the Library retained only descriptive materials relating to motion pictures. This practice changed in 1942 when, recognizing the importance of motion pictures and the need to preserve them as an historical record, the Library began to retain films. Today the Motion Picture Section in the Prints and Photographs Division of the Reference Department has responsibility for the acquisition, cataloging, preservation, and service of the motion picture collections.

The Collections

The collections contain over 50,000 titles, or more than 167,000 reels. More than a thousand titles, including television films and video tapes, are added each year through copyright deposit, purchase, gift, or exchange. The collections also include more than 300,000 stills.

Copyright Deposit. Films have been selected from copyright deposits since 1942 — feature films and short subjects for entertainment; educational, scientific, religious, and business-sponsored films; and television documentary, educational, and entertainment programs. Titles are selected to show the diversity of the American film industry and the quality of artistic achievement. Emphasis is also placed on the sociological and historical importance of the film.

Historic Collections. The Library has an unusually large number of motion pictures produced before 1915 — 3,000 titles in the paper print collection, more than 350 titles in the George Kleine collection, and several hundred titles in the American Film Institute collection. Other early films are in the collections of Louise Ernst, John Allen, and Gatewood Dunstan, among others. Viewing copies exist for most of the titles.

Major Studio Deposits. Original motion picture preprint materials (negatives, master positives, and work prints) from Columbia Pictures Corporation, Hal Roach Studios, Monogram Pictures, Paramount Pictures, RKO Radio Pictures, United Artists Corporation, and Warner Brothers have been deposited in the Library. Titles include short subjects and features. All materials are nitrate and viewing copies exist for only a small portion of the titles.

American Film Institute Collection. Copies of all films acquired by the AFI are deposited in the Library. The emphasis of this collection is on recovering American films produced between 1912 and 1942, the period during which the Library did not retain films. The AFI has also acted in partnership with the Library in arranging for the deposit of major studio collections. While much of the collection is on nitrate stock, viewing copies exist for many of the important acquisitions.

Films Seized During World War II. The collection includes more than 5,000 feature films, short subjects, documentaries, newsreels, and educational films made in Nazi Germany and several hundred films made in Japan and Italy. Viewing copies are available for many of the titles.

U.S. Government-Produced Films. The National Archives and Records Service in Washington, D.C., is the official repository for these films, as well as other Federal records, The Library has a limited collection of Government-produced films.

Preservation

The preservation of its motion picture collections is a prime concern of the Library. Film, whether in the form of paper prints, nitrate, or acetate, is one of the most fragile of all art mediums.

In 1948 the Academy of Motion Picture Arts and Sciences sponsored a project to develop a practical method of converting paper prints — which are difficult to examine and impossible to project — to acetate (safety) film. After a technique was perfected, the Academy paid for the conversion of 1,600 titles in the Library's collections and, in 1958, the U.S. Congress appropriated funds to continue the project to its conclusion in 1964.

In the early 1960's the Library began efforts to restore motion pictures which were made on highly combustible nitrate film — footage which must be stored in fireproof vaults outside the District of Columbia, some as far away as Dayton, Ohio. Its efforts were enhanced in 1970 when, with assistance from the AFI, the Library installed a sophisticated motion picture preservation laboratory in its Main Building. In the laboratory, old nitrate film is cleaned by an ultrasonic process, repaired, and transferred frame by frame to acetate stock. The film which is being converted is stored in a small fireproof vault in the laboratory. The facility is capable of converting more than two million feet of film each year.

Services

The Motion Picture Section maintains the Library's film collections for scholarly study and research. Public projection, preview, and loan services are not available. The Section staff answers written and telephone inquiries about the holdings and makes appointments for the use of the reference facilities by individual scholars. Inquiries should be addressed to: Motion Picture Section, Library of Congress, Washington, D.C. 20540. The Section is open from 8:30 a.m. to 4:30 p.m. Monday through Friday and is located in the Annex Building, Room 1046.

The viewing facilities, which consist of several 16mm and 35mm viewing machines, may be used free of charge by serious researchers only; viewing times must be scheduled in advance. The facilities may not be used by high school students; undergraduate college students must provide a letter from their professor endorsing their project.

The Section maintains a reading room with extensive card files describing the Library's motion picture holdings. The files include a shelf-list, a dictionary catalog, a nitrate film file, a directors file, and chronological and production company files for silent films. At present there is no printed catalog describing the Library's collection. The reading room also contains a basic collection of reference books on cinema subjects, film distribution catalogs, yearbooks, reviews, and trade periodicals. The greater part of such material, however, is available through the Library's general and periodical reading rooms. The Section has custody of descriptive materials (pressbooks, plot synopses, continuities, dialogue scripts, stills, and posters) for motion pictures registered for copyright after 1912.

Copies of film footage not restricted by copyright, by provisions of gift or transfer, or by physical condition may be ordered through the Section. The requester is responsible for a search, either in person or by mail, of Copyright Office records to determine the copyright status of specific works. Inquiries should be directed to: Register of Copyrights, Library of Congress, Washington, D.C. 20559.

Cataloging

The Motion Picture Section creates and maintains a catalog of all films added to the Library's collections. A pilot project is under way to automate the cataloging information and eventually to replace the various card files maintained by the Section with a single data base, from which bibliographic information could be retrieved in a variety of ways.

Publications
The Library publishes cataloging information for films and related materials, as it does for books. This information, produced by the Processing Department in three forms, covers films which are of general interest to libraries, schools, and individuals; the films are not necessarily added to the Library's collections. The data are available in the form of the printed catalog card; a book catalog, *Library of Congress Catalog – Films and other Materials for Projection* (formerly *Library of Congress Catalog – Motion Pictures and Filmstrips*), issued quarterly and in annual cumulation, and appearing as volumes in the quinquennial cumulation of the Library's *National Union Catalog*; and as computer tapes produced monthly in a machine-readable cataloging (MARC) format. The three items are for sale by the Card Division, Library of Congress, Building 159, Navy Yard Annex, Washington, D.C. 20541.

In addition, the Copyright Office prepares a semi-annual *Catalog of Copyright Entries: Motion Pictures and Filmstrips*, which lists all such materials registered for copyright in the United States, and five cumulative catalogs, entitled *Motion Pictures*, which together cover registrations for films for the years 1894-1969. Both are for sale by the Superintendent of Documents, U.S. Government Printing Office, Washington, D.C. 20402.

BETTY WHARTON

The Chamberlain and Lyman Brown Theatrical Agency Collection

TWELVE YEARS AGO Paul Myers, curator of the Theatre Collection of The New York Public Library, turned a key in a lock and let himself into several rooms that turned out to be both a Collyer brothers' nightmarish lair and a Tutankhamon tomb of treasures.

These rooms had been the offices of the Chamberlain and Lyman Brown Theatrical Agency which had operated in New York City for over forty years. The agency, which was run by two eccentric brothers, was incredibly successful and powerful. During the 1920's and 1930's they were agents for eighty percent of the most popular actors and actresses of the day, and in addition they were responsible for the beginnings of many brilliant acting careers in both the theatre and motion pictures.

The two brothers who ran this fabulous business had been inseparable; they lived together and they worked together. When Chamberlain died in 1955 the agency was really finished, although Lyman lingered on in the almost deserted offices, until 1961. When he died in March of that year there were no heirs and no one who cared or who was interested in the old place.

Several months later a distraught landlord telephoned the Theatre Collection — he needed the space — the offices were a mess; no one had swept or dusted them for years. Old photographs and posters were all over the place. Did the Library want to clear it out or should he just send in a wrecking crew and get rid of it all?

Paul Myers hurried over to 45th Street. The rooms were

indeed filled with dust, cobwebs, musty scrapbooks — and ghosts. Posters and photographs lined every inch of available wall space. In an inner office there were numberless file cabinets of correspondence, contracts and more photographs.

Paul Myers took a deep breath and went to work. For ten days he pulled the place apart, burrowed in the dirt, and hurriedly packed the usable materials in wooden crates (some three hundred of them) and sent them to the Library.

The staff was both elated and appalled. How could they begin to process the material? It was simple — they could not. All the boxes and crates were packed off to the Annex and there they remained — half forgotten by everyone.

Several years later the Theatre Collection moved into its new quarters at Lincoln Center. Here there was supposed to be space for everything. The Chamberlain Brown Collection surfaced; but again it was too unmanageable and it was quickly shunted to the basement.

Then a miracle happened. The Edward John Noble Foundation, which had helped the Theatre Library Association and American Society for Theatre Research launch their international Congress in 1969, gave the Library money for processing; monies to be used specifically for the Brown Collection. Two large tables at the end of the reading room were roped off for the special librarian and her two assistants. In November, 1973, they began working through the material box by box. It is slow, meticulous work and it is unbelievably dirty work. But underneath the grime there are treasures!

There are inscribed photographs of many of the great stars of the first half of the twentieth century. Photographs which they gave to their agents when they were young and struggling and grateful. It is sometimes hard to recognize Cary Grant because then he was known as Archie Leach; and the young Douglas Fairbanks and Elsa Maxwell and Fred Allen and Rudolph Valentino and Humphrey Bogart. The list stretches on endlessly.

And for every one of these names there are several large

scrapbooks, sometimes four or five, sometimes a dozen. In these scrapbooks are clippings from all over America that the youngsters sent to their agents. Clippings which would tell of their performances in the jobs their agents had been able to secure for them — long before they hit "the big time." And in the latter pages of these scrapbooks is a chronicle of their successes, and sometimes of their scandals and their tragedies. On the last pages there may be obituaries and finally an account of their funerals.

Perhaps the most important part of the Collection (certainly the most unique) will prove to be the correspondence files. Contracts, telegrams and letters in endless profusion tumble out of the crates. There is a tremendous amount of material concerning the stock companies across the country. In fact, there is spread before the librarians a panorama which illustrates the whole business practice in the American theatre of the period. There are also thousands of fascinating letters that give insights into the personal lives of the actors and actresses. These letters often cover a whole professional lifetime — from the early beginnings of a career, through the successful years and sometimes to a sad and lonely old age.

Fritzie Scheff was a delightful client and friend for many years and the later correspondence reflects her tremendous need and desire to work and the great efforts of Lyman to keep her working up until the end when she died almost penniless. Alice Brady writes from Hollywood about her problems with the movie studios and about an unhappy love affair. Humphrey Bogart, long before his Hollywood days, writes about his divorce from Helen Menken and how he hopes the unpleasant publicity won't have an adverse affect on his career. The early letters are signed "Humphrey." It is only in his later letters, from Hollywood, that he signs himself "Bogie."

Many of the letters reflect an extraordinarily close and warm relationship with Lyman. When they were both young and hungry for jobs, Norman Foster was in love with Claudette

Colbert. He writes that she made him spend his last salary check on railroad tickets to Richmond because she thought he owed it to his parents to go home:

> It was terrible to leave her — we've been together almost continuously for over six months. But perhaps the absence will be for the best. . . . you know how much I'm really in love with that girl. And that is the whole story.

And later:

> Can't you find a play so we can both play together? This isn't fun at all — being separated like this.

Lyman did get them a job together playing *The Barker*. After the New York run they went to London with the show and Norman Foster writes gaily from the Piccadilly Hotel:

> They are marvelous to Claudette and she has made the biggest personal hit in London. We're all upside down — no flat yet or anything because the play looks so doubtful. . . . Best to you — Claudette says 'me too.' It would be nice of Ward Morehouse to reprint a bit from the enclosed notices. I want New York to know we're still alive!

And then there is Joseph Schildkraut, who signs himself "Pepi," In 1928 he writes of his pride in his young wife, Elise, and her ". . . exquisite performance of 'Julie' in *Lilliom*! — and we are still the happiest couple in the world." In 1930 a telegram from Los Angeles announces "Elise and I are divorced."

In 1932 Peggy Wood was a lovely young musical comedy star appearing in London in *The Cat and the Fiddle*:

> Everything is going beautifully in London, and I am extremely grateful to the British public not only for their taking me back to their hearts, but for what they have done in giving me some backbone again. New York did seem to take the starch out of that.

In 1951 Gertrude Lawrence apologizes for her lateness in acknowledging ". . . your most generous thoughts and wishes . . . the actual truth is that I had no respectable notepaper on which to express my thanks and did not wish to just send a telegram. . . . Affectionately, 'Mrs. Anna' "

The Chamberlain and Lyman Brown Theatrical Agency Collection

Mrs. Leslie Carter writes berating them for their neglect of her. She could be both tough and tender. From California she telegraphed:

> AM TERRIBLY SORRY LYMAN DEAR I SHOULD LOVE TO HAVE MISS BRADY PLAY MY ZAZA BUT I CANNOT ACCEPT MR. ELLIOTS PROPOSITION STOP FRENCH AUTHORS DEMANDING TEN PERCENT IS FUNNY AND PRACTICALLY MAKES DOING BUSINESS IMPOSSIBLE AND FURTHER I WILL NOT GIVE THEM ANY AUTHORITY OF ANY DESCRIPTION REGARDING ANYTHING STOP THE DAVID BELASCO ZAZA BELONGS TO ME AND TO ME ALONE AND I SHALL PROTECT IT STOP ON MORE THAN ONE OCCASION THEY USED MY ZAZA AND THEY OWE ME MONEY FOR SO DOING STOP IF THERE IS ANY WAY YOU CAN THINK OF THAT WILL NOT STULTIFY ME OR HURT MY RIGHTS I SHALL BE GLAD TO SEND MY ZAZA TO MISS BRADY I AM TERRIBLY SORRY LET ME HEAR
>
>   MRS. C.

And then in a softer mood:

> How is the little dog? my two little ones — are gone. I have never missed anything in my life so much. Each and every corner of this great big house is filled with little white ghosts with big soft brown eyes — and it breaks my heart.
> They are buried down in the corner garden — where they loved to play — and each day I go and talk to them. . . . You know — in a way — I believe I am on the verge of melancholia.

Fred Allen is as witty and delightful on paper as he was in vaudeville and radio:

> to lyman brown
> if you're still in town
>
> your letter received
> in haste i reply
> that i cannot work either
> in june or july

during august, too
i can't be a mummer
which means, you'll agree
that i can't work this summer

i avoid summer theatres
because of one fact
it isn't the money
i simply can't act

sincerely
    (signed) Fred Allen

And so it goes, on and on and on — endlessly. The project is begun and every day is exciting.

AVI WORTIS

The Burnside Mystery
The R.H. Burnside Collection and the New York Public Library[1]

ON THE THIRTEENTH OF MAY 1952, William Matthews, a librarian on the staff of the Preparation Division of The New York Public Library, wrote a memo to George Freedley, Curator of the Theatre Collection. Matthews had learned from a Mr. Fred J. Myers that the home of R.H. Burnside in Ridgewood, New Jersey, had been bought for demolition as part of a redevelopment project, and that the house seemed to contain valuable theatrical materials. "This looks like something worth writing for," Mr. Matthews noted, suggesting that a query be directed to Mr. Burnside who, advanced in years and quite ill, was living at the Lambs Club in New York.

The house in Ridgewood turned out to be a curious place indeed. It had been built in 1892 by one Joseph F. Corrigan, a distiller whose wealth was considerable. Mr. Burnside had bought the house in 1915 and made it into the center of much theatrical social life, as well as a home for his family.

In 1952 its windows were smashed, every corner of its wood structure sagged. The paint, such as remained, was flaked and peeling. The roof leaked. It was the classic image of the Victorian haunted house. Inside it was stacked high with great piles of theatrical memorabilia, as much trodden underfoot as elsewhere. Neighborhood boys and girls made regular looting raids.

Mr. Matthews' notion that the Burnside materials were

"something worth writing for" proved to be an understatement of major proportions. Seventeen years were to pass before The New York Public Library learned just what was in that house, and there are still bits of mystery, some things not yet known, and some things only guessed.

For a beginning, who was R.H. Burnside?

The Veteran of Everything

R.H. Burnside, or to give him the name he did not himself reveal, Robert Hubber Thorne Burnside, was a singular individual in the history of the American theatre. The New York *Herald Tribune* summarized and discussed his accomplishments under the headline "R.H. Burnside, Veteran of Everything."

When Burnside died in a New Jersey nursing home in September 1952 he was eighty-two years old, and had been ailing for six years. He was born in Scotland in 1870, son of the manager of the Glasgow Gaiety Theatre. Appropriately for one whose life was to be totally committed to the theatre, he made his debut on the stage in his mother's arms. His first performing role brought him onto his own all-fours in the part of a dog in an Edward Terry command performance of *The Bohemian Girl* before the Prince of Wales, later Edward VII.

At the age of twelve Burnside left Scotland to join the Edward Terry company in London. With Terry and in other London theatres, including the Savoy, home of Gilbert and Sullivan, he served his apprenticeship. He must have learned his trade well; when still a young man of eighteen he met Lillian Russell, and she took him on as a director when she made an American tour in 1894. He staged many plays for her in the United States, and branching out from the Russell company accepted directing jobs throughout the country. It was in this way that he began his association with the Shuberts, for whom he handled a traveling company.

Burnside developed his theatrical talents in all fields, including playwriting. His first successes of note in this area were

Sergeant Kitty (1903), *The Tourists* (1906), and *Trip to Japan* (1906), light entertainments in the operetta style. He became a well-known figure in the theatrical world. Affectionately called Burny, or Zipp, he established a reputation for grand showmanship, expert storytelling with memories to fit every occasion, and much personal warmth. During his later years he turned to a variety of theatrical enterprises (including the film), ranging from production jobbing — he supplied everything for a production from typescript to costumes — to the formation of his own Gilbert and Sullivan company. When he retired from the stage Burnside had been connected in a principal role with more than three hundred productions.

Burnside's greatest fame and success came during his two periods of association with the Hippodrome, first under the Shuberts and then under Charles Dillingham. New York's Hippodrome was as much the ideal of a certain spectacular form of theatrical entertainment as it was a mammoth building with production facilities able to project a concept of theatrical art not so very different from that of Radio City Music Hall.

The Hippodrome was considered to be something of a magical place, and it certainly tried very hard to look the part. It took up the entire footage between Forty-Third and Forty-Fourth Streets along Sixth Avenue, an imposing position in the theatre district that had just settled in around Times Square. Two pseudo-Arabian towers rose high at each Sixth Avenue corner, topped with illuminated electric globes. Flags and bunting rimmed the building's edge and two signs (electric, of course) spelled out in huge letters HIPPODROME. Every one of its 5,200 seats was filled for the premier show on April 12, 1905, accompanied by the rumbling of the Sixth Avenue Elevated which rattled along in front of the theatre doors. In those days even the El had magic.

The vastness of the Hippodrome stage brought it singular fame; the apron of the stage alone was sixty feet long. The first production was *A Yankee Circus* — and indeed it was nothing less than that, with something of a plot, and a cast of six hundred actors with one hundred and fifty animals (elephants being a chief part of the act). In Burnside's heyday (1920) the Hippodrome bragged of a company of six thousand and a house count of four hundred thousand paying customers a season.

The true glory of the Hippodrome was the stage machinery and its technical possibilities. There were few spectacular events that could not be presented: battles, cavalry charges, baseball games, circuses, stag hunts, all were played there. Upon and over that stage audiences saw enacted a prediction of the air warfare yet to come — *Sensational!* was the byword for Hippodrome productions. Burnside's ability to create a dramatic pattern in this great cave of the arts was remarkable enough; his own contribution to the special effects, the Hippodrome disappearing water tank act, was nothing less than world famous.

The Hippodrome stage had a large pool, hidden when not in use, which was customarily the scene of naval battles and ice skating. Burnside's brilliant innovation was a procession of the chorus line, perhaps sixty in number, marching like so many lemmings into the pool, steadfast, unflinching, down a flight of steps into the water, never to emerge. Their actual escape? — a pathway through a secret air lock below. The effect, so it appears, was, well, *Sensational!*

Burnside first directed at the Hippodrome when it was under the management of the Shuberts, who had taken it on after the original builders and owners were bankrupted. This period came to a close when Burnside and J.J. Shubert ended an argument with fists — despite the efforts of Lee Shubert, Burnside would not return. He did return, however, when Charles Dillingham took over the management of the theatre in 1915. They had great success; Director-in-Chief Burnside's income was $400 a week. The theatre was torn down in 1939 and its site is now graced by the particular glories of New York architecture, a garage and office building.

The number of productions that bore the Burnside stamp was large, but it can hardly be claimed that his was a great qualitative venture. There is much sameness in the work, with routine and predictable plots which depend heavily on romantic illusion and coincidence. His real talent lay not in constructing a solid theatrical structure, but in brilliantly dressing a production suggestion — not so much substance as spectacular froth. It must be remembered that Burnside was working at a time when theatre was a widely enjoyed popular entertainment. While today it moves more and more into the sanctuary of a luxury fine art, theatre once had an immense, broadly based public, which lavished upon it the attention and patronage which television enjoys today by default. Burnside was able to hold together in his directorial grasp productions of enormous size, and was thought to have an uncommon sense of what the public liked. This may have been double-edged: the public got, willy-nilly, what the producers *thought* they liked. At any rate the Hippodrome productions were very popular, and from time to time quite profitable. It was an age when reputations could be built on the size of one's flops (as was often the case with Dillingham) as well as on the income from one's successes. The Hippodrome, designed as it was for such huge productions, was the cause of its own downfall. In time, and no doubt with help from the Depression, it priced itself out of existence.

The Burnside promptbooks, particularly for his Hippodrome shows, look like outlines for military maneuvers. In the days before Actors' Equity Association helped insure a living wage literally hundreds of performers could be, and were hired and fired as stage patterns demanded. Burnside developed such a reputation for handling crowds that in later years he complained that he had trouble getting shows to direct with casts of less than two hundred. He produced the 1926 Sesquicentennial in Philadelphia, and that had a cast of 2,700.

A real insight into Burnside's way of thinking and his theatrical concepts is provided by a verbatim transcript [2] of a working session with one of his collaborators, Manuel Klein. The production is *Trip to Japan* (1906), one of Burnside's successes.

BURNSIDE. . . . Now on comes the Japanese spy who addressed the Jap as "Prince Yamato!" The Jap says, "Silence." "Be Careful." Then they have a scene regarding the new airship. The spy tells the student all about them. He then says, "I have heard that the circus has been hard up. The proprietor is going to make a tour of the world, visiting various countries. This would be a great opportunity for us to send over the airships, as it otherwise would be impossible for me to come out openly and hire the circus for the reason that my purposes here (spying and stealing airships) might become known and my negotiations discovered. I don't want that so I have selected you to do it all for me.

The Young Jap, seeing an opportunity of further paying his addresses to the girl, eagerly accepts and agrees to charter the vessel to convey the circus people over. He is in love with the girl himself. He calls the proprietor of the circus down and engages in conversation with him. They go upstage.

Then the Proprietor comes down. "Ladies and gentlemen: I want to make the announcement that this company has been engaged at a great expense to go to Japan, by the Prince Yamato."

At the finish of the act, we could have some sideshows at back, the barkers, yelling, a bum band playing at the back, interrupting the barkers, etc, etc. Perhaps we could wind up the circus by having the lions break loose. It would be funny to finish up with a funny accident. Madame Loop the Loop doing her world famous stunt of falling through the roof.

KLEIN. A funny accident would be great.

BURNSIDE. Yes, and it would break up the circus all right, wouldn't it?

Now we've got to get our people off. You know, we can't finish up by sending them off saying "Oh wasn't it a lovely day." Or, "What beautiful weather we're having!" They could go off to prepare for some affair for the evening.

KLEIN. Yes, some exercises at the Seminary which are to take place. They've got to dress. Some exhibition drill at the Academy.

BURNSIDE. Or a ball. I wouldn't have a disastrous finish to the circus this time.

KLEIN. We ought to have something with lots of life.

BURNSIDE. I have it. Let them finish up with a two-step, dancing all over the lawn.

KLEIN. How about a goodbye number?

BURNSIDE. We could have a scene between the young fellow and the girl saying goodbye. Have him swell out with a magnificent voice and sing, "Farewell, Sweetheart, it's time to part. I'll be true, on the ocean blue, and think of you!"

KLEIN. Then the circus people could go off.

BURNSIDE. The boys are all going off to their (naval) stations and are saying goodbye to the girls. Or, if you take your boys to Japan, you could use the goodbye number in that scene, the boys singing goodbye to the girls before leaving.

KLEIN. Then there would be no necessity for any action at all.

BURNSIDE. That's the idea.

KLEIN. We've never had anything like that.

R.H. Burnside was very much a man of the American theatre, and his personality and accomplishments reflect its unique elements. American theatre, alone in world theatre history, has never been to any relevant degree a subsidized art. Its history is commercial history — it is a popular art, in the sense that film and television are popular forms of entertainment. Bigness has always been considered a virtue of this tradition, and R.H. Burnside was in the very symbolic center of that Bigness: the Hippodrome.

Not that his theatrical interests were limited to the commercial stage. Burnside played an active role in the Lambs Club, which he served as Shepherd for a number of years, and of which he became an honorary life member. The Lambs, in addition to its devotion to convivial sociability as a private club, produced short-run shows, called Gambols, many of which Burnside staged. He was also a charter member of A.S.C.A.P.

It is not surprising that The New York Public Library was interested in securing for its Theatre Collection the archive of a man whose theatrical activities had such great scope.

The Collection Acquired

At the time it all seemed quite clear: Mr. R.H. Burnside, of Hippodrome fame, was very ill and his home, full of theatrical records concerning one of the glories of the American theatre, was tumbling down. How was the Library to save this collection from destruction and make it available to the public in the best tradition of library service?

Acquisition — by gift or purchase, single item or great collection — is an aspect of library functioning rarely perceived by the library user, even the most learned. There is a story, and often a very good one, about the acquisition of every collection that exists on Fifth Avenue and Forty-Second Street. In a trade which has made a profession out of dignity, order, and system, acquisition quickens the pulse and brings a blush to the cheek of the librarian. A recent major addition to the Theatre Collection was rescued from a garbage pile: the romance, no doubt about it, of librarianship. The acquisition of the Burnside Collection has its own good story.

The New York Public Library is a large institution, and it should astound no one that it has its bureaucratic elements; not the least of these is the necessity to put all things down in writing. Why walk a few steps and talk when you can write a memo? — but then it must be admitted that pulp has greater retentive power than brain. As the eighteenth and early nineteenth century made of the letter a distinct literary form, so the mid-twentieth century has developed the inter-office memo into a modest, but no less potent device. No need for despair at the decline of the novel: the inter-office memo grows apace.

In the memo mentioned in the first paragraph of this article

William Matthews alerted George Freedley, Curator of the Theatre Collection, to the imminent destruction of the Burnside house in Ridgewood, as brought to Mr. Matthews' attention by a reader, Mr. Fred J. Myers. That was on May 13, 1952. On May 15 Mr. Matthews reported a visit with Mr. Burnside at the Lambs Club. Mr. Burnside was willing that the Library have the materials, which could at any rate stay in the house only until the end of May under the agreement with the contractor-owner; but a note of authorization was required. A memo from Mr. Freedley on the same day asked the Chief of the Acquisition Division to prepare such a document, and by late afternoon Mr. Matthews was again at the Lambs. In his memo of the next day, Friday, the 16th, Mr. Matthews told Mr. Freedley that Mr. Burnside was unwilling to sign the authorization until he had consulted with his daughters and lawyer; this he proposed to do over the weekend. Illness delayed this, but on Monday the 19th and again a week later (as duly recorded in separate memos), Mr. Burnside retracted his proferred gift.

Diversionary tactics ensued. The house was due for demolition at the end of the month; Mr. Burnside was ill and recalcitrant; the Library was most anxious that a large chapter of theatre history not be buried in the sub-basement rubble of a New Jersey development project. Mr. Matthews reported in regular memos during June calls from the original Mr. Fred J. Myers of Ridgewood with word that the house still stood. Mr. Myers helped institute a newspaper campaign which resulted in a *New York Times* article on August 3, another in the *Herald Tribune* on August 8, and one in the Ridgewood press two days later. On August 6 Mr. Freedley set down in a memo, confirming a verbal report of the day before, the particulars of a visit to Mr. Burnside's attorney, Mr. Louis Froelich. Mr. Froelich, convinced of the urgency and propriety of the Library's interest in the imperiled Ridgewood materials, at once dictated a letter to Mr. Burnside, who some weeks earlier had suffered a stroke and was convalescing in a Metuchen nursing home. With his letter Mr. Froelich enclosed an authorization to be signed and returned to the Library.

On August 8 Mr. Freedley addressed a letter to Mr. Matthews, who was vacationing, in which he reported the arrival in the morning mail of R.H. Burnside's signed authorization for the removal of the materials from the Ridgewood house to the Annex of the Library. And in a detailed memo of August 12 (noting such items as the loss of a loaned pinchbar, the cooperation of the local police department and Commissioner of Police, and the overnight disappearance of several dozen new shoes) the Library assistant responsible for overseeing the transferral of the Burnside Collection from Ridgewood to New York brought this chapter of the story to a close. Little more than a month later, on September 14, R.H. Burnside died. His collection and the record of his life's work had been saved.

Formalities extended for some months. On December 11 Ralph Beals, Director of the Library, requested a letter of conveyance from Burnside's son-in-law. This was delayed until July 9, 1953. The reply mentioned additional Burnside materials in Jersey City. The Library was naturally interested in these, if perhaps with an enthusiasm somewhat dampened by the enormous quantity of material already on hand. The new cache was thought to be costumes, which would not be collected by the Library. It was summer, however, with staff illness and vacation unhappily mixed; the matter was put off until the fall, and then it was agreed that these boxes be given to the Joe Jefferson Players.

At any rate, The New York Public Library had a Burnside Collection of ample proportions. Two, some reports say three, huge moving vans of Burnside material had been acquired for the Theatre Collection. The full staff at that time consisted of three librarians (including the Curator), one full-time assistant, and one or two pages. It is hardly surprising that no inventory of the Burnside Collection was prepared.

Processing and Discovery

A rough estimate of the segments of the Collection can be made in retrospect. Eighty-two cartons of materials, including non-production records in typescript and correspondence, went to the Library's Manuscript Division. Some 125 cartons, principally containing music in parts, went to the Music Division. Although exactly what remained in the Theatre Collection is impossible to determine, there must have been typescripts, manuscripts, promptbooks, scene designs, and photographs; and there were apparently a large number of published plays. These were absorbed in the normal processing procedures of the Collection over a period of six years, at the end of which Mr. Freedley wrote a congratulatory note to the head of the cataloging division.

Curiously enough the collection, large as it was, seemed of less importance than one might have supposed after six years of processing. When the Theatre Collection celebrated its twenty-fifth anniversary in 1956, and when the Collection moved to its new home at Lincoln Center in 1965, the attendant publicity made no mention of the Burnside Collection. In 1961 Mr. Freedley did recount the episode briefly in the *Dramatist's Bulletin.* He spoke of the complexities of securing legal authorization for removing the materials from the Ridgewood house, and of the looting that had brought some damage: ". . . but the vast majority of the plays were saved."

The problem was not to rest so easily. If saved, where were they? The Library's catalogs contain little mention of the Burnside Collection, and no record of a collection of plays. In 1969 a script was found — the "last" of the "Burnside scripts," according to a note written in 1959 by Mr. Freedley to the cataloging division. The script, however, had not been processed. Moreover, it had nothing to do with Burnside.

In the fall of 1968 the staff member of the Theatre Collection responsible for working through the backlog of play typescripts and manuscripts had opened an ordinary cardboard box. It was unmarked, except for the printed label which proclaimed its earlier contents to have been "Original White Horse Blended Scotch Whisky." There were no drinkable spirits in the box, but there were, among other things, typescripts by James Barrie, Conan Doyle, Somerset Maugham, and Arthur Wing Pinero; and there was a variant version of *The Importance of Being Earnest* by Oscar Wilde. Each of the scripts was stamped with The New York Public Library acquisition number 53 x 300: the three hundredth addition made to the holdings in 1953.

A check against Library acquisition records showed where these rather valuable scripts came from. They were all part of the R.H. Burnside Collection. In time about one thousand unprocessed scripts from the Burnside Collection were located. There were scripts by William Gillette, Clyde Fitch, Milne, Shaw. There was even a new Sherlock Holmes adventure, attributed to Conan Doyle, although later disclaimed by the Doyle estate. There were plays in English, French, and German; there were scripts with prompt notations; there were variant texts with author's revisions. Many of the scripts were from the Hippodrome, but the greater number were from the Charles Frohman offices. A check of bound and cataloged plays from the Burnside Collection on the shelves brought the total to some four thousand scripts, most of which were from the Frohman offices. This was clearly not so much the R.H. Burnside Collection as it was the Charles Frohman Collection.

Who was Charles Frohman? Bernard Shaw called him

The Napoleon of the Theatre

Charles Frohman, of German-Irish descent, was born in Sandusky, Ohio, in 1860. At the height of his success during the first decade of the twentieth century he was perhaps the most powerful single force in the American theatre. He was both financially and artistically successful; many of his production concepts shaped the theatre and all popular entertainments as we know them today. With his partner, Alf Hayman, Frohman was the cornerstone of the New York theatrical trust, and helped to create and make effective what was then known (and fought) as the Syndicate. He was the arbiter of theatre values for the nation. It was Frohman whose ideas about advertising shaped the credo through which the entertainment world sells itself; it was Frohman who created the star system as we know it — the star as an actor who, offstage, is yet another character, a "special person" acting in public a role in a play called "Life" (see Bogart, see Monroe).

Exactly how many theatres Frohman owned is not clearly established, but at the high point of his career he had a controlling interest in perhaps as many as two hundred. At one time he owned outright forty-two theatres, eight of them in New York City. With all this he was deliberately reticent about projecting himself personally into the public view, even to the point of its becoming an obsession. Little is known of Frohman beyond his theatrical pronouncements, and much that has been written seems repetitious, contrived, even, perhaps, invented. His delight in obscurity extended to a refusal to have photographs taken or portrait drawings reproduced in the press, although thousands of words were published about his plans and ideas. It pleased him to brag about the small number of his employees who knew him by sight.

The facts of Frohman's life are not very revealing. His involvement with the theatre began at an early age and little else seems to have interested him. The Frohman family moved to New York when Charles was still a boy, and he watched his older brothers Gustave and Daniel, who were to become producers, move into the world of the theatre. Charles's first theatrical positions were in business capacities: as ticket seller, treasurer, and advance man he toured the extensive European and American routes which were then the fashion. While still in his twenties he secured the production rights to Bronson Howard's floundering play *Shenandoah,* urged changes, brought the play around, made a fantastic financial success of it, and effectively launched his most prolific period.

Frohman organized his own stock company and built the Empire Theatre. He sent out road companies by the hundred and eventually had under contract some two thousand actors producing sixty plays a year on both sides of the Atlantic. Maude Adams, William Gillette, John Drew, Ethel Barrymore were among his stars; Belasco, Barrie, Wilde, Fitch, Galsworthy, Maugham, Gillette were among his playwrights. Frohman produced what was considered the very best of the theatre of his time, if not, in retrospect, the avant-garde. One of the few notable playwrights whom he did not produce in quantity was G.B. Shaw, who wrote in uncharacteristically flattering terms:

> Charles Frohman is the most wildly romantic and adventurous man of my acquaintance. As Charles XII became a famous soldier through his passion for putting himself in a way of being killed, so Charles Frohman has become a famous manager through his passion for putting himself in the way of being ruined.

Frohman's closest associates appear to have been James Barrie and Charles Dillingham. The trio of Frohman (producer), Barrie (author), and Maude Adams (star) was vastly successful. The association with Dillingham is less clear. He seems to have been Frohman's personal secretary, handling much of the advance work and personal contacts, although he was occasionally an independent producer even while Frohman lived. Dillingham appears to have been much involved in the arrangements for Frohman's funeral — but more of Dillingham later.

Frohman was personally involved in the production of many of his plays, working with authors, concerning himself about direction, attending to advertising and the state of his theatres. He read nothing but plays, hundreds of plays, and the walls of his office in the Empire theatre were lined with the scripts of all of his productions, successes and failures alike, bound in red leather. For Frohman the theatre was all. He seems to have lived for his opening nights, immersing himself in the detail of the plays currently in production, often as many as eight at a time.

He was short, barely five feet in height, rather rounded in girth as the years went on and described as Buddha-like. He was well respected, with a reputation for honesty and generosity; he was also said to have an hypnotic quality, a nervous tension which both fascinated and exhausted those to whom he was close. He constantly consumed sweet drinks, lemonade, peanuts, chestnuts; he sent telegrams by the hundreds; he was brief with words and had a sharp wit. Perhaps it was because he refused to show himself in a personal fashion that Frohman seems so interesting. He apparently viewed life in a totally detached way, and even said that it was not after all very important, that it was unreal. The theatre, too, was a detached phenomenon: "The theatre's business," he said, "is to present not life, but the illusion of life."

Frohman's sudden and dramatic death on the submarine-struck *Lusitania* in 1915 adds to the man's personal mystery. His manner was widely reported. He showed no fear, and was quoted as having said "Why fear death? It is the most beautiful adventure in life." The phrase, a bit enlarged, is from Barrie's *Peter Pan*, perhaps Frohman's biggest success, and certainly his favorite production. The line is Peter's as he is about to drown. Spoken by Frohman it is almost as though his death were his own final press notice, suggesting that the biggest star in Frohman's system was, after all, himself.

Twenty-one years after his death, his brother Daniel suggested that Charles Frohman's death "occurred at just about the right time."[3] His Empire was due for a collapse. It is certainly extraordinary, considering the scope of Frohman's activities, his influence and the strength of his control in theatrical matters, that at the time of his death his estate totalled no more than $451. But then Frohman liked to say that he did not have contracts with his people; he didn't believe in them.

The Frohman enterprises, however, continued for many years. Frohman's partner Alf Hayman maintained the firm, retaining the potent corporate name, Charles Frohman: "Charles Frohman Presents" was virtually a trademark. When Hayman died the organization continued, with the Empire Theatre still its center. The company was later taken over by Paramount. The theatre eventually came down in 1953. On this occasion Frohman, the theatre, its casts and plays, were widely and warmly remembered.

A description of Frohman's office at the Empire Theatre appeared in a New York newspaper column by John Whitney.

> I was up to the old offices (At the Empire) yesterday. Jim Reilly — in thirty years from office boy to general manager — was putting away some of the old documents, filing away in packages some of the old letters. He handled them reverently — and no wonder.
>
> A brief note from Maude Adams to "C.F.", a hurried flowing script of thanks . . . from Lilly Langtry. A blunt message from Drew. An Author's plea from Jerome K. Jerome. Best of all, a curt, quick message from Shaw — signed. It advised strongly against granting film rights to "Pygmalion." "For the films will kill a play with deadly certainty," he wrote.
>
> Back of Reilly, against a wall, were long shelves lined with morocco-bound volumes of every play Charles Frohman Inc. ever produced . . . . They are invaluable, scrawled with signature of great stars . . . . They are marked with author's notations, stage directions. Reilly doesn't know what to do with them, but they are of enormous value to some theatre library, some collector.

What happened to all these documents? In 1969 scripts closely related to them were located in the Theatre Collection of The New York Public Library. It is clear that The New York Public Library, on acquiring the R.H. Burnside Collection, came into possession of a large portion of the Charles Frohman archive. But these materials are not those described as having once existed in the Frohman office — there are no plays bound in red leather; there is no correspondence with actors and authors. It would be interesting to know what has become of the missing portions.

Equally interesting is the question of how the Frohman scripts and prompt-books now in the Library came to be part of the Burnside Collection. The two men never worked together: Burnside's early New York associations were with the Shuberts, rivals to the Frohman Syndicate. And certainly their natures and interests, aside from a shared passion for the theatre, were totally different. The one link between the two men was Charles Bancroft Dillingham.

Dillingham was born in 1868 in Hartford, Connecticut, the son of an Episcopalian clergyman. Not wishing to follow his father's calling he went into newspaper work, became a drama critic in Chicago, and wrote a play. Frohman came to see the play and while he did not care to produce it he seems to have taken an interest in Dillingham; in any case he offered him a job. That job led to a close relationship which developed into something of a partnership. Dillingham seems to have been Frohman's personal business secretary, advance man, and general confidant. Together they owned a large estate in Purchase, New York.

Dillingham, unlike Frohman, was the most public of showmen. Even while associated with the Frohman enterprises he functioned as an independent producer (for example, *Man and Superman*), and took over the Globe Theatre. In 1915, the year that Frohman died, Dillingham assumed the management of the Hippodrome, perhaps with funds realized from a fifty-thousand-dollar note from the Frohman estate. And this is the link: Dillingham brought back R.H. Burnside to direct the Hippodrome shows; they were also partners at the Globe.

Dillingham had spectacular ups and downs as a producer. The year before his death he went into bankruptcy with liabilities of seven million dollars. It took some time to disentangle his financial affairs, and in 1936, the year after his death, it was discovered that Dillingham had owned the rights to 122 plays not listed as assets at the time of his bankruptcy. These included a number of Frohman plays, among them

Peter Pan; and the case hinged on an unopened trunk which, as matters developed, was in the possession of R.H. Burnside, of Ridgewood, New Jersey.

Burnside's correspondence makes it clear that he had a large accumulation of materials given to him by Dillingham for safekeeping, and although the nature of the materials is not specified it is now apparent that they were largely from the Charles Frohman offices. It may well be that there were materials from the Frohman productions among the huge quantity of costumes and stage properties originally part of the Burnside Collection given to amateur groups. There are now in the Manuscript Division, besides Burnside's correspondence, some dozen letter copy-books from the Frohman offices; and the Theatre Collection has letters from the Frohman office in London to the New York office which cover the period from August 1909 to January 1910. Frohman productions may have been depicted in the costume and set designs which came with the collection. There was also apparently a large number of published plays from the Frohman offices, but they have passed into the general collections of the Library and are no longer identifiable as such.

Was it then, the R.H. Burnside Collection of Charles Dillingham papers from the Charles Frohman offices? Not quite. Some twenty cartons of Dillingham's own letters and business records came to the Library as a separate acquisition shortly after Dillingham's death. They have not yet been processed — and that is, perhaps, another story.

This historical survey introduces a check list of the promtpbooks and play scripts (in typescript and manuscript) which came to the Library with the Burnside Collection, the larger number of which were originally Frohman scripts. Some were no doubt lost in the looting of the Burnside house and other moves, but it can be estimated that about four thousand items from this source are now available in the Theatre Collection. About one thousand authors are represented in the collection, and more than two thousand titles.

There is a small number of scripts of unknown authorship and an even smaller number lacking both title and author. In many cases a title is represented by more than one script, including working copies at various stages of completion and promptbooks; detailed information of this kind must wait upon full cataloging.

1. Originally published in the *Bulletin of The New York Public Library*, LV (October 1971), 371-409, and reprinted here with the permission of the author and The New York Public Library. The published article contains changes made by The New York Public Library, not the author.

2. In the Theatre Collection, The New York Public Library.

3. *Daniel Frohman Presents: An Autobiography* (New York: Claude Kendall and Willoughby Sharp, 1935), p. 251.

A Preliminary Check List of Authors and Titles of Plays in the R.H. Burnside – Charles Frohman Collection

In this abbreviated check list, plays are listed under both the author and the translator, adaptor, lyricist, or other collaborator, without cross-references or elaboration. Plays are listed by the title found on the typescript, usually in the language of the text of the play. Occasionally, however, the title is the original title of a work which has been translated into English. In some cases, there are early versions of works which might be known by a different title; for example, Wilde's *Lady Lancing* is an early version of *The Importance of Being Earnest*. Some works are presently uncatalogued; the Theatre Collection should be consulted for further information about the typescripts.

Abbott, Elisabeth
  The 2nd, 3rd, 4th, etc.
About, Edmond François Valentin
  Germaine
Acosta, Mercedes de
  Himself
Ade, George
  Father and the Boys
  Just Out of College
  Just Out of College [revised version]
  Luck in Love
  Mrs Peckham's Carouse
  The Old Town
  U. S. Minister Bedloe
Adler, Hans
  Fahrt nach Sorrent
  A Trip to Sorrento
Agar, Herbert
  Healthy, Wealthy and Wise
Agate, James
  Dreyfus
Aide, Hamilton
  Doctor Bill
Akins, Zoe
  Déclasse
  Greatness
  Rings and Chains
  The Texas Nightingale
Alcaraz, Enrique
  My Prince
Ambient, Mark
  The Arcadians
Anderson, John
  Collision
Anstey, F. [pseud of Thomas Anstey Guthrie]
  The Brass Bottle
  Love among the Lions
  A Short Exposure
Anthelme, Paul
  L'honneur japonais
  The Honor of Japan
  The Japanese Honour
Arliss, George
  The Wild Rabbit
Armin, Walter
  Lost and Found
  Reduced Rent
  Two Against One
Armont, Paul
  The Zebra
  Le zèbre

Armstrong, Paul
  The Heart of a Thief
Arnold, Franz
  The Girl from Cook's
  In Quest of Happiness
  Mein alter Herr
Arnold, Victor
  Mein alter Herr
Artus, Louis
  La coeur de moineau
  Heart of a Sparrow
Artzybashev, Mikail Petrovitch
  Enemies
Athis, Alfred
  Le costaud des épinettes
  A Thief in the Night

Bach, Ernesta
  The Girl from Cook's
  In Quest of Happiness
Bahr, Herman
  The Concert
  The Little Dance
Baker, Elizabeth
  Chains
Baker, Robert Melville
  The Come Back
Bakonyi, Karl von
  Der kleine Koenig
  The Little King
Balint, Michael
  The Two Mihalyi Girls
Ballard, Frederick
  Us Ladies
Balimer, Oryliss W.
  Yesterday's Today
Balzac, Honoré de
  The Honor of the Family
  The Wrong Man
Bancroft, George P.
  Ballantyne's Idol
Barba, Sagi
  Artistic Temperament
Barde, Andre
  The Piano Teacher
Barker, Albert
  Tiger Hour
Barker, Edwin L.
  Tiger Hour
Barker, Harley Granville
  The Romantic Young Lady
Barker, Richard
  Ivanhoe
Barker, Richard Hardinge
  Accidents Will Happen
  According to Plan
  The Blue Diamond
  Let's Be Broadminded
  The Love Puzzle
  The Mallaby Mystery
Barker, Theodore T.
  The Mascot
Barnett, John
  Shakespeareana
  Youth a-la-Mode
Barre, Albert
  Paradise
Barrie, Sir James Matthew
  The Admirable Crichton
  The Adored One
  Alice Sit-by-the-Fire
  Dear Brutus
  The Ladies Shakespeare
  Legend
  The Legend of Leonora
  Leonora
  Little Mary
  The Old Lady Shows Her Medals
  Punch
  Quality Street
  Der Tag
  Two Kinds of Women
  The Wedding Guest
  What Every Woman Knows
  Untitled Play
Barrisre, Theodore
  Bohemia
Bartholmae, Philip
  Tangerine
Basset, Serge
  The Seniors
Bataille, Henry
  L'enchantement
  The Foolish Virgin
  Le masque
  The Scandal
  La scandale
Baum, L. Frank
  Ozma of Oz
  The Rainbow's Daughter

Beahan, Charles
   Hold Your Horses
Beatty-Kingston, William
   The Beggar Student
Beauvoir, Roger de
   The Infernal Regions of Paris
Reddington, E. F.
   To Have and to Hold
Behrman, S. N.
   Brief Moment
Beiser, Rudolph
   Lady Patricia
Belasco, David
   The Girl I Left Behind Him
   Governor Rodman's Daughter
   Madame Butterfly
   Men and Women
   Zaza
Belknap, Edwin S.
   The Better Part
Bell, Hillary
   The Social Trust
Bellamy, Frank
   I Can't Bear It
Benière, Louis
   Papillon, dit Lyonnais le Juste [?]
Bennett, Arnold
   Don Juan
   Sacred and Profane Love
Beranger, Clara
   Your Home Comes First
Bereny, Henry
   The Girl from Montmartre
Bergerat, Emile
   More Than Queen
Bergeret, Gaston
   L'assassinée
Beringer, Oscar
   The Agitator
   A Bit of Old Chelsea
Berkeley, Reginald
   The Man I Killed
Berlin, Irving
   Stop, Look, Listen
   Watch Your Step
Bernard, Octave
   La chanteur des rues
Bernard, Tristan
   A Bolt from the Blue
   Le costaud des épinettes
   Le danseur unconnu
   Les deux jumeaux de Brighton
   French As He Is Spoken
   The Hoyden
   The Little Cafe
   A Thief in the Night
   Toddles
   Triplepatte
   The Uninvited Guest
   The Unknown Dancer
Bernauer, Rudolph
   His Highness' Mistress
Bernstein, Else
   King's Children
Bernstein, Helen
   Naughty Nicholas
Bernstein, Henry
   L'assault
   The Attack
   Brother Jacques
   The By-path
   Le détour
   Frère Jacques
   Israel
   L'ossaut
   La rafale
   Samson
   The Thief
   Le voleur
Bernstein, Herman
   Vera
Berr, Georges
   Monsieur de Pre-en-Pail est serviable
   Monsieur de Pre-en-Pail Is Accomodating
   Oh! Oh! Delphine!
   Ten Minutes in an Auto
Berry, William J.
   La Valliere
Berte, Heinrich
   Creole Blood
Berton, Pierre
   La Belle Marseillaise
   Les façades
   Frique
   Yvette
   Zaza
Bibesco, Prince Antoine
   A Very Practical Joke
Bilhaud, Paul

The Best of Wives
The Glove
My Daughter-in-law
Le papillon
Paradise
The Surprise
Tit for Tat
Bipschuetz, Leopold
Edythe
Birabeau, André
A Dangerous Girl
The Orange Blossom
Birdsall, Alfred Ward
The Lady of Luzon
Biro, Ludwig
The Baron Robber
The Czarina
Eva's zwei Lügen
The Last Kiss
Der letzte Kuss
Bisson, Alexandre
Because She Loved Him So
Le bon Juge
The Captivating Florence
The Good Judge
Madame X
Mariage d'étoile
The Marriage of a Star
The Masked Ball
The Mistakes of Marriage
Mr. Wilkinson's Widows
Mouton
My Housekeeper
Nea Gouvermante
Nick Carter
The Night Boat
No Questions Asked
On and Off
Blackmore, R. D.
Lorna Doone
Blasco Ibañez, Vicente
Blood and Sand
Bloch, Bertram
Spring Again
Blossom, Henry
The Lone Star Girl
The Red Mill
Blow, Sydney
Lord Richard in the Pantry
Old Juge

Blumenthal, Oscar
The Blind Passenger
A Stage-struck Village
Bodansky, Robert
Collette
The Little King
The Fair Risette
Bolton, Guy
The Dark Angel
Grounds for Divorce
Ladies Who Listen
Out to Win
Tangerine
Three after Three
Walk with Music
Bonsergent, Alfred
Irregular
Booth, Hilliard
The Nutmeg Girl
Boucheron, Maxime
Le billet de logement
Bouchinet, Alfred
Her Father
Boucicault, Dion
London Assurance
The Luck of Roaring Camp
Zoe
Bovill, C. H.
St. Antony
Bowers, Robert Hood
The Red Rose
Boyesen, Algernon
Modern Love
The Other Mary
Bracco, Roberto
Comtesse coquette
The End of Love
Eve and the Serpents
Unfaithful
Bradley, Lillian Trimble
The Wonderful Thing
Brammer, Julius
The Bajadere
Die Bakadere
The Dancing Girl
The Laughing Husband
Bright, Addison
The Bugle Call
Brinton, Selwyn
Harlequin

Broadhurst, George Howells
  The American Lord
  The Captain
  General Crack
  The Red Knight
  That American
Broadhurst, Thomas W.
  The Holy City
Brody, Alexander
  The Teacher
Brookfield, Charles Hallam Elton
  By Proxy
  The Cuckoo
  Kenyon's Widow
  The Third Moon
  A Woman's Reason
Brown, Martin
  The Face Play — "Venus"
Brown, Vincent
  A Magdalen's Husband
Browne, Porter Emerson
  Chains
  Elaine
  Half the World
  Oil and Water
  Sex
Bruegger, Frederick
  One O'clock
Buchanan, Robert
  Alone in London
Buchanan, Thompson
  As Good As New
  Natalie
  A Woman's Way
Buchbinder, Bernard
  Paula Sees to Everything
Buhler, Hans
  The Little Girls of Davos
Burani, Paul
  Le billet de logement
Burnand, Sir Francis Cowley
  Incognita
  The Manager
Burnett, Frances Hodgson
  The Pretty Sister of José
Burnside, Kathryne
  Some Party
  Stop Thief
Burnside, Robert Hubber Thorne
  As It Happened

The Ballet of Jewels
The Battle in the Skies
Better Times
The Blue Diamond
Boncieux's Inn
The Boojam of Bangalore
The Broadway Bells
Burning to Sing
The Captain of the Guard
Cheer Up
Chin-chin
Chinese Justice
Circus Life
Crooked Crooks
Crooks Farm
The Dancing Duchess
The Darling Girls
The Double Cross
The Duke's Double
Easy Money!
The Eldest Son
Everything
Fascinating Flora
Freedom
George Washington
The Girl I Love
The Girl from Cook's
The Girl from Mexico
Girls and Boys
The Great Scotch Mystery
The Gun Man
H.M.S. Pinafore [15-minute version]
Her Ladyship
Here and There
The Hermits in Europe
The Hermits of Happy Hollow
The Hermits in Paris
The Hermits in Sardinia
The Hermits in Vienna
The Hindoo Idol
His Grace, the Duke
I'm Telling You
In the Bag
Inside the Earth
The International Cup
Jack O'Lantern
The King of Diamonds
The King of Hearts
The (K)Night of the Garter
The Love Puzzle

The Love Racket
A Loving Legacy
Merry & Bright
The Merry Duke
Miss Millions
Mr. Millions
Montgomery and Stone Show
Murder in Church
Nay, Nay, Napoleon
A Night in Town
The Nighthawk
Nothing but Cuts
Once upon a Time
The Pied Piper
Possession
Private Patsy
Professional
The Prudent King
The Queen of Hearts
Regan's Revenge
School Days
Sergeant Kitty
The Singing Society
Some Party
Sporting Days
Stepping Stones
Stop Thief
Ten Minutes in a Lunchroom
The Three Kisses
The Three Romeos
The Tidal Wave
Tip Top
The Tourists
A Trip to Japan
The Two Gun Man
The Two Romeos
Uncle Tom's Saloon
Where Shall We Go Tonight?
[Untitled work]
Bús Fekete, László
  The Two Mihalyi Girls
Bussiere, Tadena
  Exit Claudine
Byrne, John F.
  The Toy Maker's Dreams
Byron, Henry J.
  Uncle Dick's Darling
Caillavet, Gaston Armand de
  The Ambassador
  L'amour veille

L'Ane de Buridan
The Beautiful Adventure
La belle aventure
Circe
Decorating Clementine
The Doll Maiden
The Great Adventure
The Inconstant George
Jenny and Her Mother
The Labors of Hercules
Love Watches
Miquette
Miquette and Her Mother
Miquette et sa mere
La Montansier
Primrose
Les sentiers de la vertu
Venise
What Woman Wills
Caldwell, Anne
  Chin-chin
  The City Chap
  Criss Cross
  Good Morning Dearie
  A Husband by Proxy
  Jack O'Lantern
  The Lady of the Slipper
  The Night Boat
  Oh Please
  Once upon a Time
  Stepping Stones
  Stop and Go!
  Tip Top
  Uncle Sam
Caldwell, Glen
  Hitchy Koo
Calthrop, Dion Clayton
  Out to Win
Campbell, Charles J.
  The Motor Girl
Campbell, Lawton
  Fangs
Capus, Alfred
  An Angel
  The Adventurer
  Les favorites
  The Favorites
  The Flirt
  The Husbands of Leontine
  Ma femme et son mari

Les maris de Leontine
Money or Life
The Streak of Luck
The Two Schools
La veine
Your Money or Your Life
Carleton, Henry Guy
   The Butterflies
   The Trap and the Bait
Carnes, Mason
   The Better Part
Carpenter, Edward Childs
   Romeo and Jane
   The Three Bears
Carr, Comyns
   In the Days of the Duke
Carr, F. Osmand
   In Town
Carr, Joseph William Comyns
   Oliver Twist
Carr, Philip
   Shock-headed Peter
Carré, Albert
   Doctor Bill
   The Masked Ball
   Une nuit de noces
Carré, Fabrice
   My Daughter-in-law
Carré, Michel
   The Surprise
Carroll, John S.
   Blind Guides
Carson, Murray
   Rosemary
Carten, Audrey
   Fame
Carten, Waveney
   Fame
Carton, R. C.
   Hobson's Choice
   Lady Barbarity
   Liberty Hall
   Nurse Benson
   The Off Chance
   The Rich Mrs. Repton
   Robin Goodfellow
   The Squire of Dames
   A White Elephant
Cella, Louis J.
   The Brothers

Cellier, François
   A Blue Moon
Chaine, Pierre
   L'étrange aventure de
     M. Martin Pequet
   The Strange Adventure
     of Mr. Martin Pequet
Chambers, Charles Hadoon
   The Awakening
   Basil the Bold
   The By-path
   In the Days of the Duke
   Mademoiselle Brulemans's Marriage
   Passers-by
   The Saving Grace
   Suzanne
   The Tyranny of Tears
Chancel, J.
   Madame Orderly
Charnay, Robert
   My Wife
Charvay, Robert
   Mademoiselle Josette ma femme
   Mister Pickwick
Chase, Ilka
   Pierre or Jack
Chase, Marjorie
   False Dawn
Christmas, Walter
   Bird of Passage
Chevalier, Albert
   The Scapegrace
Chiarelli, Luigi
   The Mask and the Face
Chilton, Eleanor Carroll
   Healthy, Wealthy and Wise
Churchill, Winston
   Richard Carvel
Claretie, Jules
   The Million
Clark, Alec
   Finnin Hari, Secret Agent
Clark, Alexander
   Hamlet O'Hara
Clarke, Harry
   Smiling Faces
Clay, Isobel
   Holiday Island
Clemens, Le Roy
   Blue Eyes

Clive, Jocelyn
   Marriage by Purchase
Cohan, George M
   The Farrell Case
Colbron, Grace Isabel
   The Colonel
   Comtess Coquette
   His Highness' Mistress
   Madame Pompadour
   Only a Dream
   A Waltz Dream
Coleby, Wilfred T
   The Likes O' Me
Collier, William
   Caught in the Rain
   Nothing But Cuts
Collins, Wilkie
   No Thoroughfare
Conland, Francis
   Officer O'Fishent
Connelly, Marcus C.
   The Lady of Luzon
Conroy, Frank J.
   King for a Night
Cook, James Francis
   Fuss and Feathers
   A Princess of Porcelain
Coolus, Romain
   The Strike
   A Woman Passed by
Cormon, Eugène
   A Celebrated Case
Cort, Harry L.
   China Rose
Cottens, Victor de
   The Fireman on Duty
Cottrell, Harry D.
   The Judge and the Jury
Coudurier, Joseph
   L'héritier
Courtneidge, Robert
   The Babes in the Wood
   The Dairy Maids
Coward, Noel
   The Young Idea
Cox, R. Kennedy
   The King's Mate
Craven, Frank
   Get Those Papers
   The Little Stranger

Croisset, Francis de
   Arsène Lupin
   Le coeur dispose
   Le diable à Paris
   The Marriage of Kitty
   Orange Blossoms
   Pierre or Jack
Cronin, A. J.
   Hatter's Castle
Cronin-Wilson, W.
   The Waggonload
Crooker, Earle
   And the Angels Swing
   Vive le corporal
Crothers, Rachel
   Nora
   The Three of Us
   Young Wisdom
Crouse, Russel
   Hold Your Horses
Croxton, R. C.
   Xmas on the Border
Curzon, Frank
   The Balkan Princess
Cushing, Catherine Chisholm
   Between the Acts
   Jerry
   Little Partners
   Princess Pretend
Cushing, Tom
   Blood and Sand
Cutter, Rollin
   Tampering with Hearts
Cutti, Berta
   Tien-hoa

Dalrymple, Leons
   David's Adventure
Dancourt, Grenet
   L'assassinée
Dane, Clemence
   [pseud of Winifred Ashton]
   A Bill of Divorcement
   The Way Things Happen
Darnley, J. H.
   The Solicitor
Daudet, Alphonse
   The Illustrious Tartarin
Dauncey, Silvanus
   Love at Home

Davidson, John
  The Children of the King
Davies, Hubert Henry
  Bevis
  Captain Drew on Leave
  Cousin Kate
  Cynthia
  The Mollusc
  A Single Man
Davis, Dorrance
  The Bitter Bitten
Davis, Gustav
  Edythe
Davis, Richard Harding
  The Dictator
  The Girl from Home
  The Lion and the Unicorn
  The System of Dr. Gourdron and Professor Plume
  The Trap
  The Vagrant
Davis, Robert Hobard
  The Family
Dazey, C. T.
  The American Lord
  The Captain
  That American
Dean, Basil
  The Private life of Helen of Troy
Decourcelle, Pierre
  Les deux gosses
  Le petite soeur
  Ten Minutes in an Auto
  The Two Kids
De Koven, Reginald
  Robin Hood
  The Snowman
De Mille, Cecil Blount
  The Royal Mounted
De Mille, Henry Churchill
  Governor Rodman's Daughter
  Men and Women
  The Royal Mounted
Dennery, Adolphe Philippe
  A Celebrated Case
Denny, Ernest
  All-of-a-sudden Peggy
  Just like Judy!
  Kidnapped
  Man Proposes

Deslandes, Raimond
  Mame
Desvallieres, Maurice
  Champignol Despite Himself
  Champignol malgré lui
  L'hôtel du libre échange
  Le toruc de seraphin
De Sylva, George Gard
  The Bajadere
  Orange Blossoms
Deval, Jacques
  Ventose
Dickens, Charles
  Mr. Pickwick
  No Thoroughfare
  Oliver Twist
  Poor Jo
Dickey, Paul
  Miss Information
Ditrichstein, Leo James
  The Concert
  Tit for Tat
Doermann, Felix
  A Waltz Dream
Dolley, Georges
  The Orange Blossoms
Donnay, Maurice-Charles
  La douleureuse
  L'escalade
  Georgette Lemeunier
  Lovers
Donnelly, Dorothy
  Blossom Time
  The Proud Princess
Donohue, Jack
  The Understudy
Donovan, Royle
  The Kinds of Diamonds
Doremus, Elizabeth Johnson (Ward) [Mrs Charles A. Doremus]
  The Circus Rider
Dormann, Felix
  The Baroness
Dotter, Paul M.
  The Zebra
Dowling, Eddie
  Sidewalks of New York
Doyle, Arthur Conan
  Brigadier Gerard
  The Fires of Fate

The Fires of Fate
    [American version]
House of Termperly
Sherlock Holmes
The Speckled Band
Doyle, J. Neven
  The Golden Age
Dregely, Gabriel
  His Wife's Husband
Drew, F. C.
  The Maid of the San Joaquin
Dreyer, Max
  Blaubart
Drury, W. P.
  The Flag Lieutenant
Dubourg, Augustus
  New Men and Old Acres
Dumas, Alexandre, the elder
  The Black Tulip
  A Marriage of Convenience
  The Silver Key
Dumas, Alexandre, the younger
  The Friend of Women
  The Lady of the Camellias
  The Squire of Dames
Du Maurier, Gerald
  An Englishman's Home
  A Royal Rival
Dunning, James E.
  The Number 29
Dunning, Philip Hart
  Sh! Sh! Listen!
  The Understudy
Duquesnel, Felix
  The Piano Teacher
Duval, Georges
  The Dragoons of the Empress
  The Lash of the Whip
  Mr. Pickwick
  Next
  The Swan Song
Ebenhack, Arthur
  The Barking Dog
Edwards, Julian
  The Musketeers
Egerton, George
  The Attack
  The Beautiful Adventure
Elisch, Ernest
  Madame Pompadour

Ellis, Edith
  The Illustrious Tartarin
  The Truth
Ellis, Walter
  S.O.S.
Emerson, John
  The Honor of Japan
Englander, Victor
  Darling Diana
  Lucky in Love
  The Naughty Duchess
Erskine, Beatrice
  My Price
Erskine, John
  The Private Life of Helen of Troy
Esmond, Henry V. [pseud Henry Jack]
  Grierson's Way
  Impudence
  The Law Divine
  Merry Springtime
  My Lady's Chamber
  My Lady's Lord
  The O'Grindles
  One Summer's Day
  The Pedestal
  Phroso
  The Wilderness
Eysler, Edmund
  The Laughing Husband

Fabre, Emile
  Caesar Birotteau
  The Honor of the Family
  The Wrong Man
  Under Which King?
Fagan, James Bernard
  Bella Donna
Falconer, Edmund
  Too Much for Good Nature
Fall, Leo
  The Fair Risette
  Madame Pompadour
  The Siren
Farnie, H. B.
  La fille du Tambour Major
Fauler, A. N. C.
  The Tattoed Man

Fazekas, Imre
  Altona
Fecheimer, Richard
  Elsie Janis and Her Gang
Fenn, Frederick
  Love and Laughter
  Op-o-me-thumb
Ferber, Edna
  Roast Beef Medium
Fernald, Chester Bailey
  The Beautiful Mrs. Towne
  Cornelia
  The Moonlight Blossom
Ferrier, Paul
  At the Lawyer's House
  Little Bohemia
  La petite Bohème
Feydeau, Georges
  The Bud
  Champignol Despite Himself
  Champignol malgré lui
  La dame de chez Maxim
  Fil-a-la-patte
  The Girl from Maxim's
  The Girl from Montmartre
  Hortense Says "Go to hell!"
  L'hotel du libre exchange
  The Lady at Maxim's
  La main passe
  My Good Friends
Fields, Herbert
  Fifty Million Frenchmen
Fischer, Hans
  Die Vielgeliebte
Fitch, Clyde
  Barbara Freitchie
  Barbara Freitchie
    That Frederick Girl
  The Bird in the Cage
  Bohemia
  Captain Jinks of the Horse Marines
  The Coronet of the Duchess
  Cousin Billy
  The Flirt
  The Girl and the Judge
  The Girl with the Green Eyes
  Glad of It!
  Granny
  The Happy Marriage
  The House of Mirth
  The Last of the Dandies
  The Masked Ball
  Toddles
  The Truth
  Wolfville
Fleming, Carroll
  Around the world
  Pioneer days
Fleming, George [pseud of Julia Constance Fletcher]
  The Canary
  Lady Rose's Daughter
Flers, Robert de
  The Ambassador
  L'amour veille
  L'ane de Buridan
  The Beautiful Adventure
  La belle aventure
  Circe
  Decorating Clementine
  Le diable à Paris
  The Doll Maiden
  The Great Adventure
  Inconstant Gengi
  Inconstant George
  Jenny and Her Mother
  The Labors of Hercules
  Love Watches
  Miquette
  Miquette and Her Mother
  Miquette et sa mere
  La montansier
  Primrose
  Les sentiers de la vertu
  What Woman Wills
Flers, P. L.
  Le petit choc
Fletcher, Constance
  The Canary
  A Man and His Wife
Flexner, Anne Crawford
  Miranda of the Balcony
Fonson, Frantz
  Mademoiselle Beuleman's Marriage
  The Marriage of Mlle. Beulemans Suzanne

Forbes, James
   The Traveling Salesman
Ford, Corey
   Hold Your Horses
Ford, Harriet
   A Gentleman of France
Forman, Justus Miles
   The Hyphen
Forst, Emil
   Marguerite for Three
Forzano, Giovacchino
   Tien-ho
France, Anatole
   Crainquebille
Francis, W. T.
   Twirly Whirly
Frank, Paul
   Fahrt nach Sorrent
   A Trip to Sorrento
Frank, Waldo
   Dot
Frapié, Léon Eugène
   Serverité
Frappa, Jean-José
   L'homme riche
Friedmann-Frederich, Fritz
   Meyers
   The White Vest
Frith, John Leslie
   Désiré
Frohman, Ben
   Naughty Nicholas
Frondaie, Pierre
   Montmartre
   The Woman and the Puppet
Frye, Emma Sheridan
   Mars'a Van
Fulda, Ludwig
   At Sunset
   The Twin Sister
   The Volcano
   The World's Mask
Fuller, Loïe
   A Little Japanese Girl
Furneau, Michael
   The Blue Diamond
Fyles, Franklin
   The Girl I Left Behind Me
Fyles, Vanderheyden

   Because of Teddy Clyde
   The Future
Galantiere, Lewis
   Lovers, Happy Lovers
Galsworthy, John
   The Eldest Son
   Justice
   The Mob
   The Silver Box
   Strife
Gandera, Felix
   Atout . . . . coeur!
   Quick
   Quick — a serious lover
Garnier, P. L.
   Serverité
Garren, Jos. J.
   Collette
Garrick, David
   The Country Girl
Gatti, E. V.
   Creole Blood
Gavault, Paul
   The Fireman on Duty
   Francoise's Idea
   The Little Chocolate Girl
   Mademoiselle Josette, ma femme
   My Aunt from Honfleur
   My Wife
   The Richest Girl
George, Charles
   Exit Claudine
Gérard, Paul
   La Culotte
Gershwin, George
   Strike up the Band
Gershwin, Ira
   Strike up the Band
Gibson, Lawrence
   For Bitter or Worse
Gilbert, Jean
   His Highness' Mistress
   In Quest of Happiness
Gilbert, Victor
   The Blue Diamond
Gilbert, W. S.
   H. M. S. Pinafore [one-act version]
   The Wedding March

Gillette, William
   All the Comforts of Home
   Because She Loved Him So
   Clarice
   Diplomacy
   The Dream Maker
   Electricity
   The Harrowing Predicament of Sherlock Holmes
   Held by the Enemy
   A Legal Wreck
   Mr. Wilkinson's Widows
   Secret Service
   Sherlock Holmes
   That Little Affair at the Boyd's
   Too Much Johnson
Gleason, J. MacArthur
   The Fly-away
Glover, J. H.
   Let's Be Broadminded
   The Love Puzzle
Goddard, Charles
   Miss Information
Godefroy, Jacques
   Ce beau naufrage
Godfernaux, André
   Toddles
Goetz, Curt
   Hokus-pokus
   Der Lampenschirm
Goetz, E. Ray
   The Never Homes
Golden, John L.
   The Candy Shop
   Cheer Up
   Everything
Gooch, Frances Pusey
   His Wife's Case
Goodman, Jules Eckert
   The Silent Voice
   The Trap
Goodwin, J. Cheever
   The Merry Monarch
Gordon, Archibald
   That Man from Boston
Gordon, Julian
   The Blue Diamond
   The Naughty Duchess
Gordon, Leon
   Blue Eyes
Gordon, Mack
   Smiling Faces
Gordon-Lennox, Cosmo
   The Freedom of Suzanne
   The Marriage of Kitty
   Miquette and Her Mother
   Jenny and Her Mother
   Primrose
   A Woman Passed By
   Yvette
Gorsse, Henry Joseph Auguste de
   Madame Orderly
   The Runaway
Gosselin, Louis Leon Theodore
   Three Days of Glory
   Les trois glorieuses
Gostony, Adam
   Experience Unnecessary
Graham, H.
   His Wedding Day
Granichstaetten, Bruno
   Madame Serafin
Greenbank, Henry
   A Greek Slave
   Incognita
Greenbank,, Percy
   The Earl and the Girl
Greene, Clay M.
   Three Christmas Eves
Gresac, Fred
   The Marriage of Kitty
   Orange Blossoms
Grimshaw, Thomas T.
   Marooned
Gross, Franz
   In Quest of Happiness
Gross, Laurence
   Lady's Choice
Groves, Charles
   A Golden Wedding
Gruenwald, Alfred
   The Bajadere
   The Dancing Girl
   The Laughing Husband
Grundy, Sydney
   The Arabian Nights
   The Black Tulip
   A Debt of Honour
   Gypsy

A Marriage of Convenience
The Silver Key
The Snowball
Sowing the Wind
Guillemand, Marcel
  Oh! Oh! Delphine!
Guinon, Albert
  Her Father
Guitry, Sacha
  Legerdemain
  Pasteur
Gunter, Archibald Clavering
  The Fighting Troubadour
Haggart, John D.
  Compromise
Halévy, Ludovic
  The Manager
  La Périchole
Hall, Owen
  A Green Slave
Halton, Theo
  The Little Girls of Davos
  Lodge No. Seven
Hamilton, Cicely
  Diana of Dobson's
Hamilton, Cosmo
  The Beauty of Bath
  The Feathers of the Jay
  The Hoyden
  The Story of the Gadsbys
  A Thief in the Night
Hamilton, Henry
  Cheer, Boys, Cheer
  The Little Duke
  The White Heather
Hamilton, Patrick
  John Brown's Body
Harbach, Otto
  Criss Cross
  The Firefly
  Jack and Jill
  Oh Please
Harding, D. C. F.
  Leonardo
Harmant, Abel
  La carrière
Harper, Neal
  The Magic Apple
Harris, Augustus
  Cheer, Boys, Cheer

Harte, Bret
  Germaine
Harwood, H. M.
  Please Help Emily
Hastings, Basil MacDonald
  Any Woman Would
Hatvany, Lili
  The Love Duel
Haussman, John
  Lovers, Happy Lovers
Hayden, John
  Warden's Orders
Hedberg, Tor
  Modern Youth
Heijermans, Herman, Jr
  The "Hope"
Hein, Sylvio
  The Girl from Home
Hellinger, Mark
  Warden's Orders
Heltai, Eugen
  The Milliner
Hemmerde, E. G.
  A Butterfly on the Wheel
Henderson, Al
  Trovatore Ill-treated
Henderson, Isaac
  The Mummy and the Humming Bird
Hendrix, August
  Love at Home
Henmyine, Maurice
  Next
Hennequin, Maurice
  The Best of Wives
  The Commissary's Wife
  Coralie & Co
  The Glove
  An Important Case
  The Lash of the Whip
  Madame la Présidente
  Paradise
  Passionately
  The President
  Tit for Tat
  Vingt jours à l'ombre
Herbein, Paul
  The Law of Man
Herbert, Ian
  Darling Diana
  The Love Pirate

Herbert, Joseph
    The Devil and His Due
    Fascinating Flora
    The Scourge of the Sea
Herczeg, Ferenz
    The Colonel
Hergesheimer, Joseph
    The Party Dress
Hermant, Abel
    The Transatlantic
Herne, James A.
    Hearts of Oak
    The Minute Men of 1774–5
    Sag Harbor
Herriman, H. N.
    The Girl from Mexico
Hervieu, Paul
    Le destin est maître
    The Enigma
    Theroigne de Méricourt
Herzer, Ludwig
    Brautnacht
    She's a Spy
Herzog, Wilhelm
    Dreyfus
Heyward, Dorothy
    The Lighted House
Hichens, Robert
    Bella Donna
Hicks, Seymour
    The Beauty of Bath
    The Earl and the Girl
    A Lucky Little Girl
    The New Sub
Higgins, David
    Cash on Hand
Hill, Grace Livingston
    A Colonial Girl
Hillebrand, Fred
    Lambs on Parade
Hillian, B. C.
    Elsie Janis and Her Gang
Hitchcock, Robert W.
    David Harum
Hoare, Douglas
    Lord Richard in the Pantry
Hobart, George V.
    The Candy Shop
    The Girl in Grey
    Old Dutch
    The Party of the First Part
    Roast Beef Medium
    Some Party
Hodges, Horace
    Grumpy
Hollister, Len D.
    Take the Witness
Hood, Basil
    The Count of Luxumberg
    The Emerald Isle
    Love in a Cottage
    Picture in Three Panels
    The Rose of Persia
    Sweet and Twenty
Hope, Anthony
    Captain Dieppe
    Phroso
Hopkins, Arthur
    Al and Bill
Hopwood, Avery
    The Harem
Hornblow, Arthur, Jr
    Pasteur
Hornung, E. W.
    Raffles
Houghton, Stanley
    Hindle Wakes
    The Younger Generation
Howard, Bronson
    [Untitled play]
Howard, Frederick
    What Goes on Here
Hoyt, Charles H.
    A Texas Steer
Hughes, Rupert
    The Deaf Mute
Hume, Fergus
    The Little Duke

Ide, Leonard
    Concealment
Irwin, Fred
    Mister R. E. Morse
Irwin, Wallace
    The Dove of Peace
Isham, Frederick
    Jack and Jill
Ives, Alice E.
    Calanthy's Mistake

Jackson, Fred
    Nothing at All

Jacobs, W. W.
   Beauty and the Barge
Jacobson, Leopold
   Collette
   A Waltz Dream
Jacoby, Carl M.
   Chick
Jacoby, Wilhelm
   Freedom from Men
Janis, Elsie
   Elsie Janis and her Gang
   A Star for a Night
Jarno, Josef
   Die Vielgeliebte
Jay, Harriet
   Alone in London
Jensen, Thit
   The Jackal
Jeoferin, ——
   La montansier
Jermon, John G.
   Show Life
Jerome, Jerome K.
   The Disagreeable Man
   Miss Hobbs
   Robina's Web
   Tommy
Jesse, F. Tennyson
   Quarantine
Johan, Ulfstejerna
   Modern Youth
Johnston, May
   To Have and to Hold
Johnstone, Alexander
   The Red Canary
Johnstone, Calder
   Sentinel Light
Johnstone, Howard
   Tangerine
Johnstone, William B.
   The Red Canary
Jones, Edward
   The Scapegrace
Jones, Henry Arthur
   The Bauble Shop
   Cock o' the Walk
   Her Tongue
   Josephine Entangled
   The Liars
   Whitewashing Julia
   Sweet Will

Jordan, Kate
   The Next Corner
Jullien, Jules
   The Feathers of the Jay
   Love or Money!
Justus, Antonia A.
   The Gratitude of Carthage
Kadelburg, Gustav
   The Blind Passenger
   The Girl He Couldn't Leave behind Him
   The Slippery Road
   A Stage-struck Village
Kahn, Julius
   The Medicine Man
Kalisch, Burnham
   Love in Law
Kampf, Leopold
   Liberty
Kardoss, Andor
   Eva's zwei Lügen
   Venus
Kardos, Andrew
   Two and two
Karlweis, C.
   The Other One
Kastner, Leo
   Uschi
Kaufman, George S.
   Strike Up the Band
Kaufman, S. Jay
   The Shortest Play
Kebler, Richard
   The Woman Lawyer
Keroul, Henry
   The Bouilnard's
   Une nuit de noces
Kerr, Clarence Vincent
   The Dancing Duchess
   The Girl I Love
   Girls and Boys
   The Hermits in Vienna
   The Nighthawk
Kessler, Richard
   The Double Emil
Kidder, Edward E.
   The Duke's Diamonds
   Sky Farm
   The Tulip Girl
Kimball, David

The Sowers
Kipling, Rudyard
  The Story of the Gadsbys
Kistemaeckers, Henry
  La flambée
  The Spy
Klein, Charles
  Les deux gosses
  The Lion and the Mouse
  The 2nd, 3rd, 4th, etc
Klein, Manuel
  Around the World
  Ozma of Oz
Kling, Saxon
  Autumn
Knight, Percival
  Detective Keen
Knoblauch, Edward
  The Captivating Florence
  Hatter's Castle
  The Paying Guest
Kohn, Simon
  Nobody's Junior
Kornell, William
  Elsie Janis and her Gang
Kraatz, Curt
  The Double Emil
  A Double Marriage
  The Lady from the Cab
  Lodge No. Seven
  The Mountain Climber
  Olympian Games
  The Scorcher
  Theatrical Sport
  Well Born
  The Woman Lawyer
Krenn, Leopold
  The Three Wishes
Kuchler, Kurt
  A Summer Spook
Kummer, Clare
  Kisses
  Madame Pompadour
  One Kiss

Labische, Eugene
  Cousin Billy
Lachaume, Aimé
  Mam'zelle Sourire
Lackaye, Wilton, Jr
  Sad but True
Lackey, R. B.
  Angels Don't Kiss
Lamb, Arthur J.
  Bamboozleum
Landesberg, Alexander
  The Fortunate Fool
Landis, Frederick
  The Copperhead
Langer, Frantistek
  The Camel Goes through
  The Needle's Eye
Larcher, Eugène
  The Twin
Lascelles, Erinta
  Lucretia
Lathrop, William Addison
  The Man Who Never Grew Up
Laufs, Carl
  All the Comforts of Home
Lavedan, Henri
  The Duel
  The Marquis de Priola
  Servir
  Sire!
  The Taste for Vice
Law, Arthur
  A Country Mouse
Leader, James
  In Town
Leavitt, Douglas
  Show Life
Le Baron, William
  Die Bajadere
  The Dancing Girl
  The Red Canary
  The Scarlet Man
Leblanc, Maurice
  Arsène Lupin
Le Clercq, Adolphe
  Because She Loved Him So
Leighton, Isabel
  Spring Again
Leipziger, Leo
  Jung Muss man Sein
Lemaître, Jules
  The Eldest
Le Maire, George
  King for a Night
Le Marchant, Peter
  The Spy
Lengel, William C.
  The Party Dress
Lengyel, Melchior

L'ange
The Black Butterfly
The Czarina
Fräulein Charlotte
Maria
Prophet Percival
Lennard, Gwynne
The Tigress
Lenôtre, G.
Colinette
Lequel, Louis
No Thoroughfare
Leroux, Gaston
The Mystery of the Yellow Room
Le Roy, Charles
Three Husbands/One Wife
Lestocq, William
The Foundling
Jane
Levenson, Lew
The Party Dress
Levy, Jose G.
Madame la Présidente
Levy, Parke
Three after Three
Walk with Music
Lewis, Alfred Henry
Wolfville
Lewis, Cecil
Jazz Patterns
Liebling, Leonard
Lacrimosa
Lindau, Carl
The Blue Doll
Die blaue Puppe
The Three Wishes
Liorat
Cupid
Lippschitz, Arthur
Freedom from Man
Lipscott, Alan
Three after Three
Walk with Music
Lisman, Robert G.
A Very Practical Joke
Locke, William J.
The Morals of Marcus
The Morals of Marcus Ordeyne
Logan, Stanley
Quick
Logouvé,
There's Many a Slip

Lolli, Alberto Carlo
Chiffon's marriage
Lonsdale, Frederuck
The Balkan Princess
Katja the Dancer
The Last of Mrs. Cheyney
Lorde, André de
Cochon d'enfant
The Husband in Spite of Himself
The System of Dr. Gourdron and Professor Plume
Lortzing, Gustav Albert
Tsar and Carpenter
Lothar, Rudolph
Harlequin
The Harlequin King
I Love You!
Louys, Pierre
The Woman and the Puppet

MacArthur, James
The Finishing School
McCarthy, Justin Huntley
Nurse Benson
Sir Roger de Coverley
McCarty, Laurence
Once upon a Time
McCarty, Lawrence
The Lady of the Slipper
McCormick, Langdon
The Mystic Melody
MacCulloch, Campbell
Brennan of the Moor
Count of Luxemberg
Dear Doctor
The Farmer's Bootstraps
The Hard Man
Her Husband's Wife
The House of Thieves
Just before the Dawn
Love at Poker Flat
Nell of Arizona
The Soul of Francesca
MacDonough, Glen
The Count of Luxumberg
The Flower Shop
The Hero
Hitchy Koo 1920
The House
The Jolly Bachelors

Joy and Gloom
The Never Homes
The Road House
The Vendue
Where Do We Go from Here
MacGill, Patrick
  Suspense
Mack, Willard
  The Big Chance
Mackall, Lawton
  I Can't Bear It
Mackay, W. Gayer
  Dr. Wake's Patient
McKenna, Stephen
  Ninety-six Hours' Leave
McLeod, J. R.
  How's Your Health?
McLellan, C. M. S.
  Nelly Neil
  Oh! Oh! Delphine
McNally, John J.
  Fluffy Ruffles
McNeile, Herman Cyril
  Bull-dog Drummond
Malin, Henri
  Médor
Maltby, H. F.
  The Laughter of Fools
Mandel, Frank
  The High Cost of Loving
Manners, John Hartley
  The Incomparable Lover
  The Patriot
  The Wooing of Eve
Mapes, Victor
  The Mechanism Man
Marchand, Leopold
  The Carlton Magician
  Professor Dimonio
Marsh, Richard
  Monte Carlo
Markbreit, Bertha
  Her Charming Excellency
Marlowe, Charles
  When Knights Were Bold
Mars, Antony
  La marmotte
  Le torus de seraphin
Marsèle, Jean
  The Husband in Spite of Himself
Marshall, N. M.
  Bonnie Prince Charlie
Marshall, Robert
  The Alabaster Staircase
  Ali Baba
  The Fugitive
  His Excellency the Governor
  The Orange Flower
  The Noble Lord
  A Royal Family
  The Second in Command
  Shades of Night
  There's Many a Slip
  The Unforeseen
Marsolleau, Louis
  A Woman's Battle
Martinetti, Pearl
  Robert Macaire
Martínez, Sierra
  The Romantic Young Lady
  Spring in Autumn
Martin, G.
  Colinette
Martos, Franz
  Der kleine Koenig
  The Little King
Mason, A. E. W.
  At the Villa Rose
  For the Defence
  Marjory Strode
  No Other Tiger
Maugham, W. Somerset
  Caroline
  The Circle
  Grace
  Jack Straw
  Lady Frederick
  The Land of Promise
  Loaves and Fishes
  A Man of Honour
  The Mask and the Face
  Mrs. Dot
  Penelope
  Sacred Flame
  Smith
  Worthy's entire
Maupassant, Guy de
  Yvette
Mayer, Edwin Justus
  Children of Darkness
Mayer, Gaston
  The Chauffeur
  French as He Is Spoken
Mayrargue, Lucien

Ma femme et son mari
Mazuel, H. Dupuy
  L'homme riche
Mears, Stannard
  Seventeen
Medcraft, Russell
  I Can't Bear It!
Megrue, Roi Copper
  Coincidence
Meilhac, Henri
  The Cuckoo
  The Manager
  La Périchole
Meltzer, Charles Henry
  More Than Queen
Mercer, Johnny
  Three after Three
  Walk with Music
Merrelle, Edna
  Flappers Beware
Merrick, Leonard
  The Imposter
Milch, Robert
  The Jockey Club
Miles, Grace C.
  The Lion and the Unicorn
  The Vagrant
Milhaud, A.
  Cab No. 117
Millocker, Carl
  The Black Hunter
Milne, A. A.
  Belinda
Mirande, Y.
  Kisses
  One Kiss
Mitchell, Dodson L.
  Civic Pride
  The Home Breaker
  What Every Hubby Knows
Mitchell, George
  The Absent One
  Granny
Mitchell, Langdon Elwyn
  Deborah
Mitchell, Norma
  I Can't Bear It
Moeller, Philip
  Molière, or, the King Comedian
  Wretched Woman
Moller, Alfred

  Uschi
Molnar, Franz
  Anniversary
  Carnival
  The Life Guardsman
  The Midnight Supper
  The Story of a Wolf
  Von Schonichen of the Guards
  The Wolf
Monnier, Jacques
  The Twin
Montgomery, James
  The City Chap
  Stella Brady
Morel, Ernest
  The Tour of the World
Morgan, Charles
  The River Line
Morosco, Oliver
  The Judge and the Jury
Morris, Grant
  The Big Chance
Morris, Ramsay
  Edythe
  The Marriage Contract
  The Social Trust
Morse, Wollson
  The Merry Monarch
Morton, Charles
  The Orphan Girl
Morton, Howard E.
  The Dream Maker
Morton, Hugh
  The Golden Cup
Morton, Martha
  His Wife's Father
  Liberty
Morton, Michael
  Detective Sparks
  Her Father
  The Imposter
  My Wife
  On with the Dance
  The Prodigal Husband
  The Runaway
Mosconi, Charles
  The Shortest Play
Moser, Gustav von
  The Arabian Nights
  Ein Kind der Secession
Mouezy-Eon, André
  The Little Homeopath

Muñoz Seca, Pedro
  My Prince
Murger, Henri
  Bohemia
Murray, Alfred
  La perichole
Murray, Douglas
  The Great Mrs. Alloway
Murray, William B.
  Pierre or Jack

Naden, Thomas
  The Junior Partners
Najac, Émile comte
  Cab No. 117
  Divorçons
Nancey, ——
  The Zebra
Nancey, Nic.
  The Little Homeopath
Neal, M.
  The Mountain Climber
Neal, Max
  The Fig Leaf
  Olympian Games
Neilson, Francis
  A Butterfly on the Wheel
Neilson, Marie
  L'héritier
Newman, Greatrex
  Accidents Will Happen
  According to Plan
  The Blue Diamond
  Darling Diana
  The Girl from Cook's
  The Mallaby Mystery
  Naughty Nicholas
Newman, Rehba
  The King of Diamonds
Niccodémi, Dario
  The Aigrette
  Dawn, Day, Night
  La flamme
  The Prodigal Husband
Nichols, Harry
  Jane
Nordlinger, Charles Frederick
  More Than Queen
Norini, Amiel
  The Key to Paradise
Nozières, Fernand de
  Marie Gazelle

O'Dea, James
  The Lady of the Slipper
  Once upon a Time
  Uncle Sam
Oden, Clarence Doubleday
  Flapper Follies
Oesterheld, Erich
  Fräulein Charlotte
Oesterreicher, Rudolph
  His Highness' Mistress
Ohney, Georges
  Colonel Roquebrune
O'Keefe, Lester
  Nay, Nay, Napoleon
Okonkowski, George
  Madame Serafin
Ongley, Byron
  Brewster's Millions
Ord, Robert
  Dr. Wake's Patient
Ordonneau, Maurice
  The Boulinard's
  Hotel Topsy-Turvy
  The Little Godins
  The Warbler's Flight
Oxenford, John
  The Magic Toys
  The Porter's Knot

Paradels, Octave
  Good King Dagobert
Parker, Louis N.
  L'aiglon
  Beauty and the Barge
  The Bugle Call
  Chantecler
  The Duel
  The Eaglet
  Feud
  Harlequin
  Lorna Doone
  Rosemary
  Sire!
  The Sorceress
  The Swashbuckler
  The Twin Sister
  A Woman's Battle
Passeu, Steve
  L'acheteuse
  Marriage by Purchase

Pasztor, Aeped
   The Magnetic
Paull, H. M.
   Across the Herring-pond
   The New Clown
Payne, B. Iden
   Dolly Jordon
Peile, F. Kinsey
   The Little Postmistress
Pemberton, Max
   The Finishing School
Percival, T. Wigney
   Grumpy
Percy, Edward
   A Magdalen's Husband
Pertwee, Roland
   Heat Wave
   Out to Win
Pessard, Émile Louis Fortuné
   Mam'zelle Carabin
Peterkin, Julia
   Scarlet Sister Mary
Peters, Mason
   Mr. Millions
Pettitt, Henry
   Carmen up to Date
Peyssonnié, Paul
   Lulu—Tojo
Philippi, Felix
   The Great Light
Philips, F. C.
   A Woman's Reason
Phillips, Stephen
   Ulysses
Phillpotts, Eden
   A Golden Wedding
   The Secret Woman
Picard, Andre
   Youth
Pigott, J. S.
   Kitty Grey
Pigott, Mostyn
   All Fletcher's Fault
Pinero, Sir Arthur Wing
   The Amazons
   Esmond
   His House in Order
   Iris
   Letty
   Mid Channel

   The "Mind the Paint" Girl
   Preserving Mr. Penmure
   Trelawny of the "Wells"
Pirandello, Luigi
   Lazzaro
Planche, J. R.
   Love and Fortune
Planquette, Robert
   The Bells of Corneville
   Mam'zelle Quatr'sous
Playfair, Nigel
   Shock-headed Peter
Pogson, Bertha
   Alma Mater
Pollonais, Gaston
   Le couché de la mariée
Porter, Cole
   Fifty Million Frenchmen
Potter, Paul M.
   The Adventuress
   Black Sheep
   Mame
   Manon
   Poor Jo
   The Wrong Man
   Stuyvie
Pollock, Channing
   Such a Little Queen
Powys, Stephen
   Walk with Music
Poynter, Beulah
   Lena Rivers
Prada, Malcolm la
   Zadig
Pratz, Claire de
   La Belle Marseillaise
Praxy, Raoul
   The Pet of the Janitress
Presbrey, Eugene W.
   Raffles
Preval,
   Cupid
Prudden, Theodore M.
   Look Out for Squalls
Pryce, Richard
   Op-o-me-thumb

Raboteau, Leon
   Good King Dagobert

Raceward, Thomas
  Sunday
Raleigh, Cecil
  The Best of Friends
  Cheer, Boys, Cheer
  Fanny
  The Flood Tide
  The Great Millionaire
  Hearts Are Trumps
  The Sunshine Girl
  The White Heather
Ralph, B. Carpenter
  Tweeny
Ranken, Frederick
  Happy Land
Raphael, John N.
  Cochon d'enfant
  The Jester
  Madame X
  The Uninvited Guest
  The Unknown Dancer
Ravold, John
  Gentlemen of the Jury
Rawlinson, A. R.
  The Private life of Helen of Troy
Reed, Daniel
  Scarlet Sister Mary
Reeves, Arnold
  The Secret Woman
Rehfisch, Hans J.
  Dreyfus
Rennie, James
  Ten Hours
Rey, Étienne
  La belle aventure
  The Great Adventure
Rex, Richard
  The Boojam
  His Royal Highness
Rhodes, Harrison
  Captain Dieppe
  Mr. Barnum
Rice, Elmer
  For the Defence
Richardson, Abbey Sage
  A Colonial Girl
Richepin, Jean
  The Spanish Gypsy
Richman, Arthur
  Ambush
  The Awful Truth
  The Exiles
Ridley, Arnold
  Headline
Riesner, Lawrence
  Ventose
Robertson, Ian
  A Play in Little
Robertson, T. W.
  Caste
Robins, Denise
  Heatwave
Robson, E. M.
  The Foundling
Robyn, Alfred George
  Tell It to the Danes
Rohr, Louis
  Circumstance
Rollitt, George
  The Moneymakers
Rose, Edward E.
  Alice of old Vincennes
  Eben Holden
  Edward Carvel
  Phroso
  Slippy McGee
  The Spenders
  To Have and to Hold
  Under the Red Rose
  Untitled comedy
Rosen, Julius
  Neighborly Love
Rosenfeld, Sydney
  Chick
  The Girl He Couldn't Leave behind Him
  The Pretty Persian
  The Rollicking Girl
  The Slippering Road
  Three Chrismas Eves
  The World's Mask
Rosmer, Milton
  A Magdalen's Husband
Ross, Adrian
  The Count of Luxumberg
Rostand, Edmond
  L'aiglon
  Chantecler
  The Eaglet

Rostand, Maurice
   The Man I Killed
Roux, Xavier
   The Swan Song
Royle, Edwin Milton
   Dee-Lighted's Dream
Rubens, Paul A.
   The Balkan Princess
   The Sunshine Girl
Ryley, Lucette
   La Belle Marsellaise
   Mice and Men
Ryskind, Morrie
   Strike Up the Band

Sabatini, Rafael
   The Rattlesnake
St Cyr, Dirce
   Comtesse Coquette
   Unfaithful
Salten, Felix von
   The Stronger Tie
Samuels, Maurice V.
   Zadig
Sanders, Louise
   The Knave of Hearts
Sanger, Joan
   The Dark Meteor
Santley, Joseph
   Hear 'em and Weep [cinema]
Sardou, Victorien
   Americans Abroad
   Diplomacy
   Divorcons
   The Poisoning Case
   The Sorceress
   La Sorcière
Savior, Alfred
   Himself
   Ladies Who Listen
   La petite Catherine
Schanzer, Rudolf
   Die blaue Puppe
   The Blue Doll
   The Girl from Montmartre
   Madame Pompadour
   Nan, Nay, Napoleon
Schary, Dore
   Violence

Schiffer, Marcellus
   Ten Years and One Second
Schiller, Friedrich von
   The Maid of Orleans
Schlack, Emil
   The Lace Veil
Schmidt, Lothar [pseud of Lothar
   Gold-schmidt]
   Only a Dream
   A Woman's Book
Schnitzler, Arthur
   Au perroquet vert
Schnitzer, J.
   Creole Blood "The President"
Schonthan, Franz Von
   Georgina
Schweefert,, Fritz
   Marguerite for Three
Scott, Clement
   Diplomacy
Scribe, Eugene
   There's Many a Slip
Scudamore, F. A.
   Dangers of London
Searelle, Luscombe
   Mizpah
Sebesi, Erno
   Zisammenstoss
Seigneur, M. de
   Germaine
Selby, Charles
   Peggy Green
Selwyn, Edgar
   A Modern Pirate
Serard, Eugene
   Le petit moucheron
Seymour, William
   Salvianti
Shakespeare, William
   Much Ado about Nothing [John
     Drew production promptbook]
Shaw, Bernard
   Over-ruled
   The Philanderer
Sheldon, Edward
   The Proud Princess
   The Song of Songs
Sheridan, Frank
   Once upon a Time

Sherwood, Robert Emmet
   Waterloo Bridge
Shipman, Samuel
   The American Sheik
Shirley, Arthur
   The Story of a Crime
Sidney, F. W.
   Naughty Nicholas
Sidney, Frederick
   The Brixton Burglary
   Lucky in Love
Simon, Charles
   Irregular
   Zaza
Sims, George R.
   Carmen up to Data
   City of Pleasure
   Fanny
   The Story of a Crime
Skinner, Ralph McHay
   The Motor Girl
Smith, Edgar McPhail
   Higgledy-Piggledy
   A Message from Mars
   Old Dutch
   Snow
   The Stickiness of Gelatine
   Tilly's Nightmare
   Whirligig
   Whoop-dee-doo
Smith, Harry B.
   Alienation
   Babette
   The Doll Girl
   Even Steven
   Gaby
   The Girl from Montmartre
   Oh, You Gabby!
   The Paradise of Mahomet
   Rambler Rose
   The Red Rose
   Round the World
   Stop, Look, Listen!
   The Tattooed Man
   Watch Your Step
Smith, J. C.
   Lady Barbarity
Smith, Robert B.
   The Babes in the Wood
   Gaby
   The Girl from Montmartre
   Oh, You Gabby!
   The Paradise of Mahomet
   The Red Rose
Smith, Winchell
   Brewster's Millions
   The City Chap
   Love Among the Lions
Sneddon, Robert W.
   Marie Gazelle
Sothern, E. H.
   The Light That Lies in Woman's Eyes
Sothern, Harry
   The Last Appeal
Soulaine, Pierre
   L'héritier
   The Variation
Soulie, Maurice
   A Woman's Battle
Stange, Hugh Stanislaus
   The Musketeers
   Seventeen
   The Showman
Steell, Willis
   Wolfville
Stein, Grant
   Caught in the Rain
Stein, Leo
   The Doll Girl
   The Doll Maiden
   The Siren
Stein, Mariam H.
   Midnight Supper
   A Trip to Sorrento
Stein-Landesmann, Alice
   Die Schiessbude
Stephany, Victor
   Alma Mater
Stephens, Robert Neilson
   An Enemy to the King
   Miss Elizabeth's Prisoner
Stephenson, B. C.
   Diplomacy
Stewart, Grant
   Caught in the Rain
Stewart, William G.
   Fuss and Feathers

Stieber, Ferdinand
   Prophet Percival
Stoblitzer, Heinrich
   The Fig Leaf
Stoddard, George E.
   China Rose
Stolz, Robert
   Collette
Stone, Fred
   The Two-gun Man
Strange, Michael
   Clare de Lune
Strong, Austin
   The Pied Piper
   Room 33 or La Sirene
   The Toymaker of Nuremberg
   What Happened Then?
Stuart, Aimee
   Monte Carlo
Stuart, Philip
   Monte Carlo
Sturges, Arthur
   Hotel Topsy-Turvy
Sturges, Preston
   Child of Manhattan
Sturm, Hans
   I Didn't Want to Do It
Suppe, Franz von
   Boccacio
Sutherland, E. G.
   Mars'a Van
Sutro, Alfred
   The Barrier
   The Bracelet
   The Builder of Bridges
   Carey and Son
   The Clever One
   The Firescreen
   Jim
   A Maker of Men
   Mollentrave on Women
   The Perfect Lover
   The Perplexed Husband
   Price of Money
   The Two Virtues
Swan, Mark E.
   The Press Agent
Swayne, Martin
   Lord Richard in the Pantry

Swanwide, Anne
   The Maid of Orleans
Swete, E. Lyall
   Miss Elizabeth's Prisoner
Sylvane, André [pseud of Paul Gérard]
   The End of the World
Szebenyei, Joseph
   My Queen I Die for You
Szulc, Józef Zygmunt
   Le petit choc

Tallien, A.
   Love or Money!
Tanner, James T.
   Our Miss Gibbs
Tarbé des Sablons, Edmond
   Joseph Louis
   The City of Pleasure
Tarkington, Booth
   How's Your Health?
   Your Humble Servant
   Seventeen
Taylor, Charles
   The Babes in the Wood
   The Beauty of Bath
Taylor, Tom
   The House or the Home
   New Men and Old Acres
Teramond, Guy de
   La petite Zaza
Terry, J. E. Harold
   General Post
   The Rattlesnake
Terwilliger, George
   Sentinel Light
Thackeray, William Makepeace
   Esmond
Theschton, Herbert
   The Fair Risette
Thexton, Herbert
   Meyers
Theyre-Smith, Spenser
   Mrs. Hilary Regrets
Thiboust, Delacour
   Paris Asleep
Thiboust, Lambert
   The Infernal Regions of Paris
   Paris Asleep
Thimpson, A. M.

  The Dairy Maids
Thomas, Albert Ellsworth
 David's Adventure
 Dealers in Glory
 The Unknown Dancer
Thomas, Augustus
 Colorado
 The Copperhead
 De Lancey
 Don't Tell Her Husband
 The Education of Mr. Pipp
 The Harvest Moon
 Mrs. Leffingwell's Boots
 The Model
 The Other Girl
 The Pug and the Parson
 Rio Grande
 Surrender!
 Thomas Grogan
 Three Christmas Eves
Thomas, Oliver
 She's a Spy
Thompson, A. M.
 The Arcadians
 The Babes in the Wood
 The Dairymaids
Thompson, Charlotte
 Rebecca of Sunnybrook Farm
Throne, Kathyrne
 The Naughty Duchess
Thurner, Georges
 Marriage d'étoile
Thurston, E. Temple
 Charmeuse
 Driven
Trarieux, Gabriel
 Un Soir
Townsend, Ralph Milbourne
 Ponderby's Heir
Trevor, Leo
 Brother Officers
 The Flag Lieutenant
Trotha, Thilo von
 Ein Kind der Secession
Truffier, Jules
 Le papillon
Turner, Paul
 [Untitled Sketch]

Turney, Arthur
 Marooned

Unger, Gladys
 L'ane de Buridan
 A Dangerous Girl
 Decorating Clementine
 Double Exposures
 Inconstant Gengi
 Inconstant George
 Love Watches
 The Marionettes
 Miquette
 Richard Brinsley Sheridan
 The Two Schools
Urban, Erich
 Jung Muss man Sein
Urvantzov, Leo
 Vera

Vachell, Horace Annesley
 Bird of Passage
 The Case of Lady Camber
 The Chief
 Humpty-Dumpty
 His Lordship
Vajda, Ernest
 Grounds for Divorce
 The Harem
Valabreque, Albin
 Corale & Co.
 The Boulinard's
Vance, Katherine
 The Way of All Women
Vanlov, Albert
 The Dragoons of the Empress
Varney, Louis
 Cupid
Veberx, Pierre
 Brother Jacques
 Chichi
 Frère Jacques
 An Important Case
 Ma fée
 Madame La Présidente
 The Runaway
 The Seniors

A Separate Room
Vingt jours à l'ombre
Veiller, Bayard
That's the Woman
Verneuil, Louis
Get Your Man
He's Mine!
Mademoiselle ma mère
The Stranger
Viereck, George Sylvester
The Maid of Orleans
Villanyl, Andor
My Queen I Die for You
Volk, Gustav
Creole Blood
Vollmer, Lula
The Honor and the Glory

Wagner, Franz
The Lace Veil
Wall, Harry
A Lady Calls on Peter
Wallace, Edgar
The Ringer
Wallace, G. Carlton
A Thief in the Night
Walsh, Austin
Blind Guides
Walter, Eugene
The Flag Station
The Undertow
Ward, Mrs Humphrey
Lady Rose's Daughter
Warner, Anne
Men Are like That
Watanna, Onota
The Honor of Japan
Watson, Malcolm
The Coping-stone
The Haven of Content
Molly
The Swing of the Pendulum
Winnie Brooke, Widow
Webber, Pierre
The President
Webster, Alfred A.
Acquitted

Weiss, Raoul Ernst
The Room of Dreams
Weld, Arthur
What Ailed Elshender?
The Three Wishes
The Whooping Cough
Welisch, Ernst
Nay, Nay Napoleon
Madame Pompadour
West, Clarence
Cupid
Westcott, Edward Noyes
David Harum
Westervelt, Leonidas
The Circus Rider
Weyman, Stanley
A Gentleman of France
Under the Red Rose
Wharton, Edith
The House of Mirth
The Shadow of a Doubt
Whitfield, Frank
The Magic Mill
Sunrise at Dusk
Wicheler, Fernand
Mademoiselle Beuleman's Marriage
Suzanne
Wiggin, Kate Douglas
Rebecca of Sunnybrook Farm
Wilcox, Ella Wheeler
Mizpah
Wilde, Oscar
The Importance of Being Earnest
Lady Lancing
Wilkes, Thomas Egerton
Halvei the Unknown
Willemetz, A.
Kisses
One Kiss
Passionately
Williams, E. Harcourt
The Philosopher in the
  Apple Orchard
Willner, Alfred Maria
The Doll Girl
The Doll Maiden
The Fair Risette
The Fortunate Fool
The Siren

Wills, Freeman
   Rouget de l'isle
Wills, W. G.
   Esmond
Wilson, Francis
   The Bachelor's Baby
   The Pretty Persian
Wilson, Harry Leon
   How's Your Health?
   The Spenders
   Your Humble Servant
Wilson, John P.
   A Modern Pirate
   The Press Agent
Wimperis, Arthur
   The Balkan Princess
   He's Mine!
   The Laughing Husband
   Love and Laughter
Winston, Jemmie
   Boccaccio
Wise, Thomas A.
   Mr. Barnum
Wittmann, Carl Friedrich
   Tsar and Carpenter
Wodehouse, P. G.
   Get Your Man
Wolf, Pierre
   L'amour défendu
   The Marionettes
   The Stream

Wood, A. C. Fraser
   In the Eyes of the World
Woollcott, Alexander
   Legerdemain
Worrall, Lechmere
   Eve and the Serpents
Wright, Margare
   L'heure exquise
Wycherly, William
   The Country Girl

Young, Rida Johnson
   The Boys of Company B
   A Wise Child

Zamacois, Miquel
   Les bouffons
   The Jester
Zamescnik, John
   The Girl I Love
Zangwill, Israel
   Jinny the Carrier
Ziegenfelder, Jane
   Nanetta
Zilahy, Ludwig
   Der Eiszapfen
Zamrof,
   La marmotte

The American Film Institute Catalog Project

PHYLLIS ZUCKER

HIGH ABOVE the Thomas Jefferson Reading Room in the Library of Congress is a narrow attic where a team of cinema researchers is zealously working away on what is probably the most important piece of scholarship to American cinema history. In crowded quarters there thirteen young men and women are researching a nineteen-tome project — a compilation of all films (features, shorts, and newsreels) released in this country.

A major undertaking of the American Film Institute, the *Catalog* project was made possible through grants from the National Endowment for the Arts, the Ford Foundation, and the Motion Pictures Association of America. The *Catalog* could not exist without the indispensable services of the Library of Congress, which in addition to providing space, light, heat, etc., affords continuous access to its collection and reference services. Presently financed by a continuing grant from the National Endowment for the Humanities, the group has already turned out a two-part volume on the American features released between January 1, 1921, and December 31, 1930. R.R. Bowker is the publisher. The works in progress are on the Teens and the Sixties. The volumes thereafter will be produced in chronological order beginning with the Thirties and continuing into the Forties and Fifties. The earliest volume, and probably the next to be published after the feature series is complete, will contain all films released between 1893 and 1910. All other shorts and newsreels will be published separately.

What is perhaps unique about the computer-based project processed by Autographics, Inc., is that the researchers are not viewing every film — that would be impossible! — but are relying upon other primary and secondary source materials such as archival and company records, state licensing or censorship files, trade and periodical reviews and pressbooks. Approximately 85% of the 6,600 titles that appear in the first volume (1920's) *are not extant anywhere.* This emphasizes again the fact that no one had the foresight to preserve every film ever made. Until 1952 all film was printed on nitrate-based stock, which turned to dust with time and under certain temperature conditions. George Stevens, Jr., Director of the AFI, notes in the preface to the first published volume:

> Allan Dwan . . . never dreamed that another generation would have an interest in his work and consequently he kept no prints or scripts of his films.

For the 1921-30 volumes, the trade magazines were relied upon heavily for information about each film. It is not coincidental that the project is housed above the Library of Congress' Motion Picture Division which retains copies of *Photoplay, Moving Picture World, Motion Picture News, Exhibitors Trade Review, Variety,* etc. *Film Daily Yearbooks, Motion Picture News Booking Guide* and *Motion Picture Blue Book* were also used, as well as published articles in such magazines as *Films in Review* and newspapers such as the *New York Times.* These sources continue to be used in the documentation process.

Of great assistance are the copyright dossiers. If a film was registered with the copyright office of the Library of Congress (as were 9000 from 1912-1942) there is a dossier containing information such as continuities, scenarios, and sometimes publicity that was offered.

The catalogers also make use of the records of the New York State Motion Picture Commission, a censorship board which, until its dissolution in 1965, was run by the Board of Regents. The records of the Commission are all now housed in Albany, New York. The records of the Maryland Board of Censors are also consulted.

The American Film Institute Catalog Project

The documentation process is also aided by special collections, such as the George P. Johnson Negro Film Collection at UCLA which is a record of Negro film achievement for the last fifty years. In addition, the catalog project has access to a number of company records and ledgers which are a major category of original documentation.

After the research on each film is complete and the special computer form is filled out and edited, it is sent to Autographics, Inc., the computer company that services the *Catalog*. The data is keyed in by means of a MTST model 5 and then converted onto a nine-track tape where the information is stored. The tape is checked for accuracy by means of periodic computer print-outs, and when the tape is certified to be free of errors, Autographics composes camera-ready copy on a VideoComp 820 machine.

The Editorial Advisory Board of the publication is headed by George Stevens, Jr., Director of the AFI and SaliAnn Kreigsman, executive editor of the AFI. The board consists of: Eileen Bowser and Willard Van Dyke of the Museum of Modern Art; James Card and George Pratt of the George Eastman House; William K. Everson, Professor of Cinema Studies at New York University; Raymond Fielding, Professor of Communications, at Temple University; John Kuiper, Head of the Motion Picture Section, Library of Congress; Mildred Simpson, Library of the Academy of Motion Picture Arts and Sciences; Thomas R. Cripps, Professor of History, Morgan State College; and James Moore, head of the Audio-Visual Section of the National Archives. The editor for the first published volume, *Feature Films, 1921-30*, was Ken Munden, who came to the project with a distinguished career as an archivist, historian, and editor, having served fifteen years with the National Archives. The second editor was Steven Zito, a graduate of the Cinema Studies department at NYU, and now program planner at AFI's Washington theatre. The current editor is Richard P. Krafsur, a scholar in American Studies and the former editor of

Rose Bibliography, a computerized, annotated bibliography of social change in the U.S. since the Civil War.

The official title of this complex, multi-volume catalog reads *The AFI Catalog of Motion Pictures Produced in the United States.* However, commencing with the 60's volume, and thereafter, foreign films which were released in the United States will be included. (A supplement to the 20's volume will carry this additional information). "Feature length" is defined as 4,000 feet, or four reels, or approximately more than forty-five minutes in length. Each film is assigned an entry number and prefix. The use of the entry number facilitates the use of the accompanying credit and subject indexes; and its relevance to a projected cumulative index is obvious. The order is as follows: Title, production company or individual sponsoring company date, and, if any, dossier number (begins with LC notation "L.P."); audio aspects (silent, sound, sound effects); color, gauge, and length. Next are production and cast credits, including the names of characters. In a musical, there is a complete breakdown of credited song and dance numbers and composers of the musical numbers.

The genres are then noted in the vernacular of the era, e.g., "Northwest Melodrama." Dramatic or literary source including full bibliographical citation is given; and finally, a synopsis or summary in less than three hundred words. The synopsis follows the formula of "statement of situation, manner of resolution." There follows a list of subject headings by which the film is indexed, such as "Cowboys," "Divorce," "Shipwrecks," etc. To many films are added special notes indicating such things as conflicting information, "working" titles, location shooting, and miscellaneous production notes.

The index (published as a separate volume for *Feature Films, 1921-30*) is divided into two parts: Credit Index and Subject Index. The Credit Index contains a personal and corporate section and a separate section listing literary and dramatic source citations. The second part of the index volume is quite unique: it is a subject index. Within each subject category it contains, in alphabetical order, a list of the films concerned, showing for each title its year of release and the entry number in the *Catalog.*

The majority of the reviews for the first volume were praiseworthy. "It makes it a snap to trace movies . . . it's not a book you'll lug on the subway with you, but I guarantee it will keep you up nights."[1] "A genuine collector's item, a gold mine of esoterica."[2] Kevin Brownlow, author of *The Parade's Gone By,* a history of the silent period, apologized before he assaulted: "No computer —let alone a human — could possibly produce such a massive work without flaw."[3] Among them he cites that the *Blue Mountain Mystery* was misprinted along with the W's; Sidney Franklin, the director, is confused with the actor of the same name; Ben Caree was the art director on *The Light in the Dark*, not the cameraman.

Morgan State College Professor Thomas Cripps interestingly notes the the *AFI Catalog* is an aid to the "scholar of black life" in providing proof that Negroes did not only play obsequious stereotypes. One can learn that Stepin Fetchit played the first straight black love scene in Hollywood (*In Old Kentucky*, 1926.)

One major criticism that is not too unreasonable is that the researchers should have published their synopsis source, probably omitted because of space limitations. However, a project is now being contemplated by the AFI to print in a separate volume all the references for any given volume.

Another critique seems a bit problematic: indication of the present location of surviving films. The Library of Congress, while it does not have a published catalog as yet, does maintain a card file of its holdings which is open to the public.

Film scholars are encouraged to send mistakes or omissions they find to the attention of the *AFI Catalog*; corrections can then be made for a projected supplement or new edition.

After all, it is not only the researchers' fault: some companies did not list individual contributors, but simply listed the heads of departments. And if a director was changed mid-stream, the *Catalog* may only document the man who was listed in the released version.

Probably the harshest criticism came from that patriarch of film scholarship, Herman Weinberg. Perhaps he was hardest on the work merely out of exasperation after waiting so long for the birth of this type of book.

His personal friendships with filmmakers give him the right to criticize and correct. For instance, through his relationship with von Sternberg, he knew that the latter wrote the original story and screenplay for *Case of Lena Smith* which had been credited to Samuel Ornitz and Jules Furthman.

Also Weinberg's age and memory give him the distinct advantage of being able to remember what he saw and what future film historians, will never be able to see. Film scholars must not be discouraged by Weinberg's one up-manship:

> The proof is that anyone who hasn't seen a film whose plot has been synopsized in the AFI Catalog has no real idea of the quality of the film.[4]

He does, however, add:

> . . . if the cinema is your 'bride,' as indeed she must be, if you're a true buff, it means that you love her, even if she is just the tiniest bit cross-eyed. . . . That's how I feel about this book.[5]

The *AFI Catalog* is an invigorating boon to the cinema scholar who waits impatiently for future volumes.

Notes

1. Bob Salmaggi, on a Westinghouse Radio Stations Feature Story, August 26, 1971.

2. *Playboy*, December, 1971, pp. 40-41.

3. Kevin Brownlow, "*The AFI Catalog: a book review,*" *Sight and Sound* (Spring 1972), pp. 115-16.

4. Herman Weinberg, a book review of *The AFI Catalog, Film Quarterly* (Winter 1971-72), p. 62.

5. *Ibid.*

An Index to
BARRY B. WITHAM *"Mirror Interviews"* [1]

DURING THE LAST DECADE of the nineteenth century *The New York Dramatic Mirror* published a series of conversations with prominent theatrical personalities titled "Mirror Interviews." These interviews, which were conducted primarily by "A.E.B." and "Thespis," were designed to explore the "careers, views, and personal reminiscences" of major figures associated with the American stage.[2] They were not the only interviews conducted by the *Dramatic Mirror,* but as a group they are the most informative and provide the student of American theatre history with a fascinating series of first-hand recollections by many of the most important people of the day.

The interviews are not limited to performers of the legitimate theatre. They range from John Philip Sousa to Buffalo Bill and include such diverse personalities as Napoleon Sarony, a distinguished theatrical photographer; Alexander Herrmann, a famous magician; and Marie Bonfanti, a pre-eminent dancer. But their primary focus is on the major theatrical figures of the period. Daniel Frohman, William Gillette, James O'Neill, David Belasco, Maurice Barrymore and many others discuss their work, reminisce about the past and comment on the current state of the theatre.

Much of the information is trivial but a good deal of it is extremely interesting. Mrs. John Drew compares Macready, Forrest and the elder Booth as tragedians. Madame Ponisi talks about playing Juliet to Charlotte Cushman's famous Romeo, and Madame Janauschek expounds on the detrimental effects of the Combination System. John Drew discusses Augustin Daly as a stage director. James Henry Stoddart recalls what it was like to perform for Boucicault. And William Gillette jokes about a nationally endowed theatre.

The following index is designed so that individual interviews can be located without reading through entire volumes of the *New York Dramatic Mirror,* which was published weekly from 1879 to 1922, and which is still lacking a comprehensive index.

Aldrich, Louis –	June 9, 1894	Haworth, Joseph –	Nov. 7, 1896
Arthur, Joseph –	Aug. 8, 1896	Herrmann, Alexander –	Oct. 19, 1895
		Hilliard, Robert –	Sept. 5, 1896
Bangs, Frank C. –	Nov. 27, 1897	Holland, E.M. –	Oct. 26, 1895
Barker, Mary E. –	Sep. 4, 1897	Holland, Joseph –	May 2, 1896
Barnard, Charles –	July 21, 1894	Hopper, De Wolf –	Sept. 15, 1894
Barrymore, Maurice –	Jan. 18, 1896	Hoyt, Charles H. –	June 22, 1895
Belasco, David –	Nov. 9, 1895		
Bellew, Kyrle –	June 29, 1895	Jack, John –	Apr. 3, 1897
Bill, Buffalo –	June 30, 1894	Jakobowski, Edward –	Nov. 17, 1894
Bonfanti, Marie –	May 29, 1897	James, Louis –	Oct. 5, 1895
Boniface, George C. –	Oct. 2, 1897	Janauschek, Madame –	Aug. 4, 1894
Braham, David –	Dec. 31, 1898		
Brough, Lionel –	Feb. 6, 1897	Keene, Thomas W. –	Sep. 21, 1895
		Keller, Henry –	Aug. 11, 1894
Carleton, Henry Guy –	Aug. 22, 1896	Kent, Charles –	Jan. 1, 1898
Carleton, William T. –	June 6, 1896	Kidder, Edward E. –	July 25, 1896
Cayvan, Georgia –	July 11, 1896	Klein, Charles –	Dec. 12, 1896
Chambers-Ketchum, Annie –	July 10, 1897	Knowles, Edwin –	Mar. 20, 1897
Claxton, Kate –	Dec. 8, 1894		
Coghlan, Rose –	Dec. 15, 1894	Lackaye, Wilton –	Dec. 7, 1895
Cotton, Ben –	July 3, 1897	Le Moyne, William J. –	Mar. 23, 1895
Couldock, Charles –	Apr. 13, 1895	Ludlow, Kate –	July 23, 1898
Crane, William H. –	Oct. 13, 1894		
		Mackay, F.F. –	Aug. 7, 1897
Davis, Jessie Bartlett –	Nov. 21, 1896	Maeder, Clara Fisher –	Feb. 13, 1897
De Angelis, Jefferson –	Nov. 23, 1895	Markham, Pauline –	Oct. 23, 1897
De Belleville, Frederic –	Aug. 31, 1895	Marlowe-Taber, Julia –	Apr. 4, 1896
De Koven, Reginald –	Dec. 21, 1895	Mayo, Frank –	May 11, 1895
Dodson, J.E. –	Aug. 17, 1895	Modjeska, Helena –	Oct. 12, 1895
Drew, John –	Oct. 27, 1894	Mordaunt, Frank –	Feb. 16, 1895
Drew, Mrs. John –	Jan. 5, 1895	Morris, Clara –	Jan. 11, 1896
		Morrison, Lewis –	July 4, 1896
Eldridge, Louisa –	Jan. 2, 1897	Murphy, Joseph –	Feb. 8, 1896
Ellsler, John A. –	June 12, 1897		
		Nethersole, Olga –	Apr. 17, 1897
Florence, Mrs. William J. –	Aug. 21, 1897		
Freeman, Max –	Oct. 3, 1896	O'Neill, James –	Feb. 2, 1895
Frohman, Daniel –	May 26, 1894		
		Pastor, Tony –	July 27, 1895
Gillette, William –	Mar. 9, 1895	Pitou, Augustus –	Sep. 14, 1895
Goodwin, J. Cheever –	May 23, 1896	Ponisi, Madame –	Sep. 1, 1894
		Potter, Paul –	June 8, 1895
Hamilton, Theodore –	May 20, 1899		
Harrigan, Edward –	Dec. 22, 1894	Rankin, Mrs. M'Kee –	Dec. 11, 1897
Harrison, Gabriel –	Feb. 27, 1897	Rhea, Hortense –	Aug. 10, 1895

An Index to "Mirror Interviews"   155

Robson, Stuart –	Feb. 1, 1896	Stoddart, James Henry –	Nov. 24, 1894
Rosenfeld, Sydney –	Feb. 5, 1898		
Russell, Annie –	Dec. 4, 1897	Tavary, Marie –	Dec. 18, 1897
Russell, Sol Smith –	Nov. 20, 1897	Thompson, Denman –	Oct. 16, 1897
Sanger, Frank W. –	July 13, 1895	Warwick, J.H. –	May 15, 1897
Salvini, Alexander –	Dec. 28, 1895	Wheatcroft, Adeline Stanhope –	June 19, 1897
Sargent, Frank –	Mar. 21, 1896		
Sarony, Napoleon –	June 16, 1894	Wheatcroft, Nelson –	Feb. 22, 1896
Shannon, Effie –	July 9, 1898	Wheelock, Joseph –	Feb. 12, 1898
Shaw, Mary –	June 26, 1897	Wilson, Francis –	Sep. 29, 1894
Smith, Harry B. –	June 13, 1896		
Sothern, Edward H. –	Sep. 8, 1894	Yeamans, Annie –	Jan. 19, 1895
Sousa, John Philip –	July 17, 1897		

Notes

1. I would like to thank Michael Whitlatch who helped me check numerous names and dates in the preparation of this index.

2. The "Mirror Interviews" were published from May, 1894, to May, 1899. A.E.B. was probably Albert Ellery Berg, a member of the editorial staff. Thespis was an actor named John Brownell. See *New York Dramatic Mirror*, July 31, 1897.

BRIANT HAMOR LEE

Theatrical Visual Arts Ephemera: Care and Protection

THE GRAPHIC ARTS in theatre include the works of the scenic designers, costume designers, theatrical draftsmen (scenographers), as well as the efforts of publicity and advertising designers: the direct and graphic interpretation of the visual effect desired in conjunction with a particular production.

The language of the visual artist in theatre is graphic and interpretative in its passing on of a visual knowledge of the object to be presented: the play. The importance of this graphic language can be better emphasized by comparison with the similar uses made of written languages. Word languages are highly developed systems for the description and communication of ideas. Nevertheless, a written language is inadequate for the description of such abstractions as size, shape, color, and the relationship of physical objects which creates and amplifies mood, period, and style in theatrical design. The writer may suggest, evoke, and stimulate the artist with his work, but it is the visual artist who creates the actual image of the written essence. Though written language is often without adequate resources for accurate and rapid communication of shapes, sizes, and the relationships of component parts, the visual and graphic arts have long been accomplishing exactly these ends.

While the most commonly available source for the theatre historian is the script of a particular production, one of the next most readily available and useful are the visual graphics kept of that production. What better argument for the preservation of these *visual* ephemeral materials.

While I was viewing a recent touring show of classic scenic designs and posters from the collections of the *Museo alla Scala*, the archives of the La Scala Opera House, it was delightful to note the spill of a small amount of scenic paint on the corner of a couple of the renderings. They actually had been used, had been produced and worked on by one of the brilliant designers of operatic history in the scenic design studios and scenic shops of one of the world's great theatres. But, at the same time, one of the renderings mentioned was not identified with any particular production: artist — unknown, productions — unknown. What a pity! What a pity that the work of some long-buried, hardworking artist cannot be matched to any extant script. As a result, while the design is of interest as a design, it can contribute little to our understanding of the play and production for which it was intended. A curious piece of ephemera, but of little use historically.

To attempt to correct this pitiful situation for the future, this essay will deal with the protection and preservation of current theatrical graphics. Many of the techniques mentioned herein are applicable to graphics in historical collections as well. In the process of learning how to protect his artistic efforts, the theatrical artist will find that the works of art are greatly enhanced for their presentation: 1) to directors, 2) for their use in the designer's portfolio, 3) as studio or gallery art, and ultimately, 4) in some distant future historical collection.

The basic medium for the theatrical visual artist is the sketch pad or piece of paper on which his ideas are noted. That piece of paper might be good grade watercolor paper, drafting paper, tracing tissue, a notebook sheet of foolscap, a piece of paper towel, or a coffee stained paper napkin. Each of these types of sketch may be one step in the process of the development of a finished design. Paper is taken for granted. Why not? It is cheap, it is both indispensable and poorly understood. To correct this inconsistency, a considerable discussion of the qualities of paper will follow.

Paper: though it is fragile and has many enemies, it can last for centuries, if properly made and cared for. It is highly susceptible to damage by environmental conditions, to insect pests, and even to man, but the destruction may start from within, for the medium may come to the artist with internal flaws. Even the finest handmade paper is sometimes disfigured by stray fragments of wood or rusty iron, has marks from the ropes in the drying loft, or is buckled because it was hastily dried and cured. Much more serious defects result from various technical "improvements" in the paper making process which lead to chemical and mechanical breakdown of the paper or pigments on it.

Use of a good grade permanent paper is half the battle of preservation. The artist must seek out one of the many fine all-rag papers available for the finished art work, if that work is to outlive even his own lifetime. In protecting the art work, the artist or art collector should take care to see that only all-rag mats and acid-free papers are used in mounting and framing pictures. This is done simply through purchasing good quality materials from reputable art stores or sources.

Most damage to paper caused by man could be avoided with just a little extra care and common sense. Dolloff and Parkinson, in their excellent pamphlet, "How to Care for Works of Art on Paper," suggest these standards for paper handling:

1. Use clean hands to handle any work of art on paper.

2. When lifting matted or unmatted pictures or graphics, use two hands to keep from bending, creasing, or tearing them.

3. Unmatted works should never be stacked on top of each other but should be separated by smooth acid-free cover tissues.

4. For optimum protection, valuable works should be matted rather than left loose. To an artist with any pride in his own work, this means all finished art work. Less valuable pictures or documents can be kept in folders or envelopes of acid-free paper.

5. Be careful not to touch or drag anything (the corner of another mat, for example) across the surface of a picture.

Pastels, scratchboard, and soft pencil sketches are particularly vulnerable to such surface damage.

6. Never use pressure-sensitive tape (scotch tape, masking tape, etc.), gummed brown paper tape, rubber cement, synthetic glues, or heat sealing mounting tissue on any work that has sufficient value to be preserved. Each of these substances either are damaging immediately to pictures or become damaging as they break down with age.

7. Pictures, posters, or handbills glued down to old board (old prints, broadsides, drawings, graffitti, etc.) should be handled with as much care as any unmounted, brittle picture. The backing gives a false sense of strength.

8. Matted pictures should be protected with cover tissue of acid-free paper when not in use. For temporary display and protection, the entire mat can be wrapped in cellulose acetate sheeting and secured with tape on the back. Cellulose acetate sheeting should not be used for permanent storage because of its dust-attracting qualities.

9. Always open a mat by the outer edge, never by inserting a finger through the window and lifting the inner edge.

10. Works of art in mats or folders or envelopes can be stored flat in drawers or flat drawing storage boxes.

11. To carry, mail, or ship loose pictures pack them between stout boards (such as matboard, corrugated cardboard, etc.) in acid-free envelopes, never in a roll.

A discussion of the preservation of art works on paper depends also on an understanding of the inherent enemies of the medium. Such destroyers of art work as: humidity, light, heat, air pollution, and insect damage need to be detailed before a discussion of protective covering and matting can be enlarged upon.

Environment is one of the enemies of paper; humidity is a chief factor. Outside of outright water damage, which is obviously to be avoided, the chief danger of excessive humidity is the growth of molds. Since molds cannot grow unless the humidity level exceeds 70%, preventive measures must include efforts to keep humidity below that level. When hanging or storing pictures, beware of dampness on outside walls, in stone houses, in basements, and cellars. Cellars are never recommended for storage of any paper products due to the threat of flood, ground seepage of water, drainpipe backup, or a combination of elements leading to higher levels of humidity. Houses closed up for an extended length of time and air-tight cabinets or lockers may become excessively humid. They should be aired periodically and checked for signs of dampness or musty odors.

Mold growth in paper often shows up as dull rusty patches which discolor the sheet. This is called "foxing" and is caused by the chemical action of the molds on the colorless iron salts present in most papers. Mold can feed also on paper sizing and fibres, thereby weakening the sheet. It grows easily on pastels, which contain good nutrients in their gelatine binding medium. Any work of art done in scenic paint (technically, distemper) is equally susceptible since scenic glues make fine mold culturing media. Smell a souring scene paint bucket sometime and you rapidly become aware of the action of mold. Foxing is the usual result of prolonged, high atmospheric humidity, but if water itself seeps into a picture or mat, rampant proliferation of mold may completely envelop the object.

First-aid treatment for humidity and mold is to remove the object to a dry environment. Open the mat, frame, or spread out the pages so that air can freely circulate to the infested areas. Expose the object to direct sunlight for about an hour (no more) to kill the mold or, preferably, place in a closed container with a non-corrosive fungicide for two or three days. There are no fungicides which will provide permanent protection against mold if the object is returned to a humid atmosphere. For protection against mold in art works, Dolloff and Parkinson suggest:

1. Keep the humidity below 70%; about 50% is ideal; below 20% the paper will become brittle and extreme care must be exercised in its handling.

2. Do not store pictures, books or any paper ephemora in cellars or basements.

3. Avoid hanging pictures on outside walls of a house, especially if they feel cold or moist.

4. Never frame works directly against glass. Glass, by its nature will condense moisture on its surfaces, therefore to frame against it invites damage by mold growth and/or from condensation of moisture.

5. Clean storage areas, frames, mats, and bookshelves regularly, as dust contains large amounts of airborne mold spores.

6. Good circulation of air reduces the chances of mold growth. With a hanging framed piece of art work, circulation of air behind the frame is improved by attaching small pieces of cork or wood to the bottom corners to keep the frame somewhat away from the wall.

7. Never store pictures, books, or any paper article directly on the floor. Raise them on supports to allow for circulation of air.

8. Avoid leaving books and pictures in a closed room, closet, or house for extended periods of time without providing some means of circulation and/or dehumidification.

9. Fumigate infested books, pictures (but not oil paintings), storage containers, and bookcases with a volatile, noncorrosive fungicide, and be sure to correct the conditions which originally caused the mold growth.

One of the more ignored and less understood factors which can affect paper is *light,* perhaps because it is so much a part of daily experience. Art collectors, concerned with this hazard, often ask art conservators whether fading can be stopped by keeping water colors, drawings, and pigmented ephemera of other sorts in subdued light; the answer is "no!" Light, any light, fades works of art on paper; less light only means less fading. The pigments used by the papermaker to tint his product or by the artist to create his image, do not automatically stop fading when the light level drops below a certain point. More unfortunately, fading is *not* a reversible process. Placing a work of art on paper in darkness merely halts the process. It can do nothing to promote recovery or rejuvenation.

How much light should be used for viewing works of art on paper? What minimum amount of light does the human eye need to perceive all the colors in their proper relationships? The answer is one of degree. In the moonlight, when light is at an extremely low level, the eye loses all ability to perceive colors and can only distinguish tonal or black and white values. One can only conclude that there must be sufficient light for good viewing, but any excess, which will hasten fading, must be avoided. An optimum amount of light for viewing would be the same amount of light needed for casual reading, corresponding to the output of a 150 watt reading lamp at a distance of three or four feet.

In the gallery situation with a permanently hung art work, it is necessary to guard against unnecessary or excessive exposure. Museums, art collections, and historical collections control exposure by a variety of means. Extremely delicate prints and watercolors are stored for viewing by appointment only, or are protected in artificially lighted rooms in cases with cloth coverings, which the visitor can remove and then replace. Most large museums rotate selections from their holdings so that an object is never left on view for more than a few months at a time. Simply changing the position of the pictures on the wall of a house once a year or so will not only diminish the possibility of their fading but will also place them in a new perspective that will enhance their enjoyment.

Avoid hanging pictures on a wall directly opposite or adjacent to windows, since light is likely to be greater there than anywhere else in the room. Translucent curtains or louvered blinds can be used to moderate or redirect the bright light of day. Pictures should never be hung in direct sunlight, of course. Even reflected or indirect daylight carries a danger in addition to intensity. Sunlight is a source of ultraviolet light, which, though it is invisible, is even more destructive than visible light. Ultraviolet rays accelerate fading and even cause deterioration of the paper itself. Watercolors, prints, and books should never be exposed directly to these damaging rays.

While few design studios or theatre lobbies or art galleries are lit with fluorescent lighting, as incandescent more properly simulates theatrical lighting and is more easily controllable, it should be noted that there are other reasons for not exposing art works to fluorescent light. These light sources are potent in the ultraviolet wave lengths of light, thus they should be filtered with plastic sleeves which will filter out this type of light, if they are to be used at all. Offices are more often lit with fluorescent fixtures. How many hang and store art works in offices? Plexiglas sheet, or acrylic sheeting, which does effectively filter out ultraviolet light, may be substituted for glass in a picture frame with proper precautions, obviating this type of damage.

Outside of the obvious damage derived from fire, extremes of heat of any type are to be avoided. Do not expose pictures and books to heat, since high temperatures accelerate the deterioration of paper. Do not hang pictures over radiators, heating registers, or air duct vents. That marveously dramatic spot over the fireplace is doubly bad as a place to hang pictures, first, because of heat deterioration, and, second, because soot and residues produced by the fire adhere to the glass and obscure the picture.

With all the talk concerning ecology and air pollution, it should be small wonder to learn that art works suffer also. The city dweller should realize that a polluted atmosphere is one of the dangers which threatens the longevity of paper and the permanence of art works on paper. The most harmful contaminant in the atmosphere is sulphur dioxide, a gas produced by the imperfect combustion of fossil fuels such as coal, oil, natural gas, and automobile gas.

Sulphur dioxide is the major constituent of smog. It attacks paper causing discoloration, embrittlement, and eventual disintegration of the paper fibres. Upon absorption by the paper, sulphur dioxide turns to sulphuric acid, an acid which does not evaporate and leave the paper after it has formed from the gas. Severe brown stains caused by this distructive pollutant are often seen on the edges of framed pictures which have been partly or entirely exposed to the air through lack of adequate backing. Certain artists' pigments are affected adversely, also. Ultramarine blue, which is often used in watercolor painting, can be completely destroyed long before the paper itself has been even moderately discolored. Lead white, sometimes used as a highlight or as a body wash in wash drawings, reacts with sulphur dioxide to form lead sulphide, which darkens to a dirty gray or sooty black; as a result the tonal range of the picture is destroyed.

Air pollution seems to have become an inescapable hazard of urban existence. To help minimize danger from a polluted atmosphere, framed pictures should be protected with all-rag acid-free mat board, front and back, plus a backing board large enough to cover the entire mat.

Silverfish, termites, cockroaches, and worms are the most common insects which threaten paper. Silverfish are silvery or pearl-gray insects with three tail-like appendages. They are often discovered when books, papers, or frames on the floor are picked up and moved suddenly. They prefer warm, damp places, shun the light, and move so rapidly that detection is often difficult. They may cause considerable damage to paper ephemera, but are considerable threat to books as well. They will eat their way through pictures to get to flour paste and glue sizing, but also enjoy bleached wood-pulp paper by itself. Glue-size painted scenery and properties are a favorite repast, also.

While woodworms and termites are considered common enemies of wood, they will devour virtually anything made of cellulose, especially paper. Their winding, branching tunnels can cause considerable structural damage to models, books, frames, and pictures or posters which have been mounted on wooden panels. Cockroaches inhabit dark, warm, damp places and usually come out at night. While they look more ferocious than they are, they can cause considerable surface damage to parchment, leather, paper, fabrics, and any glue or paint medium which contains sugar.

Infestation by insects is best prevented by regular cleaning and by inspection of dark spaces behind and beneath books, cases, boxes, and picture frames. Particular attention should be paid to areas such as basements and attics, where traffic is minimal, and which tend to be dark and damp. Use of aerosol or powdered insecticide is necessary, should signs of these insects be present.

While the obvious causes of damage to graphic art can be prevented, and the more insidious, less obvious, causes guarded against, there is nothing more frustrating to the artist who is looking for a particular stored piece of work or drawing than to find that either negligently or carelessly it has become folded, creased, torn, or crumpled, thus obviating its usefulness.

The proper care of art work on paper, which begins with matting all produced efforts, is an ideal greatly to be desired. Unfortunately, cost is a factor in the matting of art works, but any work which merits protection merits the amount of cost expended in protecting it with a good mat.

Mats are flat pieces of cardboard or other material which have an opening or 'window' cut in them to reveal that part of a rendering or drawing it is wished to show and to help isolate them from a background. Mats may be in any color, plain, decorated, or covered with some material such as cloth or paper. "A frame (or mat) will not make or break a painting," according to Frederic Taubes in his *Studio Secrets,* "but [it] may indicate how good or bad the taste of the artist is!" For the purposes of preserving theatre graphics, and for their presentation, our discussion will be limited to mats, avoiding the equally extensive area of picture framing.

Until they can be matted, theatre graphics should be stored flat, with interleaves of good grade acid-free paper. Certain ephemeral types of graphics may not need matting, but anything of an artistic or visual nature must be protected in this manner until it can be matted. Ephemeral material should be stored flat and in envelopes of acid-free paper. The perennial "standard" red cardboard envelope with a stringtie is actual very destructive because of the high acid content of its paper, yet for years has been used for the storage of unmatted art works.

White or off-white mats are most commonly used and will be found most suitable for renderings and theatre graphics. There are a variety of alterations which can be done to a standard white/off-white mat to make it more appropriate to framed-art-on-the-wall kinds of presentation, but for most theatrical display and portfolio uses, a simple mat is recommended. At this point in the discussion the basic techniques of matting will be explored.

Sense of proportion must be exercised in the making of a good mat. Until enough experience has been gained, the following rule should be observed: *Always make the bottom of the mat slightly wider than the top and sides!* This is necessary in order to compensate for the optical illusion which makes the bottoms of mats (which have all equal sides) appear narrower. The eye normally travels from top to bottom and must have more area to rest at that point. In the case of rigid, standard mat sizes — as in a uniform portfolio or a traveling graphics show — it may not always be possible to have the bottom wider than the sides, but it must always be wider than the top, even if only slightly.

The first requisite for mat cutting is a good knife. Paper dulls a cutting edge quicker than any other material; therefore, the knife should be thin and of high quality steel, to take and hold an edge as long as possible. Commercially available razor knives, cartoon knives, mat knives, or carpet knives, having rigid changeable blades, are the best solution to the knife problem. Remember that it is easier to use a new knife blade than it is to cut a new mat over again because one side may have been spoiled by a ragged edge.

Next to the knife in importance is a good straight-edge. Mats will never satisfactorily be cut without one. If possible, a metal straight-edge — long enough to handle the largest size mat to be cut — should be procured. Lacking the metal kind, secure a good quality, metal-edged ruler as long as necessary. Wooden or plastic rulers or tee-squares are inappropriate for mat cutting since one can as easily cut them as the mat.

The third requirement is to have a fresh surface under the mat for each cut to be made. This will help eliminate ragged edges and slipping. Scrap pieces of smooth cardboard are suitable, and sufficient quantity of them should be kept on hand for the purpose.

To prevent the straight-edge from slipping while cutting, adhere one or more strips of masking tape to its bottom. Thin felt or light sandpaper cemented to the bottom will also provide the necessary friction. The straight-edge should be kept clean at all times. It is wise to hang it up, by one end, when not in use to avoid damage to the edge and contact with grease or paint.

Provided good proportion follows throughout, slight differences in mat sizes are not noticeable. For the average rendering, a mat which is *about* 3" wide at the top and sides and 3½" on the bottom will look best. The word 'about' is used advisedly because sometimes it occurs that ½" or ¼" one way or the other will not harm the finished appearance and may result in considerable savings over a period of time in mat board, backing board, etc. Consider also the ease of marking and cutting a mat 16" long compared to one 15 and ⅞". In addition, there is a great deal less possibility for error when cutting a mat if one uses the larger fractions of inches in measurement. These remarks refer to the overall measurements of the mat as the opening will be cut to the exact size for viewing the art work.

Having determined the size of the opening in the mat, add 3" to the edge to produce the total width, and and 3" to the top and 3½" to the bottom for the overall height of the mat. Given that overall size, cut the mat with square edges. Lightly mark the surface of the mat for the picture window. Then, lay the mat on the cutting surface with a strip of cardboard or scrap matboard underneath the first line to be cut. This provides a cushion the matknife can penetrate without cutting or damaging the table surface. Place the straight-edge approximately ⅛" away from the line toward the outside edge of the mat. Insert the matknife at about a 45° angle, resting the edge of the blade against the steel edge of the straight-edge. Pull the knife steadily and smoothly along, trying to maintain the same blade angle for the entire length of the cut. Regular matboard should cut through with one pass of a sharp, rigid blade, leaving a clean cut bevel edge. Double-thick matboard may require three or more passes over the same cut. It will be found that after the four sides of a window are cut, the center may still adhere at the corners. Slip the matknife blade through the cut and complete it at the corners with the same angle as the rest of the bevel. Ragged edges on the bevel can usually be removed by sandpapering lightly on the reverse side of the mat with fine sandpaper.

After cutting the mat, cut a piece of *backing* board of the same matboard to use behind the picture and mat. This arrangement is called a *hinged* or *folder* mat, and is formed simply by attaching a second sheet of matboard to the back of the cutout mat with gummed-paper hinges. Hold the picture in position in the mat by attaching it to the backing board, not to the mat, with two hinges affixed to the upper edge of the art work. Never paste the corners of a picture directly to the backing board. Hinging allows the picture to hang freely in the mat, permitting the paper to expand and contract without stress as atmospheric conditions vary. When attaching a picture to its mat, never use 1) pressure sensitive tapes of any kind, e.g., masking tape, scotch tape, etc., 2) cheap brown paper, gummed paper wrapping tape, 3) synthetic glues, i.e. Elmer's, etc., or 4) rubber cement. Use only a good quality acid-free gummed paper tape.

Gummed paper tape may be cut into strips ½" in width, of whatever length is demanded by the size and weight of the art work to be supported. The strips are folded in half and applied, first to the picture and then to the backing board. For especially large works use short lengths of gummed cloth tape, which is stronger than paper tape. Gummed paper and cloth tape hinges are simple and quick to use and can be easily removed for changing of mats. A hinge should be no wider than necessary for satisfactory adhesion. Thus, to keep a picture from slipping down in a mat, the *length* of the hinge, measured along the upper side of the picture, is more important than its width. There is unfortunately no better rule of thumb for tape hinge sizes than experience; though for most theatrical renderings one might start with a hinge ½" by 1" in length. When matted the art work may be displayed in a variety of ways.

Labeling of matted theatrical graphics is of extreme importance for their future use, as well as for their continued use by the artist. Each matted work should be identified on the back of the backing board with a legend, preferably typed, which lists the following information: 1) *Artist*, (designer, photographer, graphic artist, etc.), (dates born and died); 2) *Production name*, (act, scene, etc.), (or theatre season, company, etc.); 3) *Description of item*, (rendering, handbill, photograph, etc.); 4) *Location of production*, (city, theatre, address, or in case of unproduced designs: 'studio work'); 5) *Dates of Production*, (dates of production run; in case of studio work — date of completion of the work); 6) *Medium*, (watercolor, pastel, etc., or photograph, daguerreotype, xerography, etc., or letterpress, photo offset, etc.); 7) *Miscellaneous details*, (other production details and staff: producers, directors, other designers, etc.).

Obviously, depending upon the type of material in the mat or envelope on which such a legend would appear, the rank ordering of necessary information in that legend might differ. At the moment, there is no standardized format for a theatre history collection's information legends, thus the above is suggested as a means to have all necessary information preserved for later codification in a collection.

Once an art work or piece of theatrical ephemera has been matted and identified, there are many important uses for it. After immediate use with the production for which it is intended, the first and most desired use would be display in some appropriate gallery, lobby, collection, or "green-room" connected with the working theatre. The comments above concerning protecting and hanging art work apply in this kind of display situation, as well. There appears to be a healthy, growing trend toward the propagation of the traveling theatre graphics show, as, for example, the touring Production Show sponsored by the American Theatre Association, and the traveling show of designs from the Southern Illinois Theatrical Designs Competitions. Individual museums and art galleries are becoming more interested in open, invitational, and juried theatrical graphics shows as well, e.g., a show being sponsored by the Art Museum of Northern Arizona State University in the winter of 1974.

Recently, there has been a growing interest expressed by commercial art galleries in displaying and selling theatrical graphics and art works. The minimum protection needed for this kind of show or display situation is the addition of a cellophane or cellulose-acetate sheet overleaf to protect the mat and work.

Another major use of the theatre graphics collection is incorporation into the artist's own portfolio. Any working scenic designer, costume designer, theatrical photographer, or theatrical graphic artist must have a portfolio of his work. The common practice is developing among theatrical artists for the designer to have 35 millimeter (2" x 2") slides of the portfolio available for first exposure to a prospective employer. But when the designer arrives for the personal interview, the portfolio must be there: matted, labeled, protected, and preserved until it is needed again.

Ultimately, the collected works of the artist would make an invaluable addition to the archives or historical collection of the production company or companies with which that artist was associated. But theatrical companies are as ephemeral, or more so, than theatrical artists; thus a safer depository would be a regional art or theatrical collection where record of the artist's life and work would be protected and preserved, and, thus, would endure.

Bibliography

Cunha, G.D.M. *Conservation of Library Materials*. Metuchen, N.J.: The Scarecrow Press, 1967.

Dolloff, F.W., and R.L. Parkinson. *How to Care for Works of Art on Paper*. Boston: Museum of Fine Arts, 1971.

Harrison, L.S. *Report on the Deteriorating Effects of Modern Light Sources*. New York: The Metropolitan Museum of Art, 1953.

Horton, C. *Cleaning and Preserving Bindings and Related Materials*. Second revised edition. Chicago: American Library Association, 1969.

International Council of Museums. *Climatology and Conservation in Museums*. Paris: UNESCO, 1960

___. *Problems of Conservation in Museums*. London: Allen and Urwin, 1969.

Langwell, W.H. *The Conservation of Books and Documents*. London: Pitman, 1957.

Library of Congress. *Papermaking: Art and Craft*. Washington: Library of Congress, 1968.

Mayer, Ralph. *Artist's Handbook of Materials and Techniques*. New York: Viking Press, 1957.

Minogue, A.E. *The Repair and Preservation of Records*. Washington: National Archives, 1943.

Plenderleith, H.J. *The Conservation of Antiquities and Works of Art.* New York: Oxford University Press, 1956.

Watrous, J. *The Craft of Old Master Drawings.* Madison: University of Wisconsin Press, 1967.

Zigrosser, C., and Christa M.A. Gaehda. *Guide to the Collecting and Care of Original Prints.* New York: Crown Publishers, 1965.

Additional information may be found in the following journals:

Art and Archaeology Technical Abstracts. Published semi-annually at the Institute of Fine Arts, New York University, for the International Institute for Conservation of Historic and Artistic Works, London.

Library Quarterly. Published by the University of Chicago Press.

Restaurator. Published by Restaurator Press, P.O. Box 96, DK-1004, Copenhagen K, Denmark.

Studies in Conservation. Published quarterly by the International Institute for Conservation of Historic and Artistic Works, London.

RICHARD STODDARD
FRANCES KNIBB
KOZUCH

The Theatre in American Fiction, 1774-1850: An Annotated List of References

NOVELISTS HAVE OFTEN been attracted by the color and glamor of the theatre. To the novelist of the first half of the nineteenth century, the playhouse was a microcosm of urban life: people of all classes crowded together, glowing gaslights, noise, music, liquor bars, strong emotions, the sense of losing oneself in the throng. To the dime novelist, the theatre was a place of danger and temptation, a resort of seducers, a rendezvous for adulterers. To the society novelist, the theatre (or more likely the opera house) was a showplace where the aristocrat might first "bring out" his daughter; where the city dandies carried opera glasses not to view the performance but to inspect the belles in the boxes; where one observed the latest fashions in dress and singers. The theatre was a touchstone that proved the character of the hero or betrayed him: a good man found innocent amusement at the playhouse, while a weak man was fatally tempted by the liquor bar and the prostitutes.

These fictional interpretations of the uses and abuses of the theatre were based on fact. The bars, the whores, the dandies were real enough — they can be documented from non-fictional accounts. But the novelists add something rarely found elsewhere: a flavor, an atmosphere, a sense of being there, plus details of audience behavior, social customs, popular opinion, and other elusive data.

In search of such material (and anything else that might be of interest to theatre historians), we have examined more than 1,800 fictional publications issued in the United States before 1851. Our bibliographical guide was Lyle H. Wright's *American Fiction, 1774-1850* (2nd rev. ed., 1969), the first volume of a three-volume bibliography covering all American fiction to 1900 (with the exception of juveniles, Sunday School tracts, jestbooks, and similar publications). Very nearly all the titles listed by Wright are available on microfilm. In fact, two publishers, Research Publications, Inc., and University Microfilms, Inc., have undertaken to issue microfilm collections based on Wright's bibliography.[1] The very availability of these microfilms suggested the present survey to us. Many university libraries have purchased one or the other of the microfilm collections, making accessible to a large number of theatre researchers a new, rich, and unexplored territory.

About 98% of the titles in Wright's first volume are now available on microfilm (Research Publications American Fiction Collection). We examined all of them — 1,815 items. Of these, we found approximately 350 which include more than a passing mention of the theatre. From this preliminary list we have selected for annotation 116 titles — those which seem informative enough to be useful to theatre historians.[2] The earliest item in our selection was published in 1795, and the great majority (98 of 116) were published in the years 1830-1850. Clearly, the list will be most useful to researchers interested in mid-nineteenth-century theatre, but we have retained the dates 1774-1850 in our title to indicate that we surveyed the fiction of the entire period.

Our list identifies a great variety of materials: scenes in the pit, the boxes, and the galleries; glimpses of life backstage and in the green room; descriptions of theatres in London, Boston, New York, Philadelphia, Mobile, and many other places — even on a man-o'-war. Some novelists attack the immorality of the theatre; others defend the value of a well-regulated stage. Many kinds of theatrical activities are represented: hippodrama, opera, dancing, circus, Shakespeare, melodrama, and other forms. Some of the more journalistic accounts include biographical details and anecdotes about performers, as well as discussion of critics, plays, acting style, and scenery. Among the entries are works by prominent literary figures (James Fenimore Cooper, Washington Irving, Herman Melville) and by theatre professionals (William Dunlap, William B. English, Joseph M. Field, Mrs. Anna Cora Ogden Mowatt Ritchie).

Much of the material identified here is not fictional at all — at least, not in the sense of "imaginary." The authors describe real actors and theatres. They discuss plays actually performed on the American stage. Many of the playhouse scenes have the ring of authenticity, of remembered experiences. In fact, novelists writing in the period 1830-1850 often insisted in their prefaces that they were devoted to "truth" — that their intention was to reflect actual conditions.

Such assertions of truthfulness are particularly characteristic of novelists writing about urban society. These "city novels" will prove valuable to researchers interested in the theatre as an urban institution. A strong "urban consciousness" appears for the first time in American fiction and drama in the late 1840's. It is reflected in plays such as Benjamin Baker's *A Glance at New York* (1848) and in many of the novels we examined. The novelists present the theatre as a prominent part of the pageantry of urban life. To think of the city was to think of playhouses, balls, concerts, richly-dressed ladies promenading on the avenue, shops glistening with expensive wares. The theatre itself — brilliantly illuminated, crowded, fraught with temptations — epitomized the spectacle of the city.

Researchers will also find the list useful in documenting *tableaux vivants,* amateur "spouting clubs," "living statues," and similar theatrical activities that are seldom treated in nonfictional accounts. We have an extensive description of privately-staged *tableaux vivants* from no less an authority than Mrs. Mowatt Ritchie (item 2120), a long short story about amateur Thespians (item 1911), and numerous attacks on the salacious exhibitions of "Model Artists" posing statuesquely in tights (e.g., item 979). The novels also reflect theatrical fashions such as the rage for Italian opera and the "Elsslermania" of the 1840's.

Even more important, the novels provide documentation of audience behavior in American playhouses — a particularly ephemeral aspect of theatre history. We learn that spectators at working-class theatres cried "Hoist that rag!" and "Hats off!" at curtain time; that newsboys who attended the Chatham Theatre in New York customarily claimed the front benches of the pit, and even carved their names into them; that frolicking men-about-town dallied with the *demi-mondaines* in the gallery bar; that the opera house was as much a place in which to be seen as to see. These and similarly elusive impressions can help fill out and vivify the picture of the early American theatre.

Some of the items in our selection were published in more than one edition. In such cases we have listed the editions included in the microfilms issued by Research Publications, Inc. We have generally adopted the short-title form used in the *Revised Index* to the Research Publications collection, which follows Wright in arranging entries by author (or title in the case of anonymous works) and numbering the entries consecutively. Occasionally we have supplied a somewhat fuller name or title from Wright. To assist readers searching for specific information, we have added an index of selected subjects and proper names mentioned in the annotations.

It should be noted that in his bibliography Wright included collections comprising both fiction and non-fiction. Consequently, some of the materials we found are not fiction, but rather essays and journalistic accounts. Only a foolish consistency would have dictated omitting them.

Preceding each entry is the item number in Wright's *American Fiction*, Volume I, which we have included to assist readers using microfilms.

110   Arthur, Timothy S. *The Maiden.* Philadelphia, 1845.
Long conversation between two young women — one rather flighty, the other solemn — about the morality of the theatre, describing the emotional effect of certain scenes in Auber's opera *Fra Diavolo,* censuring the immodest dancing costume worn by Madame Celeste and Fanny Elssler, and indicating the girls' parents' attitudes towards the theatre: "Your father and mother take you to the theatre! Goodness! Mine would as soon take me to my grave." (pp. 42-54; see also pp. 63, 92, 121.)

193a Asmodeus, *pseud. The Jenny Lind Mania in Boston.* Boston, 1850.
Satirical attack on P.T. Barnum's exploitation of the Swedish Nightingale and on Bostonians for paying as much as ten dollars for a ticket. Biographical details on Jenny Lind, description of Barnum's publicity devices, an auction of tickets, the excitement of Bostonians at her arrival, her visit to the Harvard University Observatory, a list of Boston notables who attended her concerts. On p. 27 is a caricature wood engraving of Barnum.

195   *Atlantic Club-Book, The.* 2 vols. New York, 1834.
"Steam," a fantasy by William Cox about a future society in which *Hamlet* is acted by steam-powered robots: "Unfortunately in the grave scene, owing to some mechanical misconstruction, Hamlet exploded, and in doing so, entirely demolished one of the gravediggers"(I, 47-48). Theodore S. Fay's story "The Little, Hard-Faced Old Gentleman," concerning the editor of a theatrical weekly, *The North American Thespian Magazine,* who badgers a newspaper editor for a puff (I, 117-29). A moral tale by John Howard Payne, the actor and playwright (I, 191-96). N.P. Willis' journalistic "A Night at the French Opera," describing Maria Taglioni in Auber's *Le Dieu et la Bayadère* (I, 309-12). "The Author," a story by Theodore S. Fay, including a chapter, "The Play," about an eccentric author's experiences in writing a play and having it produced; satire on ghosts, dungeons, and spectacle in melodrama, specimen of wretched blank verse, notes on the performance (II, 72-82).

212   Averill, Charles E. *The Secrets of the Twin Cities.* Boston, 1849.

Attempting to seduce the hero, a wicked woman stages *tableaux vivants*, starting with a sentimental deathbed scene and working up to a voluptuous tableau of Venus and her nymphs (pp. 96-99).

304a Bennett, Emerson. *The Prairie Flower.* Cincinnatti, 1850. (Research Publications copy, labeled 304, is really 304a.)

Vivid description of a fire during a performance at the National Theatre, New York (pp. 15-18).

330 Bloomfield, Obadiah Benjamin Frankiln, *pseud. The Life and Adventures* .... Philadelphia, 1818.

In the forward, the author (an American) says he wrote a tragedy produced by Kemble at Drury Lane and well-received by the audience, but the London critics murdered it (pp. v-vii). Brief mention of G.A. Steven's *A Lecture on Heads* (p. 93). Scene in an unidentified theatre, referring to a performance of *Richard III* by Thomas A. Cooper ("inferior to Cooke and Kemble in that character"), noting that the performance lasted four hours (pp. 110-12).

407 Briggs, Charles F. *The Adventures of Harry Franco.* 2 vols. New York, 1839.

Scenes at unidentified New York theatres, commenting on the prostitutes in the gallery bar, second-rate *entr'acte* entertainment, "the rude and ribald language of the people in the pit," the ungainliness and scanty costume of an opera dancer (I, 52-56, 110-14). Mention of an amateur Thespian club (I, 83) and of a restaurant called "The Terrapin Lunch" located under the American Museum in New York (II, 49).

478 Cannon, Charles J. *Scenes and Characters from the Comedy of Life.* New York, 1847.

Country boy's description of his first visit to a theatre, a performance of *Richard III* with battles featuring "as many as half a dozen on a side," mentioning Richard's hump and one outsized leg (pp. 68-75). Miscellaneous references: the fine distinctions made by those morally opposed to the theatre; a performance of J.S. Knowle's *The Wife* at an unspecified New York theatre; praise of the acting of Mrs. Emma (Wheatley) Mason; general remarks on the opera (pp. 110-13). More comments on opera, calling it "unhealthy excitement" (pp. 133-34, 137-38). A character quotes from *Macbeth* "in the harsh tones of Macready" (p. 182).

494 Caruthers, William A. *The Kentuckian in New-York.* 2 vols. New York, 1834.

Conversation about a brawl in an unidentified circus in Baltimore (I, 62, 65-67). Brief description of Castle Garden in New York (I, 179-80). Scene at an unidentified theatre in New York during a performance of an Italian opera, with remarks on the audience and the performers, including naive comments by a Kentucky backwoodsman (I, 215-23). Scene at the Park Theatre, New York, with remarks on the audience, the practice of calling for national songs from the band, the performance of a comedy featuring a character named Nimrod Wildfire, plus the afterpiece *Paul Pry;* again, comments by the backwoodsman (II, 101-108).

495 ———. *The Knights of the Horseshoe.* Wetumpka, Alabama, 1845.

Description of Williamsburg, Virginia, as it appeared c. 1714, mentioning a small theatre on the public square and noting: "We have undoubted authority — both traditional and historical — for the assertion, that a Theatre existed at the time stated, though overlooked, if not denied, by Dunlap" (p. 112). [This note may be the earliest published reference to the history of the Williamsburg Theatre (1716). William Dunlap's *History of the American Theatre* (1832) identified the first theatrical performances as those of the Hallam company in 1752, also at Williamsburg.] Brief mention of an unidentified actor at this theatre (p. 115).

521 Child, Mrs. Lydia. *Letters from New-York.* New York, 1843.

Remarks on Macdonald Clarke, a well-known New York eccentric, who eloped with a Park Theatre actress named Miss [Mary Anne] Brundage, later known on the English stage as Mrs. Burrows (pp. 88-92). A concert and pyrotechnical exhibition at Castle Garden in New York (pp. 153-56). An exhibition of American Indians at the American Museum in New York in March, 1843 (pp. 247-57).

529 ———. ———. Second Series. New York, 1845.

Discussion of the violinist Ole Bull, including an anecdote about his playing "Yankee Doodle" on request from an American audience (pp. 22-27, 228-33, 272-79). Notes on exhibitions by a New York animal-tamer and menagerie-operator named Driesbach (p. 109). Places of recreation in New York, including the Italian Opera House, Castle Garden, Niblo's Garden, Vauxhall, Barnum's American Museum, the Park Theatre (which "retains a sort of vanishing likeness of gentility"), and the Bowery Theatre (pp. 170-76).

546 Clark, Willis G. *The Literary Remains of the Late Willis Gaylord Clark*, ed. Lewis Gaylord Clark. New York, 1844.
Brief notes: one knee band for Richard III (p. 29); the lyric poetry in *Romeo and Juliet* (p. 92); Charles Kemble skating on the Schuylkill River (p. 100); amateur Thespian clubs (p. 121); Shakespeare's prologues (pp. 180-81); the murder of Lord Sandwich's mistress, Miss Reay, at Covent Garden Theatre in 1779 (pp. 292-94). Shakespeare and his contemporaries (pp. 313-14). Essay "The Snake Eater" about an exhibition in a Mississippi town: a man appears to eat, then disgorge, a rattlesnake; flushes "purple" to heighten the effect (as Junius Brutus Booth could do, at will); the trick explained (pp. 350-58). Essay "Dramatic Alterations" about distortions of history in alterations of *Richard III* (pp. 359-63).

554 Cobb, Joseph B. *The Creole*. Philadelphia, 1850
Private boxes at New Orleans theatres (p. 53). Scene at the opera house in the Rue Française, New Orleans, including the appearance of General Andrew Jackson, with remarks on audience behavior (pp. 59-63).

573 Conkey, Mrs. M. *The Perennial Flower*. New York, 1841.
Actresses said to lack wifely virtues (p. 83). Country boy newly arrived in New York is led into dissipation and near-ruin by visiting the theatre, "that wretched haunt of infamy" (pp. 142-47).

579 Cooper, James Fenimore. *Afloat and Ashore*. 4 vols. in 2. Philadelphia, 1844.
Amusements in New York in 1799, mentioning Rickett's Circus; a lion "kept in a cage quite out of town, that his roaring might not disturb people"; and the John Street Theatre, "a very modest Thespian edifice" (I, 113). Scene at the Park Theatre, New York, around 1800, including comments on audience behavior, seating arrangements, Thomas A. Cooper, and James Fennell (II, 201-210).

715 ———. *Satanstoe*. 2 vols. New York, 1845.

Regret that America has no native drama to record social customs, (I, 9). Exhibition of a lion and a monkey in New York in 1757 (I, 77, 82). Interesting remarks on the Nassau Street Theatre in New York, mentioning Hallam's company, and on the building of a second theatre [on Cruger's Wharf?] in the city (I, 92). In New York in 1757 a group of military officers produce *Cato* and *The Beaux' Stratagem* at a theatre apparently located in William Street: notes on Cato's costume (an altered dressing gown), audience behavior, the playhouse, the playing of Syphax and Juba in blackface with woolly wigs, the acting of Othello on the American stage as a "non descript" rather than a Negro, the beauty of Addison's sentiments, the ladies' discomfort at the coarseness of *The Beaux' Stratagem* (I, 95-96, 98-99, 105, 113-21).

771   Cox, William. *Crayon Sketches.* 2 vols. New York, 1833.

Mainly essays rather than fiction. "A few of the Inconveniences of Seeing Shakspeare Acted," including remarks on typical *Macbeth* productions and on stage versions of *Richard III* and *King Lear* (I, 41-54). "Prize Tragedies," on the low state of tragedy in America, mentioning Edwin Forrest's prizes for plays like J.A. Stone's *Metamora* (I, 154-60). Praise of the design of the Park Theatre, New York (I, 195). "The Drama As It Is," defending melodrama and spectacle, pooh-poohing the hue and cry over the "decline" of the legitimate drama in America, suggesting revivals of old "sterling comedies" (II, 26-35). "Old English Comedies," attacking the farcical comedies of Thomas Morton, Richard Peake, and John Poole, promoting judiciously-pruned versions of the comedies of Wycherley, Congreve, Vanbrugh, and Farquhar (II, 94-98). "An Evening at the Theatre," discounting the moral influence of the stage, defending the pleasures of play-going, among which is the study of audience types and audience behavior (II, 107-115). "London Theatres," with remarks on Covent Garden, Drury Lane, the Haymarket, Astley's, and general comments on the minor and "minor-minor" theatres with their blood-and-thunder productions of melodrama; comparisons to the Park, Bowery, and other New York theatres (II, 128-35). Essays, each three to seven pages, on English, American, and European performers, including remarks on the following: the opera singer Mrs. [Elizabeth?] Austin, actors John Barnes and Thomas Barry, singer-actress Clara Fisher, actors Mr. and Mrs.

Thomas Hilson, ballet-master Hutin and the French Ballet, singer Lydia Kelly, actress Frances Kemble, actor John Liston, opera singer Giuditta Pasta, actor [Henry?] Placide, singer Peter Richings, actress Mrs. Sharpe, danseuse Maria Taglioni, actress Mme. Vestris, danseuse Mme. Ronzi Vestris, and actors Mrs. [Sarah?] Wheatley and [Jacob?] Woodhull (II, 144-220; cf. remarks in the Preface).

801 Curtis, Newton M. *The Matricide's Daughter.* New York, 1847.
First in a trilogy (see also Nos. 811 and 813) of short novels in which the hero and heroine take to the stage (rare in novels published before 1851). Here, the heroine acts for only a season, then falls ill, but the novel includes one informative scene at the Park Theatre, New York, in the 1830's, mentioning the effect of the music ("rapture") and acting ("she caused them to weep or smile at pleasure"), the rolling curtain, and footlight illumination that increased when the performance began (pp. 89-90).

811 ———. *The Star of the Fallen.* New York [1847].
Sequel to the preceding. The hero, an American, travels to London and turns actor. The manager of the Haymarket Theatre hires him, puffs him in the papers, rehearses him in a new play, plies him with liquor on opening night ("the common beverage of all of us, when we have arduous parts to perform"), and engages him at fifty guineas a night following his successful debut. After touring England, he is engaged by an English agent for the Park Theatre, New York. *Passim;* see especially pp. 71-75, 80-85.) Back in New York, the heroine recovers and returns to the stage of the Park Theatre (pp. 102-103).

813 ———. *The Victim's Revenge.* New York, 1848.
Sequel to the preceding, and last of this trilogy of novels. Several theatrical scenes: the hero and heroine are cast opposite each other at the Park Theatre, New York; their appearance together (pp. 55-58) is a triumph. As in the previous parts, the stage life is rather fanciful.

821 Dana, Richard Henry. *Poems and Prose Writings.* Boston, 1833.
Essay "Kean's Acting," published originally during one of Edmund Kean's American tours, including remarks on his Lear, Hamlet, Richard III, Othello, and Sir Giles Overreach (pp. 420-37).

851 *Desultoria: The Recovered Mss. of an Eccentric.* New York, 1850.

Unusual description of a performance of *Hamlet* as reflected in the facial expressions of a young woman in the audience, with additional remarks on audience behavior and on the play (pp. 68-88).

852 *Diary of a Pawnbroker, The.* New York, cop. 1849.

Slight, but a fine example of the novel which shows a young man ruined by taking one false step: going to the theatre. A clerk, though warned against "the wicked company" and "the demoralizing effects of many of the scenes," goes to the playhouse, meets a seductress, and is snared (pp. 96-98). Extravagance, disease, poverty, and drunkenness follow.

852a Dix, William G. *An Imaginary Conversation between William Shakespeare and His Friend Henry Wriothesly, Earl of Southampton. Also, an Imaginary Conversation between the Same Mr. Shakespeare and Mr. Richard Quyner.* Boston, 1844.

Foreword laments the corrupt state of the drama but predicts it will be turned to good use presenting church history and promoting religion. In the first conversation, Shakespeare talks about the playwright's common sense and imagination; in the second, about the subjects and the moral qualities of his plays. [Historical presentism throughout. Curious and dull.]

865 *Drunkard, The.* By the Author of the Moral Drama of the Same Name. Boston, [1844.] 38 pp.

Clearly an exploitation of the enormous success of the melodrama *The Drunkard,* generally attributed to William Henry Smith.

875 Dunlap, William. *Thirty Years Ago; or, The Memoirs of a Water Drinker.* 2 vols. New York, 1836.

The best American theatrical novel published before 1851, and one of the best ever. Clearly based on Dunlap's experiences as manager of the Park Theatre in New York. The main character is a young man named Spiffard who is stage struck in New York, travels to England, trains himself as a burletta singer, and makes his debut at an amateur theatre in London. Successful, he turns professional and tours England, making such a name for himself that Thomas A. Cooper engages him for the Park Theatre. Other real-life actors who appear are George Frederick Cooke and Thomas Hilson. Numerous comments on acting and dramatic literature (both American and English), the social lives and daily routine of actors, and the morality of the theatre. Backstage and auditorium scenes at the Park Theatre. Shakespearean similes and allusions throughout. Highlights: an excellent description of a young man's introduction to the theatre, with remarks on a performance of *Othello* (I, 75-79); a description of Spiffard's wife as Lady Macbeth (II, 18-21); and many biographical details about George Frederick Cooke (II, 115-36, 145-52, 168, 207-13, 217, 220).

880   Durell, Edward H. *New Orleans as I Found It*. New York, 1845.
Remarks on French opera in New Orleans, which drew fashionable audiences on Sunday evenings; description of an unidentified theatre in New Orleans Street, commenting on the dress and behavior of the audience; reflections on dance as an art and descriptions of the Sylphide, Cachucha and other dances (pp. 52-55, 58-60).

881   Durivage, Francis A. *Angela; or, Love and Guilt*. Boston, 1843.
Brief but unusual comments on the decline of the drama, attacking the "declamation des jambes" and horses in melodrama, praising the acting of Junius Brutus Booth (with particular notice of his Pescara in Massinger's *The Duke of Milan*); description of the debut of a female singer who, though beautiful, lacked "a stage face" (pp. 15-16).

887   ———, and George P. Burnham. *Stray Subjects, Arrested and Bound Over*. Philadelphia, 1849. (Research Publications copy, labeled 886, is really 887).
"Familiar Lectures on Shakspeare," a course in Shakespeare-Made-Easy, being comic accounts of *Macbeth*, *Othello*, and *Romeo and Juliet* (pp. 33-44). A poem, "Love in the Bowery," including these lines: "I took her to the Bowery — / She sat long side of me — /They acted out a piece they called/ 'The Wizard of the Sea.'/And when the sea-fight was fetched on,/Eliza cried 'hay! hay!'/And like so many minutes there/ Five hours slipped away" (p.108). [The speaker is plainly a Bowery B'hoy.] Comic story "Tom Links, the Showman," about a menagerie operator who owns a bear with a predilection for mixed drinks (pp. 114-20). Brief satirical remarks on the inflated style of theatrical newspaper advertisements and playbills (p. 148) and on the conventions of melodrama (pp. 165-166).

The Theatre in American Fiction, 1774-1850; 185
An Annotated List of References

891   *Easy Nat; or, Boston Bars and Boston Boys.* Boston, 1844.
      Description of a "Thespian" (amateur) theatre in Boston called the Forrestians' Theatre (after Edwin Forrest), with remarks on a performance at which the spectators indulge in typical shouts such as "hyst that rag" (raise the curtain), mewing, barking, etc. (pp. 12-14, 24-25).

910   English, Thomas Dunn. *1844; or, The Power of the "S.F."* New York, 1847.
      A New York policeman searches the theatres to find a certain pickpocket. Scene at the Bowery Theatre, including a long parody of a sensational playbill; description of the crowded house, with standees in the orchestra pit and on the stage; remarks on audience behavior, especially that of the pittites (pp. 227-32).

917   English, William B. *Rosina Meadows.* Boston, 1843.
      Scene at the Tremont Theatre, Boston, during a Christmas night performance of *The London Merchant,* mentioning the apprentices sent by Boston merchants to learn a lesson and referring to the gallows scene; comments on audience behavior and the whores in the third tier (pp. 22-23). [English was an actor and manager in Boston. Wright lists a number of other novels by him.

935   Fay, Theordore S. *Hoboken.* 2 vols. New York, 1843.
      Scene at the Park Theatre, New York, mainly interesting for its remarks on audience behavior (I, 64-71, 75-77). Brief mention of a performance by Maria Taglioni at the King's Theatre, London (II, 120).

941   ___. *Sydney Clifton.* 2 vols. New York, 1839.
      Scene in an unidentified New York theatre, mentioning [Henry?] Placide and Edwin Forrest, remarking on audience behavior (I, 112-20).

953   Field, Joseph M. *The Drama in Pokerville.* Philadelphia, 1847.
      Comic stories. "The Drama in Pokerville," about a strolling company's visit to a small town, where they perform *Pizarro* "with a new precipice"; notes on costumes, acting, crude scenery and effects, audience behavior (pp. 9-92). "'Old Sol' is a Delicate Situation," concerning events at Ludlow and Smith's theatre in Mobile, Alabama, when some spectators protest a

bawdy gag by Sol Smith in a performance of *A Roland for an Oliver* (pp. 112-17). Opposite p. 116 is an excellent illustration of Smith on the stage with the leader of the protestors. "The Gagging Scheme," satirizing actors, scenepainters, a down-on-their-luck strolling company, and clerical opposition to the theatre in a small town (pp. 118-28). "Establishing the Science," about mesmerizers who give exhibitions in small towns (pp. 129-33). "Ole Bull in the 'Solitude'," concerning the violinist's stormy ride on the prairie near St. Louis, including an illustration (pp. 134-38). "A Night in a Swamp," about Sol Smith's company and how they "make do" on a trip from Georgia to Alabama, with an illustration of Smith disguised as a clergyman (pp. 188-93). "A Resurrectionist and His Freight," describing a joke played on a country bumpkin by the comic actor Tom Placide (pp. 197-200). [Field was an actor and manager in the Midwest.]

964   *Florence de Lacey.* New York, 1845.
      Scene in an unidentified New York theatre [probably the Park], with remarks on the acting of [Tyrone] Power and Edmund Kean; the social function of the playhouse; and the "buffooneries," melodrama, and vaudevilles popular on the American stage (pp. 44-46).

972   Forbes, Gerritt Van H. *Green Mountain Annals.* New York, 1832.
      Scene in an unidentified theatre: a country boy is enchanted with the music, the acting, the Greek Revival drop curtain, the tragedy *Metamora* (pp. 33-39). Remarks on the unhealthy influence of the theatre on the young man's character (pp. 50-51).

977a *Fortunes of a Young Widow, The.* New York, 1850.
      A country boy at the theatre, and how he is corrupted by it (pp. iii-iv). Arguments for and against the theatre, citing such plays as "Don Caesar de Bazan" [i.e., Hugo's *Ruy Blas*] in favor of it (pp. iv-v). Comments on the prostitutes in the third tier of the Park Theatre, who had taken up the wearing of immodestly short dresses called "pantalettes" (p. 41; cf. the illustration on p. 43). Audience behavior in theatres (pp. 45, 58). Crude wood engraving by T.C. Boyd showing the stage of an unidentified New York theatre as viewed from a private box (p. 56). Conversation about the moral influence of the theatre, including re-

marks by a worldly woman who defends the stage as a school of life and praises "the beautiful exemplars of true womanly character" in Shakespeare's plays (p. 59). Scene in an unidentified New York theatre, mentioning a garden scene with real flowers, actresses' use of a lamp-blackened pin as an eye-brow pencil, the liquor bars, and the whores in the third tier (pp. 59-62). Incidental mention of Blake, the Park Theatre treasurer, who had apprehended a counterfeiter (p. 65, note). Suggestion that daughters of fashionable families were sometimes "brought out" at the opera (p. 68).

978 Foster, George G. *Celio; or, New York Above-Ground and Under-Ground.* New York, cop. 1850.
  Conversation about the way a new opera singer must promote her talents to the New York newspaper editors (pp. 71-72). The singer's debut at the [Astor Place?] opera house, the reaction of the fashionable world, the vindictiveness of some critics, envy and depravity among opera performers and green-room habitues (pp. 77-83, 97-108). A party at the cottage of an opera star, most of the guests being performers; a game called "Musica Magica" (pp. 115-20). [The author was himself a theatre and music critic in New York.]

979 ———. *New York by Gas-Light.* New York, 1850.
  Like Foster's *New York in Slices* (item 980), this is a mine of curious information, closer to yellow journalism than to fiction, about underground and night-time life in New York City. Remarks on Barnum's American Museum with its Drummond Light and chromatic wheel, a rendezvous for adulterers (pp. 7-8, 20-21). "Model Artist Exhibitions," those presentations of "living statues" brought to America by one Frimbley, an English dancing master, and carried to lewd extremes by "Doctor" Collyer's "model men and women" (pp. 12-17). Description of the patrons of a Negro dance hall, "wild with excitement, like Ned Buntline at Astor Place" (p. 74). "Theatres and Public Amusements," including descriptions of the Park, Broadway, Astor Place, Bowery, Chatham, Olympic, Niblo's, and Franklin theatres, as well as Mager's Concert Hall, identifying their patrons, with passing remarks on Charlotte Cushman, the opera manager Max Maretzek, the opera singer Giuseppe Forti, and the *demi-mondaines* of the third tier (pp. 82-92). Comments on the Bowery B'hoy, referring to F.S.

Chanfrau's portrait of him in Benjamin Baker's *A Glance at New York* (pp. 101-109). More on prostitutes and depravity in New York theatres (pp. 111-12). Remarks on working-class theatres (p. 123).

980 ———. *New York in Slices.* New York, 1849.
Wood engraving "Broadway," by Durand after Mayr, showing the exterior of Barnum's American Museum (p. 6). Discussion of Bowery B'hoys and volunteer firemen in New York, referring unfavorably to F.S. Chanfrau's portrayal of the B'hoy in Benjamin Baker's "Mose" plays [such as *A Glance at New York*] (pp. 43-48, including an illustration of the B'hoy, p. 46). "The Theatres," mentioning Niblo's Garden, the Broadway Theatre, and the Park Theatre, commenting on newspaper puffing, prostitutes, the substitution of cheap novelties for standard dramas such as those of Shakespeare ("He don't draw"), policemen in theatres, liquor bars, and immorality (pp. 89-93, including an illustration of fashionable spectators in a box, p. 91). "Behind the Scenes," discussing the indecency of many plays, the immodesty of stage costumes, immorality among actors and green-room habitues; suggesting reforms; referring to Chatham, Olympic, Broadway, Burton's Chambers Street, and Park Theatres, as well as the Astor Place Opera House (pp. 100-103). Remarks on the New York newsboys' passion for the theatre, especially the blood-and-thunder dramas at the Chatham and Olympic theatres and the acting of [J. Hudson] Kirby, famous for his death scenes (p. 105). Description of the Bowery Theatre on holiday evenings, with a vivid picture of audience behavior (p. 120).

984 Foster, Mrs. Hannah. *The Boarding School.* Boston, 1798.
One of the earliest items of theatrical interest. Lessons for young ladies, including a cautionary tale about a girl whose parents encourage her to cultivate music and dancing; growing vain of her talents, she elopes with an actor, takes to the stage, falls into bad company, becomes "a complete courtezan," hastens the death of her parents, and ends in wretchedness (pp. 42-45). Admonition to avoid immoral books and plays (p. 78), and a few more unfavorable comments on the theatre (pp. 157-58).

986 ———. *The Coquette.* Boston, 1797.
Another eighteenth-century item (cf. the preceding entry).

Mention of a performance of *Romeo and Juliet* in Boston in 1797, commenting on the depressing effect of the funeral scene on a woman's sensibility (p. 167). Brief but interesting remarks on a Boston "circus" [Lailson's Boston Ampitheatre in Haymarket Place], said to be "a place of fashionable resort of late, but ... inconsistent with the delicacy of a lady... especially, when the performers of equestrian feats are of our own sex" (p. 168).

999   Fox, Mary Anna. *George Allen, the Only Son.* Boston, 1835.

A young man of respectable family visits the theatre for the first time. "His mind was enervated by the music, and still more by the dancing of the very beautiful, bewitching actress...." From the theatre, "the transition was easy to a gambling house," from thence to "forgery, robbery, and finally murder." (*Passim,* especially pp. 64-67, 91.)

1067   Greene, Asa. *Travels in America.* New York, 1833.

Satirical and descriptive comments on the Park Theatre, New York, referring to the respectability of the pit and a riot caused by the anti-American slurs of the English singer [Joshua R.] Anderson; mentioning actors [John] Povey, [Henry?] Placide, and Frances Kemble (pp. 48-52). Amusing explanation for the conversion of a Chatham Street (New York City) theatre into a church (p. 64).

1071   Griffith, Mrs. Mary. *Camperdown.* Philadelphia, 1836.

Story "Three Hundred Years Hence," a clever feminist satire about life in 2135, with remarks on theatres and actors; e.g., "All our actors now are men and women of education, such as the Placides, the Wallacks, the Kembles, the Keans, of your day.... In your day, out of the whole theatrical corps of one city, not more than six or seven, perhaps, could tell the meaning of the *words* they used in speaking, to say nothing of the *sense* of the author" (p. 78-79).

1133   Hart, Joseph C. *Miriam Coffin.* 2 vols. New York, 1834.

Attack on the exaggeration and empty glitter of melodrama, including an amusing "scenario" (I, 134). Extensive description of a nautical melodrama about an American ship and its crew, as produced at Drury Lane in the mid-eighteenth century, starring the actress-dancer Nancy Dawson. Her fitness for breeches parts ("fine ample hips, small knee, tapering calf, delicate ankle, and a foot almost Chinese"); her performance as a she-dragon and a goddess of the sea; the view from a stage box; the reactions of the naive American crew, who are present at the performance; anachronistic description of scenery and effects; and an account of how Nancy, in a fit of jealous pique, clamps a padlock on the mouth of one of the crew, an incident which is called "fact" in a footnote (II, 45-64).

1138 Hawes, William P. *Sporting Scenes and Sundry Sketches.* ed. William H. Herbert. 2 vols. New York, 1842.
Comic remarks on various commentators' interpretations and punctuations of Othello's line "Put out the light, and then put out the light" (II, 149-58).

1149 Hawthorne, Nathaniel. *Twice-Told Tales.* Boston, 1837.
Historical-fictional story "The May-Pole of Merry Mount," including descriptions of May Day mumming and Morris dancing at the colonial settlement of Mount Wollaston, near Boston (pp. 75-94). The preface suggests that Hawthorne found his material on mumming in Joseph Strutt's *Sports and Pastimes of the People of England* (1801), rather than in native documents and traditions.

1286 Ingraham, Joseph. *Eleanor Sherwood.* Boston, 1843.
Two city sharpers persuade a rich country boy to visit the Chestnut Street Theatre in Philadelphia, hoping to tempt him into vice and fleece him. Remarks on the morality of the theatre, the classes of spectators at the Chestnut (whores in the third tier, kept mistresses in the pit, "Africans" in the heavens, etc.), audience behavior, the country boy's fascination, the liquor bar (pp. 14-15). Another scene at the Chestnut, describing the thrilling performance of Miss Sheriff [i.e., Jane Shirreff] in Rooke's opera *Amilie* and vividly recreating the "confusion, voices, oaths, blasphemy, lewdness and lust" in the third tier (pp. 38-42).

1301 ———. *Harry Harefoot.* Boston, 1845.
Scenes in the Washington Gardens, Boston, a city resort [later the site of a theatre] with shady promenades, lighted for nighttime strolling, and a liquor bar (pp. 33-38). Brief mention of Theatre Alley, a narrow and dismal street [running behind

the Federal Street Theatre in Boston] (p. 46). A brief scene at the [Federal Street] Theatre, condemning the loose women in the third tier (p. 54).

1341 ———. *Rodolphe in Boston.* Boston, 1844.
Scenes at the Tremont Theatre, Boston, during a performance of an unidentified opera including a character named Zenella, played by Fanny Elssler; remarks on costumes, audience behavior, and the exclusion of Negroes from the box circle (pp. 20-25, 32-47).

1349 ———. *The South-West.* 2 vols. New York, 1835.
A few remarks on Shakespeare's humanity (I, 25-26). Discussion of New Orleans theatres, including a description of James H. Caldwell's American Theatre on Camp Street (comparing it to Northern theatres) and of the French Theatre, or Théâtre d'Orléans (I, 219-225). Brief comments on the theatre in Natchez, Mississippi (II, 40).

1429 Irving, Washington. *The Letters of Jonathan Oldstyle.* New York, 1824.
Letters II-VII include Irving's well-known observations on the acting, plays, scenery, lighting, costumes, audience behavior, orchestra, liquor bar, furnishings, and decorations at the Park Theatre, New York, plus some animadversions on drama critics. The only clearly identifiable actor is an unnamed "portly gentleman" discussed in Letters II, IV, and VI; he is obviously John Hodgkinson. Letter II, i, satirizes a chauvinistic afterpiece called *The Tripolitan Prize.*

1430 ———. *The Sketch Book of Geoffrey Crayon.* 7 pts. New York, 1819-1820.
"The Boar's Head Tavern, Eastcheap," with remarks on *Henry IV, Part 1,* and Falstaff (Part III, pp. 217-42). "Stratford-on-Avon," including a description of the house where Shakespeare was born, an old man's memories of Garrick at the Shakespeare Jubilee ("a short punch man, very lively and bustling"), Shakespeare's tomb, his deerpoaching, and the influence of the country on his sensibility (Part VII, pp. 51-89). Remarks on the singing of a song from *Gammer Gurton's Needle* at gatherings of a London men's club (Part VII, pp. 106-108). Brief note on quasi-theatrical amusements at Bartholomew Fair (Part VII, p. 110).

1449 ———. *Tales of a Traveller.* 4 pts. Philadelphia, 1824.

"Buckthorne," a comic story about a young gentleman's adventures, including a stint as an actor in a strolling company playing at country fairs in England, with remarks on the crude acting style of the booth theatres and the rollicking life of the actors (Part 2, pp. 69-117). "The Strolling Manager," another humorous treatment of an itinerant English troupe, including satire on fashions in acting Shakespeare (Part 2, pp. 187-212).

1468 Jerauld, Mrs. Charlotte. *Poetry and Prose.* Boston, 1850.

Mentions lectures by [Richard Henry] Dana on "Macbeth, Shakespeare in [sic] the Supernatural, and Hamlet," given in the winter of 1842 (p. 50). Story "Emma Beaumont" about a girl of good family who reluctantly goes on the stage to support her widowed mother (pp. 197-208). Episode in a short story, "Caroline," about a girl forced to become an actress to support her child (pp. 298-311).

1490 Jones, Justin. *Hasserac.* Boston, 1849.

Scenes at an unidentified Boston theatre, including the debut of a Boston lady as Ophelia in *Hamlet*, with the third scene of Act I [Polonius's admonitions?] cut at her request; some details about her acting style (pp. 92-96).

1511 Judah, Samuel B. *The Buccaneers.* 2 vols. New York, 1827. (Research Publications copy, labeled 1509, is really 1511.)

Gratuitous and bitter attack on the character of actors (alleging drunkenness and debauchery), the liquor bar and prostitutes in theatres, and the theatre in general as "the very hot bed of vice" (II, 16-19).

1535 Judson, Edward Z.C. *Three Years After.* New York, 1849.

Vivid description of a New York working-class theatre, Novelty Hall on Centre Street, with remarks on the smell and appearance of the auditorium, audience behavior, and the music and crude scenery of melodrama (pp. 42-44).

1590 Knapp, Samuel L. *The Bachelors.* New York, 1836.

An American major in England meets Richard Brinsley Sheridan and Tom Moore, who, thinking him a "raw Yankee," try to "smoke" him. In an amusing exchange, touching on the drama in England and America, the Yankee gets the best of Sheridan (pp. 44-48).

1592a ———. *The Polish Chiefs.* 3rd ed. 2 vols. New York, 1835.

A Yankee character comments naively on plays he sees in London: *Macbeth* ("Duncan should have looked out for a better guard"), *Hamlet*, and *The School for Scandal* (II, 110-13). Similar eccentric opinions of opera (II, 119-20).

1677 Lippard, George. *'Bel of Prairie Eden.* Boston, 1848.

Scene at the Walnut Street Theatre, Philadelphia, with a sensational description of a "lascivious" dancer, remarks on audience types (including the whores), and mention of a pocket-picking (pp. 73-77).

1741 M'Cabe, John C. *Scraps.* Richmond, Va., 1835.

In a poem, "Richmond," the author recalls the horror of the burning of the Richmond Theatre in 1811 and mentions two of the victims (pp. 37-39). Notes to the poem describe the fire and identify some of the victims (p. 190).

1781 Mallory, Daniel. *Short Stories and Reminiscences.* 2 vols. New York, 1842.

"Recollections of New York" includes a discussion of the Grove Theatre [Bedlow Street], near Corlaer's Hook, where bad plays by one "Winchell" [John Minshull] were performed (I, 47-48). Remarks on a porter house in Nassau Street operated by the actor John Hogg, and on the Shakespeare Tavern, kept by a brother of the actor John Hodgkinson (I, 48-50). "Gen. Washington's Marquee" includes comments on the actors in the Philadelphia-Baltimore company, who performed in Washington, D.C., during the summer; mentions William Warren, William Francis, Thomas Burke, John Duff, and supplies interesting information on Joseph Jefferson, noting that he was an avid fisherman, a respectable scenepainter, and a skilled theatre mechanic, as well as an actor (I, 166-68, 171).

1787 Mancur, John H. *Constance; or, The Debutante.* Philadelphia, cop. 1846.

A ballet story. The heroine, a French girl, is apprenticed to the ballet company at the Académie Royale de Musique in Paris. She makes her professional debut in Paris and later appears in England. Description of her debut at the Haymarket Opera House, London, with some discussion of management policies and public tastes in ballet. Pestered by peers, beaux, and rakes, she marries a childhood sweetheart and retires from the stage.

1792 ———. *La Meschianza.* New York, 1844.

Military theatricals at the Southwark Theatre, Philadelphia, in the winter of 1777-1778, mentioning scene painting by Major John André and Captain Oliver Delancey (pp. 320-24). Description of an elaborate *fête champêtre,* "La Meschianza," planned by André and others and held in honor of General William Howe at an estate near Philadelphia, May 18, 1778 (pp. 360-70).

1821 *Mary Beach; or, The Fulton Street Cap Maker.* New York, 1849.

Slight but significant episode in which a city libertine takes a newly-arrived country girl to the theatre. He is pleased to find that she is enchanted with her first play, since he believes that the experience will help him to seduce her: "Frank did not venture to take any more liberties with her that evening, but contented himself with letting the theatre do its work" (pp. 42-43).

1829 Mathews, Cornelius. *The Career of Puffer Hopkins.* New York, 1842.

An auctioneer of books does a "hard sell" on a Bowery Theatre melodrama called *Brimstone Castle:* satirical description of the plot (pp. 38-39). Conversation with a theatrical "lightning-maker," with satire on the fondness of the pittites for spectacular effects (pp. 66-68, 212). Description of Vauxhall Gardens in New York and of a ball held there (pp. 216-17). [The author edited a theatrical periodical called *The Prompter's Whistle.*]

1832 ———. *Moneypenny.* New York, 1849.

Scene at the Chatham Theatre, New York, a favorite resort of newsboys, describing audience behavior, the auditorium, the plot of a romantic melodrama, and the boys' insistence on sensational death scenes like those of [J. Hudson] Kirby (pp. 62-65).

1837 ———. *The Various Writings of Cornelius Mathews.* New York, 1843.

Includes his play *The Politicians* (pp. 117-50), with a preface commenting on the need for dramas on American subjects and the need for a copyright law; condemning frivolous foreign plays which make up most of the repertoire; and refuting the idea that American society furnishes no materials for comedy (pp. 119-20). Brief mention of Theatre Alley behind the Park Theatre, New York, and a balloon ascension at Castle Garden (pp. 314-15). Lectures and essays promoting an international copyright and discussing the relation between English and American literature and drama (pp. 353-70).

1838 Mattson, Morris. *Paul Ulric*. 2 vols. New York, 1835.
Scene at an unidentified theatre, perhaps in Philadelphia, with brief comments on the music, the audience, the costume of Romeo. Scene in a class taught by Mr. Wire, who prepares gentlemen (such as the stage-struck hero) for "the stage, pulpit, senate, or bar." After being tutored by Mr. Wire, the hero buys costumes and props (including a jeweled dagger to kill himself in *Othello*) and hires an agent who arranges his debut. Brief description of his successful appearance as Richard III, after which his father dissuades him from this "miserable and iniquitous life" (I, 60-81).

1871 Melville, Herman. *White-Jacket*. New York, 1850.
Chapter XXIII, "Theatricals in a Man-of-War": description of an amateur production by sailors to while away idle hours in port, including a transcription of their playbill, notes on the performance (a nautical drama called *The Old Wagon Paid Off!*), and remarks on the enthusiastic behavior of the sailor-audience (pp. 110-17). Comments on the books in the ship's library, including "glorious old dramas" by Marlowe, Jonson, "the magnificent, mellow old Beaumont and Fletcher," and "St. Shakspeare" (pp. 200-201). Topical allusions throughout — some theatrical.

1882 Mitchell, Donald. *The Lorgnette*. 2 vols. (24 nos.) New York, 1850.
Throughout, references to and discussions of opera, the Astor Place Opera House in New York, and the customs of opera-goers (see especially Vol. I, Nos. 7 and 9). Comments on P.T. Barnum and Jenny Lind (Vol. I, No. 6, and Vol. II, Nos. 10-11).

1911 Moore, Horatio N. *Fitzgerald and Hopkins*. Philadelphia, 1847.
Engraved title-page shows a curtained stage cluttered with

props. Text comprises two stories, "Alonzo F. Fitzgerald; or The Autobiography of a Spouter" (pp. 7-46), and "The Hopkins Family; or, English Immigrants and Itinerant Players" (pp. 48-166). The former is a humorous treatment of teenagers' amateur theatrical clubs ("spouting societies"), including accounts of their crude theatres, performances, audience behavior, and a fanciful wood engraving illustrating a performance of J.S. Knowle's *Virginius* (opposite p. 16). "The Hopkins Family" recounts the adventures of a strolling company and contains satirical descriptions of performances in a converted livery stable in a small Eastern town. [One of the best of our finds, amusing and refreshingly free of moralizing.]

1913 Moore, John McDermott. *The Adventures of Tom Stapleton.* New York, 1850.

Amusing account of low life in New York, including some theatricana: verses to the minstrel song "Zip Koon" (p. 42; cf. p. 67); a conjuror's exhibition (p. 83); and a description of a theatrical hoax at the Chatham Theatre, caricaturing extravagant newspaper advertisements and the credulity of New York theatre-goers (pp. 85-89).

1921 Morris, George P. *The Little Frenchman and His Water Lots.* Philadelphia, 1839.

Passing mention of a Saratoga Springs concert by singers Miss Elizabeth Hughes, Charles Horn, and John Sinclair (p. 50). Anecdote about the first performance of J.S. Knowle's *The Hunchback,* starring Charles and Frances Kemble (pp. 105-108). Biographical remarks on the playwright Mordecai M. Noah, describing the faultiness of the actors at the premiere of Noah's *She Would Be a Soldier,* mentioning actors [Catharine?] Leesugg, John Barnes, and others, and praising Noah's generosity when the Park Theatre in New York was destroyed by fire (pp. 108-111). Anecdotes about actors John Barnes, Thomas Hilson, and Charles Gilfert (pp. 112-16, 122-25). Illustration of a New York street scene, including a large placard with a theatrical advertisement (p. 138).

1926 Motley, John L. *Merry-Mount* 2 vols. Boston and Cambridge, 1849.

Quasi-theatrical May-Day pageantry and mumming at Merry-Mount, near Boston, in the early seventeenth century (I, 167-72, 177-86).

1945 Neal, John. *Errata.* 2 vols. New York, 1823.

A long conversation about Shakespeare, one party defending his plays, the other attacking them as immoral (not one "could a modest woman read aloud, in company; not one *ought* she to sit out, upon the stage") and singling out *Othello* and *Romeo and Juliet* as failures (II, 66-70). Discussion of various interpretations of the portraits in the closet scene in *Hamlet* (II, 80-82). A character named Hammond the Dwarf describes a crude performance by a strolling company in Virginia and recounts his experiences playing Glenalvon in *Douglas* and Zanga in Edward Young's *The Revenge,* mentioning an actor "who had a knack of snapping his eyes, and making faces, like George Frederick Cooke" (II, 194-98).

1946 ———. *Keep Cool.* 2 vols. Baltimore, 1817.

Scene at an unidentified New York theatre during a performance of *Hamlet,* with some remarks on acting style, stage business, and audience behavior (I, 186-92).

1949 ———. *Randolph.* 2 vols. [Baltimore?] 1823.

Indecency in the plays of Beaumont and Fletcher, Mrs. Centlivre, and Shakespeare, as well as Sheridan's *The School for Scandal,* "the greatest outrage upon decency I know" (I, 218-19). Some general comments on Shakespeare (II, 42). Brief remarks on the author's one tragedy [*Otho*] (II, 180). Excellent discussion of Thomas A. Cooper's acting and of acting in general, using Richard III as an example of various styles (II, 261-63). Brief remarks on Edmund Kean, Talma, Mrs. Siddons, Junius Brutus Booth, James and Henry Wallack, Mr. and Mrs. John Duff, and William Pelby (II, 263-66).

1951 Neal, Joseph Clay. *Charcoal Sketches.* Philadelphia, 1838.

Comic story "Garden Theatricals" about the catastrophic debut of an amateur Hamlet at the Tivoli Theatre, Market Street near Broad Street, Philadelphia, commenting satirically on the performances, acting styles, and audiences at this minor playhouse (pp. 114-29).

1981 *Oran, the Outcast.* 2 vols. New York, 1833.

Edwin Forrest in *Metamora* (I, 25-26). Low women at the Park Theatre, New York (I, 26-27). Master [Joseph] Burke, "the Irish Roscius," as Young Norval in *Douglas* and as Dr. O'Toole in *The Irish Tutor* (I, 107-108). A conversation about the theatre in New York, mentioning a number of actors and opera singers, discussing ghosts in Shakespeare, and criticizing the actors at the Park Theatre (I, 171-77). Guests at a masquerade ball dressed as dramatic characters (I, 189, 191, 196-97).

2021 Paulding, James K. *A Sketch of Old England.* 2 vols. New York, 1822.

The low state of the theatre in England, including remarks on the plays of Byron, Barry Cornwall [Bryan W. Proctor], and Charles R. Maturin; the British taste for swordplay and protracted death scenes such as those of Edmund Kean; the vulgar style of comic acting; the superiority of the French theatre to the British (I, 211-26). Robert W. Elliston's unauthorized production of Byron's *Marino Faliero;* brief remarks on Byron's *Cain* (II, 103-108).

2063 Porter, William T. (ed.). *A Quarter Race in Kentucky.* Philadelphia, 1847.

Humorous story "Uncle Billy Brown — 'Glorious,' " describing a boisterous amateur performance in a Mississippi village — a vivid picture of audience behavior in rural America (pp. 110-16).

2108 Rees, James. *Mysteries of City Life.* Philadelphia, 1849.

Brief scene in an unidentified theatre, describing it as the resort of wealth and fashion (pp. 116-17). Nostalgia about the theatre in the period 1800-1820, when actors were artists and plays were both agreeable and instructive — as contrasted with the vulgarities of the present (pp. 125-26). The poor plight of playwrights at the mercy of newspaper critics (pp. 317-18). The immorality of the theatre: the liquor bars, prostitutes, Dr. Collyer's "Model Artist" exhibitions, and indecent plays such as *Jakey's Marriage* (pp. 377-80). [Rees wrote *The Life of Edwin Forrest* (1874).]

2114 *Revelations of Asmodeus.* New York, 1849.

Brief remarks on the opera as an upper-class pastime (pp. 8, 13). Passing reference to a panorama exhibition (p. 10). Discussion of "Model Artist" exhibitions, tracing them to risqué tableaux vivants presented by the idle rich in New York (pp. 50-52). Biographical remarks on P.T. Barnum; gossip about an unnamed actor [apparently Edwin Forrest] who, though married, was accustomed to sleeping with his leading ladies while on tour; similar revelations about an unnamed circus singer (pp. 72-76).

2120 Ritchie, Anna Cora (Ogden) Mowatt. *Evelyn.* 2 vols. Philadelphia, 1845.

Informative episode about the preparation and presentation of a series of tableaux vivants by a party of fashionable ladies and gentlemen, including a description of the stage, the use of a lace scrim, lighting, postures, costumes, music, and the moralistic protests of one of the guests (1, 85-100). [The author was a well-known actress and playwright.]

2126 Robb, John S. *Streaks of Squatter Life.* Philadelphia, 1847.

Brief mention of humorous Western stories by the actor-manager Sol Smith (p. viii). Humorous story "A Spiritual Sister" concerning a Mormon woman who mistakes Sol Smith for a brother of her church (pp. 67-70, including an illustration showing Smith and the woman). Story "Natural Acting!" concerning Dan Marble's performance at Grand River, Michigan, while marooned by a storm (pp. 83-87).

2242 Rowson, Mrs. Susanna. *Charlotte's Daughter.* Boston, 1828.

Memoir of the author, mentioning her appearance at theatres in Philadelphia and Boston, discussing her plays (pp. 3-20).

2256 ———. *Trials of the Human Heart.* 4 vols. Philadelphia, 1795.

The list of subscribers includes the names of a number of actors at the Chestnut Street Theatre, Philadelphia (pp. v-vi). Preface contains autobiographical details about the author's father and her youth in Massachusetts (pp. xv-xviii). (Cf. the preceding entry.)

2276 Sands, Robert C. *The Writings of...* 2 vols. New York, 1834.

General remarks on the tragedies of Aeschylus, Sophocles, and Euripides (I, 10-11, 15). Comment on an article by Sands, "Ghosts on the Stage," explaining that opinions therein attributed to President Thomas Jefferson are "poetic license" (I, 15-16). Brief scene at a theatre in Washington, D.C., describing audience behavior (II, 198-99). Essay "Ghosts on the Stage," an imaginary conversation with President Jefferson about ghosts in *Hamlet, Macbeth,* and Aeschylus's tragedies (II, 267-74). "Prologue to Waldimar, A Tragedy," promoting native drama in America (II, 363-65).

2278 Sanford, Ezekiel. *The Humours of Eutopia.* 2 vols. Philadelphia, 1828.
A foolish English schoolmaster-spy teaches an elementary lesson about the theatre to a pre-Revolutionary American schoolgirl (I, 86-89). The schoolmaster describes, then re-enacts, David Garrick's Richard III (I, 92-94).

2373 Sedgwick, Mrs. Susan. *Alida.* New York, 1844.
Tableaux vivants in fashionable society: arrangement of the stage, costumes, music, performance (pp. 129-33).

2410 Simms, William Gilmore. *Border Beagles.* 2 vols. Philadelphia, 1840.
Informative conversations about actors and acting, including stories about "C-----ll" [James H. Caldwell], manager of the American Theatre, New Orleans (*passim,* especially Vol. I, Chaps. III, V, VII-IX).

2433 ———. *The Prima Donna.* Philadelphia, 1844.
Debut of a foreign singer at an unidentified New York theatre (pp. 13-15). The singer's history; satirical remarks on an unidentified pantomime actor (pp. 16-18). A green-room scene at the same unidentified theatre (pp. 18-19).

2449 Sly, Costard, *pseud.* [possibly the actor Henry James Finn]. *Sayings and Doings at the Tremont House.* 2 vols. Boston, 1833.
The view of the Tremont Theatre from the Tremont House hotel in Boston (I, 10). Reference to the custom of crying "The Pit's Full" (I, 153). English and American actors and theatre, discussing Charles Kemble and his daughter Frances and a number of others, many of them members of the Tremont Theatre company (II, 11-20). Comic memoirs of an Italian opera singer, including remarks on rehearsal customs, backstage scenes, portraits of opera-house characters, and a description of a performance in a provincial Italian opera house (II, 65-81). Spitting on the stage (II, 147). Doggerel about two Boston actors, [George H.] Barrett and [Henry J.] Finn; praise of Charles Kean's acting (II, 264). More on the Tremont Theatre actors, including Barrett, Finn, Mr. and Mrs. [William Henry?] Smith, and [George] Andrews (II, 264-66).

2456 Smith, I. Anderson. *Blanche Vernon, the Actress.* New York, 1846.

Description of a performance in an unidentified New York theatre, with comments on audience behavior (p. 33). A newspaper editor discusses how he solicits bribes from actors by threatening to print scandalous stories about them (pp. 34-36). The heroine's reasons for becoming an actress; her encounter with the hero while tending a sick woman; her marriage and retirement from the stage (pp. 47-56). [One of the few pre-1851 novels with an actress as the central character. The subtitle, "A Romance of the Metropolis," makes a typical connection between the theatre and urban life. The pleasures of the city are contrasted to the dullness of rural life (see, e.g., p. 31)].

2461 Smith, Richard Penn. *The Actress of Padua and Other Tales.* 2 vols. Philadelphia, 1836.
In the preface Smith explains that "The Actress of Padua" is an adaptation of a Victor Hugo play, *Angelo, Tyran de Padoue* (I, iii). Three-act play *The Daughter,* based on part of Mme. de Genlis's novel *The Siege of Rochelle* (I, iv; II, 89-137). "The Actress of Padua," a story about a mid-sixteenth-century actress; includes no scenes in theatres (I, 1-73). Brief praise of William Dunlap, calling him the best American playwright (II, 20). Story "The Man with a Nose," including a character who is apparently a tragedian (II, 20-37). [The author was also a playwright.]

2462 ———. *The Forsaken.* 2 vols. Philadelphia, 1831.
British military theatricals in Philadelphia in 1777-1778, with scene painting by Major John André and Captain Oliver Delancey; an officer reminisces about playing the ghost of Hamlet with floured face and truncheon (II, 72-78). [This documentation of André's and Delancey's scene painting at the Southwark Theatre pre-dates William Dunlap's record of it in his *History of the American Theatre.*] Detailed description of a *fête champêtre* ["La Meschianza," or "Mischianza"] held in Philadelphia in May, 1778, to honor General Howe and to celebrate the arrival of General Clinton: officers and ladies in costume, tilting, swordfights, and quasitheatrical spectacles (II, 214-19, 222-23).

2490 *Squints Through an Opera Glass.* New York, 1850.
Opera in New York, discussing the Astor Place Opera House, audience types and their behavior, opera critics (Richard Grant White, Henry C. Watson, James F. Otis, George G. Foster, Regis de Trobriand [probably Philippe Régis Denis

de Keredern, comte de Trobriand], John S. Dwight, and one Masseras), and opera singers (Zerlina Bertucca, Novelli Masetto, [Teresa] Truffi, [Giuseppe] Forti, [Sesto] Benedetti, Amalia Patti, and Signors Leporello and Beneventano).

2498 Stephens, Mrs. Ann. *High Life in New York.* New York, 1843.

Informative naive-Yankee-style description [à la Jonathan in Royall Tyler's *The Contrast*] of a visit to the Park Theatre, New York, to see Madame Celeste, including comments on the arrangement and appointments of the house, the drop curtain, the audience, scenery, dancing, acting, and lighting (pp. 44-48).

2500 ———. ———. Complete in One Number. New York, 1845.

Description of a visit to the Park Theatre (pp. 44-48, identical to the preceding item, q.v.). The unsophisticated Yankee hero has an interview with Fanny Elssler (pp. 72-75), then attends one of her performances at the Park Theatre and comments on the auditorium, drop curtain, her dancing, and life backstage and in the green room (pp. 79-84). Another visit to the Park, with remarks on a new drop curtain and on an affecting play concerning a character named Grandpa Whitehead (pp. 110-11). Again to the Park, describing the redecorated auditorium (pp. 113-16). Description of a concert by the singer [Jeanne] Castellan at an unidentified concert room (pp. 127-29).

2508 Stone, William L. *Tales and Sketches.* 2 vols. New York, 1834.

Story "The Mysterious Bridal" including a scene at the John Street Theatre in New York [possibly adapted from information in William Dunlap's *History of the American Theatre*, published two years before the novel], with remarks on Lewis Hallam, Jr., Thomas Wignell, Mr. and Mrs. John Henry, Joseph Jefferson, and other actors (II, 148). "Setting the Wheels in Motion," a record (compiled from printed accounts and private reminiscences) of quasi-theatrical pageantry in New York following the adoption of the U.S. Constitution in 1788, noting that William Dunlap appeared in a procession carrying the banner of the Philological Society (II, 174-82). Account of festivities in New York after the election of Washington as president, including the hanging of transparencies on "the Theatre, then situated at the corner of Fly-Market-slip" (II, 202).

2586 Thompson, William T. *Chronicles of Pineville.* Philadelphia, 1845.
Humorous story "Great Attraction! or, The Doctor Most Oudaciously [sic] Tuck In," about a performance in a small Georgia town by a company of touring equestrians, with remarks on the reactions of the townspeople and on the performance (including the intrusion of a drunken "spectator" wearing layers and layers of clothing who turns out to be [William?] Harrington, the leader of the company) (pp. 11-38). The frontispiece illustrates a scene during the performance, showing the clown, in motley, mounted on a horse.

2592 ———. *Major Jones's Sketches of Travel.* Philadelphia, 1848.
Brief remarks on Fanny Kemble and the sad lessons she has learned [on a Georgia plantation] (p. 94). Bumpkin's description of Balfe's opera *The Bohemian Girl* as performed at the Chestnut Street Theatre, Philadelphia, in 1845, by the "Segwin" [i.e., Seguin] Troupe, with remarks on the public's taste for opera, audience behavior, and the performance (pp. 97-103). Brief remarks on a performance of Donizetti's opera *The Daughter of the Regiment* at the Olympic Theatre, New York (pp. 118-19).

2615 Tuckerman, Henry T. *The Italian Sketch Book.* Philadelphia, 1835.
Pyrotechnics in a religious ceremony in Florence: an artificial dove is driven along a wire stretched from the altar of the cathedral to a point in the cathedral square (pp. 82-83). Remarks on a performance of Bellini's *Norma* in Florence — mainly a plot summary (pp. 84-87). General remarks on opera, especially Italian opera (pp. 179-85).

2617 ———. ———. 3rd ed. New York, 1848.
Theatre and opera in Florence, with special attention to Carlo Goldoni (pp. 37-38). Essay "The Cantatrice" about an unidentified Italian singer (pp. 114-21). Story "The Thespian Syren," set in Edinburgh, Scotland, about a law student who falls in love with an actress; description of her as Virginia in a play about the Appius and Virginia story (pp. 240-57). A performance in Milan by the opera singer Maria Malibran (pp. 355-56). General remarks on opera, especially Italian opera (pp. 368-72; identical to item 2615, pp. 179-85).

RICHARD STODDARD
FRANCES KNIBB KOZUCH

2618 ———. *Rambles and Reveries.* New York, 1841.
Comments on Vittorio Alfieri's youth in Turin (pp. 64-65). Theatre and opera in Florence, with special attention to Carlo Goldoni (pp. 113-15; identical to item 2617, pp. 37-38). Story "The Thespian Syren" (pp. 118-38; see item 2617). Essay "Characteristics of Lamb," discussing Charles Lamb's writings on the drama, especially Shakespeare (pp. 339-44). Remarks on "eye-language" in Shakespeare, quoting lines about the way eyes convey and betray emotions (pp. 375-78).

2649 Waln, Robert, Jr. *The Hermit in America on a Visit to Philadelphia.* Philadelphia, 1819.
An orgy of Shakespeare-quoting at a supper party (pp. 108-13). The theatre in Philadelphia, mentioning the Olympic Theatre and describing a performance at the Chestnut Street Theatre, with remarks on acting and audience behavior (pp. 195-203).

2651 ———. ———. 2nd Series. Philadelphia, 1821.
"Philadelphia Amusements," including a short history of the theatre in Philadelphia (Quaker opposition, a converted warehouse on Water Street, a theatre at Cedar and Vernon Streets, the South Street [Southwark] Theatre, the Chestnut Street Theatre, the Olympic on Walnut Street, and the Tivoli), plus remarks on concerts, pleasure gardens, the Museum and a note on plays disguised as "moral lectures" at the Broad [i.e., Board] Alley Theatre in Boston (pp. 63-82). [This is surely one of the earliest published records of the history of the theatre in an American city.] Ironic remarks on those who compare American theatre and drama unfavorably to those of Europe (pp. 162-64).

2691 Weir, James. *Lonz Powers.* 2 vols. Philadelphia, 1850.
Conversation between the manager of the Nashville (Tenn.) Theatre and others about the low state of theatre business, the personal lives of actors, and the attractiveness of a new actor in *Othello* (II, 184-92). Scene in the Nashville Theatre, with remarks on the appointments of the house, audience behavior, and a performance of *Othello* in which an actor (said to be modeled on a real actor named M'Glocklin) becomes so involved in playing the title role that he actually stabs himself dead at the end of the play (II, 197-210).

The Theatre in American Fiction, 1774-1850;   205
An Annotated List of References

2731   Willis, Nathaniel P. *Complete Works.* New York, 1846.

A collection of essays, fiction, and poetry (much of which first appeared in newspapers), plus Willis's two plays. Frequent references to and discussions of the theatre and opera, especially in the section called "Ephemera." The following is only a selection.

Opera in London, discussing dancers Maria Taglioni, Fanny Elssler, and Mlle. Augusta, as well as singers Pauline Garcia, Maria Malibran, and Giulia Grisi (pp. 532-33). Description of a London dinner honoring William Charles Macready, with remarks on Sir Edward Bulwer-Lytton and the actor Charles M. Young (pp. 536-37). A private concert in London presented by the opera singers Giulia Grisi, [Giovanni] Rubini, [Luigi] Lablache, [Antonio] Tamburini, and [Nikolai] Ivanhoff (pp. 550-52). Descriptions of Stratford-upon-Avon and Charlecote, mentioning the recent use of Shakespeare's birthplace for a butcher shop and describing the house where he lived in retirement (pp. 560-65). A visit to a Washington, D.C., theatre by a party of Indian chiefs, including the Indians' comments on the acting of [Tyrone?] Power (p. 572). A visit to a New York menagerie and lion-training exhibition operated by one Driesbach (p. 586). A concert by Mme. [Jeanne] Castellan, comparing her singing to Malibran's (pp. 596-97). The dwarf Tom Thumb at Barnum's American Museum (pp. 605, 623). The opening of a new season at the Park Theatre, New York, with remarks on the appointments and decorations of the house and on a drop curtain including a portrait of Macready (pp. 621-22). Ladies' dress at the opera in New York (pp. 624-25). Macready as Macbeth (p. 627). Comparison of Edwin Forrest and Macready as Richelieu (p. 638). Macready as Werner, supported by Charlotte Cushman (p. 645). Description of Palmo's new opera house in New York (pp. 663-65). Willis's verse plays *Tortesa the Usurer* (pp. 865-82) and *Bianca Visconti* (pp. 883-95).

2757   Wood, Mrs. Sally. *Julia and the Illuminated Baron.* Portsmouth, N.H., 1800.

Slight, but early, reference to the theatre in Boston [probably the Federal Street Theatre], comparing it favorably to theatres in London, praising the acting of John Hodgkinson, and defending the value of a well-regulated playhouse (pp. 84-85).

RICHARD STODDARD
FRANCES KNIBB KOZUCH

2760 Woodworth, Samuel. *The Champions of Freedom.* 2 vols. New York, 1816.

At a fashionable masked ball in Boston, a masque is presented (complete with elaborate decorations, machinery, and costumes) in which American Liberty repels attacks by Ambition, Avarice, and other assailants (I, 128-47). Scene at the Richmond (Virginia) Theatre on the night in 1811 when it was destroyed by fire (I, 166-73). Remarks on the aftermath of the fire (I, 178). Scene in an unidentified New York theatre [probably the Park] during a performance of *The Point of Honor, or, School for Soldiers* and *Huzza for the Constitution*, plus a hornpipe by Master Whale, "the Infant Vestris," with remarks on audience behavior (II, 50-53). [The author was a popular playwright.]

Index of Selected Subjects and Proper Names

Acting (see also the names of individual actors), 494, 771, 875, 953, 972, 1071, 1429, 1449, 1490, 1838, 1911, 1945, 1946, 1949, 1951, 2021, 2410, 2449, 2498, 2649, 2691
Aeschylus, 2276
Alfieri, Vittorio, 2618
Amateur theatre, 407, 546, 891, 1871, 1911, 2063
Amilie, 1286
Anderson, Joshua R., 1067
André, Maj. John, 1792, 2462
Andrews, George, 2449
Angelo, Tyran de Padoue, 2461
Astor Place Riot, 979
Audience behavior in theatres, 193a, 407, 494, 554, 579, 715, 771, 851, 875, 880, 891, 910, 917, 935, 941, 953, 977a, 979, 980, 1067, 1133, 1286, 1341, 1429, 1535, 1832, 1871, 1882, 1911, 1913, 1946, 1951, 2063, 2276, 2456, 2490, 2498, 2586, 2592, 2649, 2691, 2731, 2760
Augusta, Mlle., 2731
Austin, Mrs. Elizabeth, 771
Ballet, 771, 1787
Balloon ascension, 1837
Baltimore (Md.)
    Philadelphia-Baltimore Company, 1781
    Unidentified theatre, 494
Barnes, John, 771, 1921
Barnum, Phineas T. (see also New York City: American Museum), 193a, 1882, 2114
Barrett, George H., 2449
Barry, Thomas, 771
Bartholomew Fair, 1430
Beaumont and Fletcher, 1871, 1949
Beaux' Stratagem, The, 715

The Theatre in American Fiction, 1774-1850; **207**
An Annotated List of References

Benedetti, Sesto, 2490
Beneventano, Signor, 2490
Bertucca, Zerlina, 2490
Bianca Visconti, 2731
Blake, Mr., 977a
Boar's Head Tavern, 1430
Bohemian Girl, The, 2592
Booth, Junius Brutus, 546, 881, 1949
Boston (Mass.)
   Board Alley Theatre, 2651
   Federal Street Theatre, 1301, 2757
   Jenny Lind's popularity, 193a
   Lailson's Boston Amphitheatre, 986
   Tremont Theatre, 917, 1341, 2449
   Unidentified theatres, 986, 1490
   Washington Gardens, 1301
Bowery B'hoys, 887, 979, 980
Brimstone Castle, 1829
Breeches parts, 1133
Brundage, Mary Anne, 521
Bull, Ole, 529, 953
Buntline, Ned, 979
Burke, Joseph, 1981
Burke, Thomas, 1781
Burrows, Mary Anne (Brundage), 521
Byron, George G., Lord, 2021
Cain, 2021
Caldwell, James H., 1349, 2410
Castellan, Jeanne, 2500, 2731
Cato, 715

Celeste, Mme., 110, 2498
Centlivre, Susannah, 1949
Chanfrau, F.S., 979, 980
Charlecote Hall, 2731
Circus and menageries, 494, 529, 546, 579, 715, 887, 986, 2114, 2586, 2731
Clarke, Macdonald, 521
Collyer, "Doctor," 979, 2108
Congreve, William, 771
Conjuring, 1913
Contrast, The, 2498
Cooke, George Frederick, 330, 875, 1945
Cooper, Thomas A., 330, 579, 875, 1949
Copyright law, 1837
Cornwall, Barry, 2021
Costume, theatrical *(see also* Opera: Immodest costumes), 715, 953, 980, 1341, 1429, 1838
Critics, dramatic and musical, 330, 978, 1429, 2108, 2490
Cushman, Charlotte, 979, 2731
Dana, Richard Henry, 821, 1468
Dance *(see also* Ballet and the names of individual dancers), 880, 1677, 1787, 2498
Daughter, The, 2461
Daughter of the Regiment, The, 2592
Dawson, Nancy, 1133
Delancey, Capt. Oliver, 1792, 2462
Dieu et la Bayadère, Le, 195
Douglas, 1945, 1981

Drama, American, 715, 771, 875, 964, 1429, 1590, 1837, 2276, 2651
Drama, English, 771, 875, 1590, 1837, 2021, 2618
Driesbach, Mr., 529, 2731
Drunkard, The, 865
Duff, Mr. and Mrs. John, 1781, 1949
Duke of Milan, The, 881
Dunlap, William, 2461, 2508
  History of the American Theatre, 495, 2462, 2508
  Thirty Years Ago, 875
Dwight, John S., 2490
Elliston, Robert W., 2021
Elssler, Fanny, 110, 1341, 2500, 2731
English, William B., 917
Equestrian drama (*see* Circus)
Euripides, 2276
Farquhar, George, 771
Fennell, James, 579
Field, Joseph M., 953
Finn, Henry J., 2449
Fires in theatres, 304a, 1741, 2760
Fisher, Clara, 771
Florence (Italy), 2617, 2618
Forrest, Edwin, 771, 891, 941, 1981, 2114, 2731
Forti, Giuseppe, 979, 2490
Foster, George G., 978, 979, 980, 2490
Fra Diavolo, 110
Francis, William, 1781
French theatre, 2021
Frimbley, Mr., 979
Gammer Gurton's Needle, 1430
Garcia, Pauline, 2731
Garrick, David, 1430, 2278
Georgia, performance in, 2586
Gilfert, Charles, 1921

Glance at New York, A, 979, 980
Goldoni, Carlo, 2617
Grand River (Mich.), 2126
Green-room scenes, 978, 980, 2433, 2500
Grisi, Giulia, 2731
Hallam, Lewis, Jr., 2508
Hallam, Lewis, Sr., 715
Harrington, William, 2586
Henry, Mr. and Mrs. John, 2508
Hilson, Mrs. Thomas, 771
Hilson, Thomas, 771, 875, 1921
Hippodrama (*see* Circus)
Hodgkinson, John, 1429, 1781, 2757
Hogg, John, 1781
Horn, Charles, 1921
Hughes, Elizabeth, 1921
Hunchback, The, 1921
Hutin, Monsieur, 771
Huzza for the Constitution, 2760
Immorality of the theatre (*see* Liquor bars; Morality of the Theatre; Prostitutes)
Indians, American, 521, 2731
Infant Vestris, 2760
Irish Tutor, The, 1981
Ivanhoff, Nikolai, 2731
Jackson, Gen. Andrew, 554
Jakey's Marriage, 2108
Jefferson, Joseph, 1781, 2508
Jefferson, Thomas, 2276
Jonson, Ben, 1871
Kean, Charles, 1071, 2449
Kean, Edmund, 821, 964, 1071, 1949, 2021
Kelly, Lydia, 771
Kemble, Charles, 546, 1921, 2449
Kemble Family, 1071

The Theatre in American Fiction, 1774-1850; 209
An Annotated List of References

Kemble, Frances, 771, 1067, 1921, 2449, 2592
Kemble, John Philip, 330
Kirby, J. Hudson, 980, 1832
Lablache, Luigi, 2731
Lamb, Charles, 2618
Lecture on Heads, A, 330
Leesugg, Catharine, 1921
Leporello, Signor, 2490
Lighting, stage, 801, 1429, 2498
Lind, Jenny, 193a, 1882
Liquor bars in theatres, 977a, 980, 1286, 1429, 1511, 2108
Liston, John, 771
Living Statues (*see* Model Artist Exhibitions)
London (England)
 Astley's Ampitheatre, 771
 Covent Garden Theatre, 546, 771
 Drury Lane Theatre, 330, 771, 1133
 Haymarket Theatre, 771, 811, 1787
 King's Theatre, 935
 Minor theatres, 771, 875
London Merchant, The, 917
Ludlow, Noah, 953
Lytton, Edward Bulwer-Lytton, Lord, 2731
McGlocklin, Mr., 2691
Macready, William Charles, 478, 2731
Make-up, theatrical, 977a
Malibran, Maria, 2617, 2731
Marble, Dan, 2126
Maretzek, Max, 979
Marino Faliero, 2021
Marlowe, Christopher, 1871
Masetto, Novelli, 2490
Mason, Mrs. Emma (Wheatley), 478

Masseras, Mr., 2490
Mathews, Cornelius, 1829, 1832, 1837
Maturin, Charles R., 2021
Melodrama, 195, 771, 865, 881, 887, 964, 980, 1133, 1535, 1829, 1832
Menageries (*see* Circus)
Merry-Mount, 1149, 1926
Meschianza, La (*fête champêtre*), 1792, 2462
Mesmerism, 953
Metamora, 771, 972, 1981
Michigan, performance in, 2126
Military theatricals, 715, 1792, 2462
Minshull, John, 1781
Minstrelsy, 1913
Mississippi, performance in (*see also* Natchez), 2063
Mobile, Ala., Theatre, 953
Model Artist Exhibitions (Living Statues), 979, 2108, 2114
Moore, Tom, 1590
Morality of the theatre (*see also* Liquor bars in theatres; Prostitutes), 110, 478, 573, 771, 852, 875, 953, 972, 977a, 978, 979, 980, 984, 999, 1286, 1468, 1511, 1821, 1945, 1949, 2108, 2120, 2651, 2757
Morton, Thomas, 771
Mount Wollaston (Mass.), 1149
Mumming, 1149, 1926
Nashville, Tenn., Theatre, 2691
Natchez, Miss., Theatre, 1349
Negroes, 715, 979, 1286, 1341

New Orleans (La.)
  American Theatre, 1349, 2410
  Opera House in the Rue Française, 554
  Théâtre d'Orléans, 1349
  Unidentified theatres, 554, 880
New York City, 579, 771, 1913, 1921, 1981, 2490
  American Museum, 407, 521, 529, 979, 980, 2731
  Astor Place Opera House, 978, 979, 980, 1882, 2490
  Bowery Theatre, 529, 771, 887, 910, 979, 980, 1829
  Broadway Theatre, 979, 980
  Burton's Chambers Street Theatre, 980
  Castle Garden, 494, 521, 529, 1837
  Chatham Theatre, 979, 980, 1832, 1913
  Cruger's Wharf Theatre, 715
  Franklin Theatre, 1781
  Grove Theatre, 1781
  Italian Opera House (cf. Palmo's Opera House), 529
  John Street Theatre, 579, 2508
  Mager's Concert Hall, 979
  Nassau Street Theatre, 715
  National Theatre, 304a
  Niblo's Garden Theatre, 529, 979, 980
  Novelty Hall, 1535
  Olympic Theatre, 979, 980, 2592
  Palmo's Opera House, 2731
  Park Theatre, 494, 529, 579, 771, 801, 811, 813, 875, 935, 964, 977a, 979, 980, 1067, 1429, 1837, 1921, 1981, 2498, 2500, 2731, 2760
  Ricketts's Circus, 579
  Unidentified theatres, 407, 478, 494, 941, 964, 977a, 1067, 1946, 2433, 2456, 2508, 2760
  Vauxhall Gardens, 529, 1829
New Way to Pay Old Debts, A, 821
Noah, Mordecai M., 1921
Norma, 2615
North American Thespian Magazine, The, 195
Old Wagon Paid Off!, 1871
Opera, 478, 494, 771, 880, 978, 1341, 1592a, 1882, 2114, 2449, 2592, 2615, 2617, 2618, 2731
  Amilie, 1286
  Astor Place Opera House (*see* New York City)
  Dieu et la Bayadère, Le, 195
  Fra Diavolo, 110
  Immodest costumes, 110, 407
  Italian Opera House (*see* New York City)
  Opera House in the Rue Française (*see* New Orleans)
  Palmo's Opera House (*see* New York City)
Otho, 1949
Otis, James F., 2490
Panorama, 2114
Paris (France), Académie Royale de Musique, 1787
Pasta, Giuditta, 771
Patti, Amalia, 2490

The Theatre in American Fiction, 1774-1850; 211
An Annotated List of References

Paul Pry, 494
Payne, John Howard, 195
Peake, Richard B., 771
Pelby, William, 1949
Philadelphia (Penna.), 1781, 2651
 Chestnut Street Theatre, 1286, 2256, 2592, 2649, 2651
 Museum, 2651
 Olympic Theatre, Walnut Street, 2649, 2651
 Southwark Theatre, 1792, 2462, 2651
 Tivoli Theatre, 1951, 2651
 Unidentified theatres, 1838, 2651
 Walnut Street Theatre (*see also* Olympic Theatre), 1677
Pizarro, 953
Placide Family, 1071
Placide, Henry, 771, 941, 1067
Placide, Thomas, 953
Point of Honor, The, or, School for Soldiers, 2760
Politicians, The, 1837
Poole, John, 771
Povey, John, 1067
Power, Tyrone, 964, 2731
Proctor, Bryan, W., 2021
Prompter's Whistle, The, 1829
Prostitutes in theatres, 407, 917, 977a, 979, 980, 1286, 1301, 1511, 1677, 1981, 2108
Puffing in newspapers, 195, 811, 980
Pyrotechnics, 521, 2615
Revenge, The, 1945
Richelieu, 2731
Richings, Peter, 771
Richmond, Va., Theatre, 1741, 2760

Ritchie, Anna Cora (Ogden) Mowatt, 2120
Roland for an Oliver, A, 953
Rowson, Susanna, 2242, 2256
Rubini, Giovanni, 2731
Ruy Blas, 977a
Saratoga Springs (N.Y.), 1921
Scenery and scene-painting, 953, 972, 1133, 1429, 1535, 1781, 1792, 1829, 2462, 2498, 2500, 2731
School for Scandal, The, 1592a, 1949
Seguin Troupe, 2592
Shakespeare William, 546, 771, 852a, 875, 977a, 980, 1349, 1430, 1449, 1468, 1871, 1945, 1949, 1981, 2618, 2649, 2731
 Hamlet, 195, 821, 851, 1468, 1490, 1592a, 1945, 1946, 1951, 2276, 2462
 Henry IV, part 1, 1430
 King Lear, 771, 821
 Macbeth, 771, 875, 887, 1468, 1592a, 2276, 2731
 Othello, 715, 821, 875, 887, 1138, 1838, 1945, 2691
 Richard III, 330, 478, 546, 771, 821, 1838, 1949, 2278
 Romeo and Juliet, 546, 887, 986, 1838, 1945
Sharpe, Mrs., 771
She Would Be a Soldier, 1921
Sheridan, Richard Brinsley, 1590
Sheriff, Miss, 1286
Shirreff, Jane, 1286
Siddons, Sarah, 1949
Sinclair, John, 1921
Smith, Richard Penn, 2461

Smith, Sol, 953, 2126
Smith, William Henry, 865, 2449
Sophocles, 2276
Spouting clubs (see Amateur theatre)
Stratford-upon-Avon, 1430, 2731
Strolling companies, 953, 1449, 1911, 1945
Tableaux vivants, 212, 2114, 2120, 2373
Taglioni, Maria, 195, 771, 935, 2731
Talma, F.J., 1949
Tamburini, Antonio, 2731
Theatres (see individual cities: Boston, New York, etc.)
Thumb, Tom, 2731
Tortesa the Usurer, 2731
Tripolitan Prize, The, 1429
Trobriand, P.R.D. de K., Comte de, 2490
Truffi, Teresa, 2490
Vanbrugh, Sir John, 771
Vestris, Mme., 771
Vestris, Mme. Ronzi, 771
Virginia, performance in, 1945

Virginius, 1911
Waldimar, 2276
Wallack Family, 1071
Wallack, Henry, 1949
Wallack, James, 1949
Warren, William, 1781
Washington, D.C., Theatre, 1781, 2276, 2731
Watson, Henry C., 2490
Werner, 2731
Whale, Master, the Infant Vestris, 2760
Wheatley, Mrs., 771
White, Richard Grant, 2490
Wife, The, 478
Wignell, Thomas, 2508
Wildfire, Nimrod (dramatic character), 494
Williamsburg, Va., Theatre, 495
Willis, Nathaniel P., 2731
Woodhull, Jacob, 771
Woodworth, Samuel, 2760
Wycherley, William, 771
Yankee heroes, 1592a, 2498, 2500
Young, Charles M., 2731

Notes

1. While the University Microfilms collection is still incomplete, the Research Publications collection is finished and — more important — is easier to use. See our "Working with Wright's *American Fiction* in Microfilm," *Microform Review*, II (April 1973), 93-96.

2. The excluded titles generally contain trivial or obviously fanciful material, but we will be happy to furnish a list of them (with page references) to anyone who is interested. Write to Prof. Richard Stoddard, Department of Drama and Theatre, University of Georgia, Athens, Ga. 30602.

JAMES P. PILKINGTON

Vanderbilt Television News Archives

THAT TELEVISION IS a prominent factor in contemporary culture is as axiomatic as the fact that the sun rises in the east. Few, if any, facets of life are untouched by it. Year after year surveys attest to the American public's reliance on television for information about national and international events that exceeds not only in degree but also in quality the public's reliance on other media. Unquestionably, television is an important phenomenon.

For many years, because of the impossibility of retaining television in replayable form, of catching its "moonbeams in your hand," television had to be accepted as ephemera, a shadow show of the moment. So established was this attitude that by 1957, when video tape became a reality, few, if any, outside the industry recognized the opportunity, indeed the obligation, to use this new electronic capability for the regular, systematic preservation of this highly effective, and affective, medium. As had been the case, libraries continued their regular, systematic accumulation of traditional forms — newspapers, magazines, books — but not television, though it flickered all around them. In many cases this neglect was recognized and lamented but, for good reason, accepted. Other media, those printed, accumulate quite naturally. Television does not. If it is to be retained, effort and money must be expanded for its preservation. When video tape and video tape recorders became fact, the expense of their use was even more exorbitant than is now the case. And too, nearly everyone interested in research, reference, and study, was oriented to printed materials.

Within the television industry, of course, this was not entirely the case. Video tape was put to use as soon as it was perfected, but not essentially for historical, academic purposes, such as those served by the countless collections of printed materials in the countless libraries around the world. Industrially the use of video tape was for industrial purposes. And even in the television industry, the most commercial of enterprises, economy dictated the reuse of tape, resulting in the erasure of many things initially recorded.

Until the summer of 1968 nowhere in the United States was a library systematically preserving any aspect of television for future public reference.

During that summer a Nashville insurance executive, Paul C. Simpson, persuaded Vanderbilt University in Nashville, Tennessee, that steps needed to be taken to rectify this situation. Admittedly not strides, these steps began cautiously with funds supplied by Mr. Simpson for the rental of three video tape recorders and the unauspicious taping of the network evening news telecasts as aired in Nashville. Housed in the Joint University Library on the Vanderbilt campus, the unnamed little enterprise at first consisted of three rental machines, two table tops in a rare-book room, two volunteer recorder operators, (Simpson and Frank P. Grisham, now director of the Joint University Library) and a three month supply of 1-inch video tape. The project was to record the evening newscasts, and the political conventions, during the period of the Presidential election campaign of 1968, which turned out to be of landmark importance in American political history. On August 6, 1968, Vanderbilt's "television collection" consisted of the previous night's news: the evening news telecasts, and the three networks' coverage of the first night of the Republican Convention of 1968.

From this point the collection has grown daily until it totals more than 3,000 hours of news programs, including the evening news and such special programming as the Democratic and Republican Conventions of 1968 and 1972 (all three commercial networks), the Watergate hearings as televised, and television coverage of such major events as the Nixon trips to Russia and Red China and the signing of the treaty ending the Vietnam War.

When the collection was opened for use in 1971 it was named the Vanderbilt Television News Archive, and work began to develop an access system to the material that, up until then, had been recorded and, placed on the shelves, essentially unviewed. Since then the program of the Archive has broadened to the monthly publication of an index to the news, *Television News Index and Abstracts* (commenced with January 1, 1972) and the development of policies and procedures for use of the collection not only at Vanderbilt but also on a nationwide basis.

Considering the three network evening telecasts, with their audiences in the 50 millions, the nearest the nation has come to a national newspaper, the Vanderbilt Television News Archive operates as nearly as possible in accord with lending library practices. Materials may be viewed in the Archive by anyone so desiring for a charge of $2 per viewing hour. Duplicates of the programs may be rented at a charge of $15 a tape hour. Compilations of items, to the user's order, can be made at $30 a tape hour. Typically, a student or other person interested in a subject will use the 3600-hundred subject-entry index to the abstracts in order to choose the items for compilation and send the order to the Archive, specifying the tape format compatible with his player. The compiled tape is then made to specification. There is a choice of three formats: 1 inch Ampex; ½ inch EIAJ-1; ¾ inch U Matic Cassette. Besides the compilation or duplication charge; the user deposits with the Archive money to cover the cost of the tape: $50 per hour for 1 inch; $25 per hour for ½ inch; $35 per hour for ¾ inch. This deposit is refunded when the tape is returned in reusable condition. No material is sold. None can be duplicated or re-broadcast. Length of time the tapes may be kept is determined by the need of the user. Besides being available on video tape, the material is also available on audio-cassettes. Rental charge for straight duplicates is $5 per tape hour, plus a deposit of $1.50 for an hour of tape. As with the video tapes, the audio tapes are for rental only, cannot be duplicated or rebroadcast. If the user is interested in tapes for periods earlier than those for which published indexes exist, rough, longhand abstracts are available for that part of the collection (1968-1971). These may be used in the Archive or copies sent to the user at a charge of 10¢ per xerox page. Under a grant from the Ford Foundation work is underway for the abstracting and indexing of the early years of the collection such as the years 1972 and 1973. It is anticipated this work will be completed in 18 months.

Presently the *Television News Index and Abstracts*, which has a circulation of about 400 copies a month, is being published without charge. Copies of the publication for 1972 and the first six months of 1973 are available on microfilm for $180. This includes an annual index for 1972. As implied, the *Index/Abstracts* is primarily designed for use with the tapes. The abstracts are digests of the items on the programs, and not transcripts. Authoritative use of the material involves reference to the tapes. This is stressed. Tapes recorded since January, 1971, show across the screen the network, date and time to the nearest ten-second interval of each item. This information is recorded as the broadcasts are recorded.

Since the publication of the *Index/Abstracts* was begun, use of the collection has well demonstrated the widespread interest in the material. During the first 11 months of 1973, nearly 50 studies have been done by local students, and 65 have involved use of material outside the Archive. The subject interest of the users has been as widespread as the news itself and the geographical distribution from coast to coast and border to border. Significant among the users was the New York State Special Commission on Attica, which used the Archive for its study of the evening news coverage of the prison revolt.

Besides growth in use of the tapes since the Archive was opened, marked interest has been shown in the *Index/Abstracts,* the circulation of which has more than doubled since the first mailing. While distribution is not officially restricted, the Archive prefers to send it to places on college campuses where it will get the most exposure — preferably the college library. But mailings are also sent to specific departments of colleges if this is deemed necessary for best use.

The Archive is administered through the Joint University Libraries by a committee of three: Robert A. McGaw, Secretary of the University, chairman; Mr. Simpson, administrative consultant; and Mr. Grisham, library director.

For further information about Vanderbilt Television News Archive write:

James P. Pilkington, *Administrator*
Vanderbilt Television News Archive
Joint University Libraries
Nashville, Tennessee 37203

LAWRENCE W. LICHTY

Sources for Research and Teaching in Radio and Television History

THERE SEEMS TO BE a growing interest in old radio programs for both nostalgia and for serious research. In large part it is the former that has made materials available for the latter — particularly for entertainment programs. There now also seems to be more understanding of the need to preserve and make available television programming.

Many colleges offer courses in film history and there is a flourishing industry renting materials for these courses. Only a few colleges have a course in broadcasting history and the materials are harder to get.

Somebody's law states: "The number of errors in any piece of writing rises in proportion to the writer's reliance on secondary sources." Too much writing about the history of broadcasting — particularly programming — has relied on secondary sources and recollection. Thus, it is especially necessary that the scholar be able to hear and see past broadcast programs. Until recently there were virtually no organized sources of programs. The situation has improved but it is not good.

In what follows I have tried to outline some of the major sources of broadcast programs — for use in teaching and in research — treated here in the following order: university collections, government libraries, networks and industry collections, audio tapes and discs for sale or trade, and films for rent and sale.[1]

UNIVERSITY COLLECTIONS

Milo Ryan Phonoarchive, University of Washington

During World War II Seattle station, KIRO, recorded many of the CBS news programs and broadcast them to the Pacific Northwest on a delayed basis. These recordings were stored in the transmitter building on an island in Puget Sound where the even temperature and humidity provided good conditions for preservation. This was the major portion of this collection begun by Professor Milo Ryan in 1957. The collection was named for him after his retirement in 1970.

The majority of this collection is news, public affairs, and special events, 1940-1945, but there are other materials including entertainment programs. In all there are more than 5,000 programs listed in a 600-page catalog. Supplements are available.[2]

Mass Communications History Center and Center for Theatre Research, University of Wisconsin-Madison

First known as the H.V. Kaltenborn Collection, the Mass Communications History Center of the Wisconsin State Historical Society was organized in 1955. Audio recordings, films and video tapes make up only a small part of this large collection which includes many manuscripts, scripts, audience mail, press releases and other materials — especially from news broadcasters and the National Broadcasting Company. While this is one of the largest collections of historical materials relating to broadcasting outside the major broadcasting organizations themselves and the federal repositories, recorded materials are limited. Of more than 3,000 tapes and discs most relate to public affairs and special events.

Other television material is held by the Wisconsin Center for Theatre Research. (See additional information by Kay Johnson in this volume.) Specifically, there are films, scripts and many other materials related to syndicated Ziv TV programs.

The materials of MCHC and WCTR do not circulate but can be used by scholars by appointment.[3]

NATAS-UCLA Television Library

In conjunction with the National Academy of Television Arts and Sciences the University of California, Los Angeles, collection is one of the fastest growing. There are now more than 2,000 titles in the collection, mostly commercial TV programs, including the entire *Hallmark Hall of Fame* series. Other motion picture and radio materials are also available at UCLA; for example, a massive Jack Benny group. (For additional information see the article by Anne G. Schlosser in this volume.)

Some may be interested in the large collection of hillbilly, country western, and other folk music, mostly from commercial recordings in the John Edwards Memorial Foundation also at UCLA.[4]

Vanderbilt Television News Archive

A new but most useful collection is housed at the Joint University Libraries, Nashville. (See additional information by James P. Pilkington in this volume.) It includes video tape recordings of the three national network evening broadcasts since August 1968. This repository is especially helpful because the material is available for viewing at a very reasonable cost and may be rented in several formats. Audio-only cassettes are available, and monthly abstracts and indices are printed.[5] In short, this is a very valuable and useful collection and hopefully can be continued indefinitely. This material is duplicated at Stanford University at the Hoover Institution.

Miami University-WLW Collection

Established by Crosley (now Avco) Broadcasting most of the materials are from WLW, Cincinnati. This station did a

Sources for Research and Teaching 221
in Radio and Television History

great deal of local programing and originated programs for all four networks at various times. Included are more than 1,500 programs most from 1936 to 1961, including many important war-time programs and a good balance of entertainment features.[6]

Michigan State University

The Michigan State University Collection, supervised by Professor Arthur Weld, contains about 200 hours of broadcast material — a good balance of entertainment and news programming. A catalog is available.[7] Much of this collection is duplicated at Temple University, Philadelphia.

Public Television and National Instructional Television Library

A large collection of instructional television programs and many important Public Broadcasting Service programs, especially documentaries, can be rented from the audio-visual library at Indiana University.[8] Some of this material is duplicated at regional educational TV libraries, and at local ETV stations.[9]

Important Collections at Other Universities

There are a number of collections that are fairly large or that specialize in specific types of material that should be noted here.

The National Voice Library, at the Michigan State University Library, is a very large collection primarily of early phonograph material.[10] Stanford has a large collection of phonographs in the Archive of Recorded Sound.[11].

The Northwestern University Radio Archive Project has more than 15,000 discs most of which have not been cataloged.[12] The Ohio State University has more than 5,000 discs and tapes, mostly programs submitted to the Institute for

Education by Radio and Television.[13] The University of Illinois has more than 3,000 discs mostly programs of WILL. The Center for the Study of Popular Culture at Bowling Green (Ohio) State University has some radio and TV materials and reportedly 30,000 records. Allen Funt's *Candid Microphone* and *Candid Camera* are at Cornell University. More than 600 radio tapes, and some TV programs are available at the University of North Carolina. At the University of Texas there are some British and Canadian dramas and the Hoblitzelle Theater Arts Library has some broadcasting materials. Professor Marvin Bensman is building an impressive collection of radio programs, and has produced a list of collectors, at Memphis State University. The University of Southern California has materials donated by Marlo Thomas, Jimmy Durante, George Burns, *Peyton Place* and *Star Trek*. Yale has a large collection of phonograph records in the Historical Sound Recordings Program. At Columbia there is no significant program collection, but nearly 100 interviews with radio pioneers and others in the broadcasting industry.[14]

About three-fourths of all radio-television-film departments in universities have some collection of radio and TV programs. Most have audio tapes of radio programs but nearly half also have discs, video tapes, or kinescopes. These collections are generally small — most fewer than 50 programs — and few have any budget or staff.[15] Recent technology, especially cassette video tape has meant that more universities and high schools are video taping programs off the air and building libraries of these materials.

GOVERNMENT COLLECTIONS

National Archives

There is a wealth of material literally buried in the National Archives. It is impossible to list all the material that may eventually be of value to scholars in broadcasting. The largest number of radio programs is probably in the sound recording

Sources for Research and Teaching   **223**
in Radio and Television History

section of the Audio Visual Archives Division. There are nearly 50,000 recordings many from federal agencies but including some broadcast programs.[16] There are many speeches by government officials; special collections on World War II, black history and Indians; and important collections related to theatre, photography, and other media.

The Social and Economic Records Division has the files of the Commerce Department, Federal Radio Commission and Federal Communications Commission. These include some recordings.[17] There are separate record groups for the Office of Censorship, Office of War Information, and the Foreign Broadcast Intelligence Service with World War II recordings including many shortwave broadcasts of enemy propaganda.[18]

Additional information, including some recordings, can be found in the record group for the Federal Trade Commission. The National Archives is now (June 1974) holding all CBS TV news and documentary programs on an experimantal basis. Hopefully this will continue and this material made available at all NA regional centers.

Presidential Libraries

Six presidential libraries are administered by the National Archives and include a great deal of broadcast material related to those presidents and other news and public affairs broadcasts.[19]

Library of Congress

The Recorded Sound Section of the Music Division of the Library of Congress is said to contain nearly 400,000 recordings — some are radio broadcasts. There may be as many as 100,000 discs from the Office of War Information.

In the motion picture section there are a number of entertainment and documentary programs on film. Each TV series that is copyrighted submits a list of programs for each year; the

Library generally asks for copies of one or two episodes from each series for the files. Most documentaries are requested but not all in fact are delivered. For both sound recordings and films the files of the Library of Congress must be consulted. In 1971 the Senate considered a bill to establish a repository for all network news programs in the Library of Congress but it was not passed.

Smithsonian Institution

The Smithsonian is a valuable resource on the technological history of broadcasting but has very few programs.[20]

INDUSTRY

Only a very limited amount of historical material is actually available from broadcasting networks and stations. There are a large number of documentary films from the networks in circulation by commercial film distributors (see below) but only a very few entertainment programs are available.

Program records at ABC apparently are almost nonexistent. At CBS the program analysis office and the CBS news library can make information available to a limited number of scholars. The NBC reference library has files on programing and microfilms of some scripts. Both CBS and NBC have many discs, tapes, kinescopes, and video tape recordings but these are not available for use. CBS recently installed a computerized retrieval system for all items on news programs but it is apparently only for internal use.

A number of ABC documentary programs, after 1972, can be purchased or rented from ABC Media Concepts.[21] Earlier ABC programs are distributed by McGraw-Hill, International Film Bureau, Carousel Films, and others. Some NBC documentary and news features are available from NBC Educational Enterprises for lease or purchase.[22] Many special events, discussion programs, and public affairs broadcasts are available for purchase from the Pacifica stations.[23].

Nearly two-thirds of all radio stations on the air before 1940 say that they have retained some historical material and one-third have recordings. A majority of all TV stations have some films, kinescope recordings or video tapes of possible historical value.[24] Many say that they will permit teachers and scholars to use some of this material. Teachers of communications and other performing arts should take the lead in seeing that that these materials eventually are placed in repositories where they can be used by students and researchers.

Broadcast Pioneers Library

Since 1971 the Broadcast Pioneers Library has been located in the National Association of Broadcasters' building in Washington. The collection includes nearly 1,000 tapes but most are oral history interviews with broadcasters — there are very few programs. However, this is a good source of other material on broadcasting history.[25]

Other Collections

Pacific Broadcast Pioneers are also building a collection to be housed in Los Angeles but no catalog or access to the collection is now available. The Country Music Hall of Fame, Nashville, is primarily a tourist attraction and has only a very few broadcast programs. Eastman House, Rochester, has an excellent motion picture collection, is worth a visit, but has few broadcast acquisitions.[26]

TAPES AND DISCS FOR SALE AND TRADE

The largest source of radio programs is various individual collectors and firms that now sell tapes of programs.

Radio Yesteryear has more than 2,000 programs available for purchase.[27] Various special offers also are made from Radiola on long play records.[28]

Old Time Radio, Inc., Joe Hehn, claims more than 25,000 complete broadcasts are available. You can order from a catalog or (for a fee) ask for research on specific programs. It is a good service for researchers or teachers looking for a specific program series.[29]

Mar-Ben Sound Company has a collection of more than 3,000 programs for sale.[30] The Great Radio Shows, Inc. has a large catalog, particularly of drama and comedy programs.[31]

A number of record shops have tapes and discs of radio programs, and audio recordings of TV programs for sale. Some offer special catalogs of radio programs available on LPs.[32]

Commercial Records

A few radio programs and a great deal of documentary sound material is on regular phonograph records. Much of this can be used in class lectures and for short program excerpts. Some typical titles include: "Great Moments in Boxing," Coral 57325; "Campaign 56," Folkways 5505; "Great Debates of 1960," Spoken Word; "War of the Worlds," Audio Rarities; and "Man on the Moon," Warner-Seven Arts. Many speeches are available on phonograph.[33]

Individual Collectors

The richest source of old radio programs is other program collectors who wish to trade. At this writing there is no really good way to find out who has what. It is a matter of building your own collection, trading, and constantly corresponding with other collectors to find new programs.[34]

FILMS FOR SALE AND RENT

Very few TV entertainment programs are now available for classroom or research use. However, note that many older TV programs are in rerun especially in early and late hours and on independent stations. These can be assigned to students to watch and taped.

Some used film dealers do have old TV films for sale.[35]
A number of TV documentaries are now rented by educational film distributors or available from university or state audio-visual libraries. These can usually be located by checking a number of catalogs for the titles you want, or going through catalogs for examples. Read descriptions carefully as sometimes titles are changed. Unfortunately these documentaries are sometimes cut to shorter lengths — butchered would sometimes be a better word.[36]

Conclusion

The number of available sources of radio programs is growing. The recent success of several TV programs will encourage distribution — for example, a collection of *Show of Shows* distributed to theatres and *CBS News Retrospective*. More universities and other schools will build their own collections, taping with the new less expensive cassette machines off the air.

There are a number of impressive collections at universities; others have great potential. Yet there is still no general source of radio programming of various types for any extended period of time that is readily available to teachers and scholars. Many historians and other academics outside radio-television-film departments still do not regard broadcast programs — even news — as proper grist for their scholarly mills.

If you should find a new source of radio[37] or TV programs take the initiative to see that it is preserved and eventually given to some library or museum. Those of us who teach broadcasting history and need these records for our research must see that the record of broadcasting is preserved. No one else will do it for us.

Notes

1. I have visited most of the major university and government collections described here. Recently I have tried to update this material by correspondence and phone calls. Thus, I am indebted to a number of librarians, individual collectors, colleagues, and others who have provided me with information. Particularly, I wish to acknowledge the help of A. William Bluem, Christopher H. Sterling, Marvin Bensman, David H. Culbert, and Kenneth Lichty, my father, who supplies me with a constant flow of newspaper and magazine clippings.

   To the best of my knowledge this information is up-to-date as of June 1974. If you have additions or corrections please write me.

2. Milo Ryan, *History in Sound: A Descriptive Listing of the KIRO-CBS Collection of Broadcasts of the World War II Years and After, in the Phonoarchives of the University of Washington*, University of Washington Press, 1963. For supplements and other information write Donald G. Godfrey, Curator, Milo Ryan Phonoarchive, School of Communications, University of Washington, Seattle, WA 98195.

3. For a partial list of the Mass Communications History Center collections write State Historical Society, 816 State Street, Madison, WI 53706. For a list of TV programs available, and feature films, write Wisconsin Center for Theatre Research, 6039 Vilas Hall, University of Wisconsin, Madison, WI 53706.

4. For a catalog, nominal charge, write NATAS-UCLA Television Library, University of California, Macgowan Hall, Los Angeles, CA 90024. JEMF has no published catalog but issues a quarterly journal; The John Edwards Memorial Foundation, Inc., Folklore and Mythology Center, University of California, Los Angeles, CA 90024.

5. Administrator, Vanderbilt Television News Archive, Joint University Libraries, Nashville, TN 37203.

6. A computerized (KWIC) catalog has been produced. John D. Herschberger, "Miami University Broadcasting Service Crosley Broadcasting Corporation ET Archive Catalog," Miami University, 1965. There are also two theses on the process of cataloging such a collection: John D. Herschberger, "The Arrangement and Cataloging of the Miami University Broadcasting Service Electrical Transcription Archives," MA Thesis, Miami University, 1965; and Ward S. Lea, "A System of Cataloging Designed for the Record Library of the Miami University Broadcasting Service," MS Thesis, Miami University, 1965. For further information write Broadcasting Service, Miamity, Oxford, OH 45056.

7. Catalog of the Michigan State University Collection of Classic Radio Programs, Television and Radio Department, Michigan State University, East Lansing, MI 48824.

8. Write National Instruction Television Library, Indiana University, Bloomington, IN 47401.

9. For example, Great Plains National Instructional Television Library, Lincoln, NB 68501.

10. For some of this material see "Hark the Years" Capitol 23334; or the ETV program *Spin Back the Years.*

11. "History—Served Up On A 'Platter'," *Lost Angeles Times*, March 6, 1972.

12. Michael Biel, "Northwestern University Radio Archive Project," Preliminary Catalog, November 1971.

13. University Archivist, The Ohio State University, Columbus, OH 43210.

14. *The Oral History Collection of Columbia University*, Oral History Research Office, 1964. Butler Library, Columbia University, New York, NY 10027. Also see "The Early Days of Radio," *American Heritage*, August 1955.

15. Survey by Lichty based on returned questionnaires from 86 departments, September 1967, reported in "A Brief Survey of Some Sources of Radio and Television Programs for Teaching and Research in Broadcasting History," Association for Professional Broadcasting Education annual meeting, Washington, D.C., March 22, 1969. For a more current survey see Ruth Schwartz, "Preserving TV Programs: Here Today — Gone Tomorrow," *Journal of Broadcasting*, 17:3 (Summer 1973), pp. 287-300.

16. Mayfield S. Bray and Leslie C. Waffen, "Sound Recordings in the Audio-Visual Archives Division of the National Archives," 1972, Mayfield S. Bray and William T. Murphy, "Motion Pictures in the Audiovisual Archives Division of the National Archives, 1972, and Select List of Sound Recordings: Voices of World War II, 1937-1945, National Archives General Information Leaflet No. 21, 1971, revised 1973.

17. Albert W. Winthrop, "Records of the Federal Communications Commission," The National Archives, General Services Administration, 1956.

18. Henry T. Ulaska, "Records of the Office of Censorship," The National Archives, General Services Administration, 1953; and Walter W. Weinstein, "Records of the Foreign Broadcast Intelligences Service," The National Archives, General Services Administration, 1959. For general information see "List of National Archives Microfilm Publications," and "Publications of the National Archives and Records Service," National Archives and Records Service, Washington, D.C. 20408.

19. "Audiovisual Holdings of the Presidential Libraries," National Archives 1972, and write for a description of each library — Hoover to Johnson.

20. The American Film Institute is helping preserve motion pictures but to date has not included television film in its collection.

21. *ABC Media Concepts Film Catalogue,* and supplements, 1330 Avenue of the Americas, New York, NY 10019 or 1001 N. Pointsettia Place, Hollywood, CA 90046.

22. *NBC Educational Enterprises 16 mm Film Catalog,* annual, 30 Rockefeller Plaza, New York, NY 10020.

23. *Pacifica Programs,* annual, and "Latest Additions," Pacifica Tape Library, 2217 Shattuck Avenue, Berkeley, CA 94704. Most programs are produced by the Pacifica stations — KPFA, Berkeley; KPFK, Los Angeles; WBAI, New York; KPFT, Houston — or the stations' Washington News Bureau.

24. Based on a survey by Lichty, 1967; returned questionnaires from 184 (24%) radio stations on the air before 1940 and 185 (31%) of TV stations.

25. An inventory of materials is available, write Catherine Heinz, Director, Broadcast Pioneers Library, 1771 N Street, NW, Washington, D.C. 20036.

26. For a list of many libraries with special materials and collections see Anthony Jruzas, *Directory of Special Libraries,* Gale Research Company. Also see "A Preliminary Directory of Sound Recordings Collections in the United States and Canada," prepared by Committee of the Association for Recorded Sound Collections, Rodgers and Hammerstein Archives, Lincoln Center, 111 Amsterdam Ave., New York, NY 10023.

27. Radio Yesteryear, Box H., Croton-on-Hudson, New York, NY 10520, catalog, $1.00, "mini-catalog" and other material on request.

28. Radiola, Box H, Croton-on-Hudson, New York, NY 10520, ask for information on "releases." The material and catalog from Radio Yesteryear is also available from Sights and Sounds of America, Box 616, Nassau, DE 19969.

29. Old Time Radio, Inc., 618 Commonwealth Building, Allentown, PA 18101, $1.00 for catalog; also see John Dunning, "The Fantasy World of Joe Hehn," *Cavalier,* December 1973, pp. 46-50.

30. Mar-Bren Sound Co., 420 Pelham Road, Rochester, NY 14610; see catalog 1969, and supplements 1-4.

31. The Great Radio Shows, Inc., P.O. Box 254, Woodinville, WA 98072.

32. For example try Ray Avery, Rare Records, 417 East Broadway, Glendale, CA 91205; Arnold's Archives, 1106 Eastwood, S.E., E. Grand Rapids, MI 49506; and Ray Morser, 1394 Third Ave., New York, NY 10021.

33. For current listings see Schwann Long Playing Record Catalog, monthly. Helen Roach, *Spoken Records,* The Scarecrow Press, 1966. Marlene J. Hager, "A Bibliography of Recorded American and British Public Address, *The Speech Teacher,* XVIII:2 (March 1969). Collections such as "Hear It Now" Columbia and a "I Remember Radio" Longines Symphonette might be helpful to some.

34. For a list of dealers, collectors, magazines, and other information get "Collectors' Contact Guide," $1.00, by Paul Jackson, 204 S. MacArthur, Springfield, IL 62704. I should note here that there are some unscrupulous traders and dealers who misrepresent their programs, exaggerate quality, or do not deliver at all. Get to know the person you are dealing with, try a small trade or order first, represent your own collection and intentions correctly, and warn others of any unsavory characters you encounter.

35. For example try Blackhawk Films, Davenport, IA 52808 or Wonderland, 6116 Glen Tower, Hollywood, CA 90028.

36. Particularly see catalogs from McGraw-Hill for a number of ABC, CBS and NBC documentaries. It is not possible to list all the film distributors here, it is best to get in touch with the nearest university or state film library. Also, see Serley Reid, "Directory of 3,600 16 mm Film Libraries," U.S. Department of Health, Education and Welfare, Washington, D.C., 1959. Many city libraries have films for loan or can arrange rental from distributors.

37. If you do find discs of radio programs treat them carefully. Glass discs (mostly WWII) will break very easily, even sudden cold can crack them. Aluminum base records get moldy and will crack if washed. Paper based records may flake. Dub records immediately onto good audio tape, with the proper needle. Consult an expert if you have any questions. After dubbing save and store the discs. Write the Library of Congress for "Preservation and Storage of Sound Recordings."

Volumes I and II will be indexed in Volume II.

Note: Requests for information about subscriptions and/or purchase of annual volumes of *Performing Arts Resources* should be directed to: Theatre Library Association, 111 Amsterdam Avenue, New York, N.Y. 10023.